To~
Lydia
Enjoy the stories of
a small community
that was truly exceptional!

But,
Pat Rose

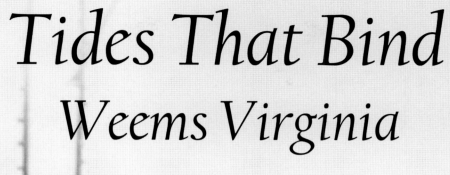

Tides That Bind
Weems Virginia

Patricia L. Rose

Author
Patricia L. Rose

Publisher
Wayne Dementi

Cover and Graphic design by:
Dianne C. Dementi

Cover photograph colorization by:
Katie Rose

Author photograph by:
Martine Rose

Dementi Milestone Publishing, Inc.
Manakin-Sabot, VA 23103
www.dementimilestonepublishing.com

Cataloging-in-publication data for this book is available from The Library of Congress.

ISBN: 978-0-9981471-4-7

Printed in the USA

Attempts have been made to identify the owners of any copyrighted materials appearing in this book. The publisher extends his apology for any errors or omissions and encourages copyright owners inadvertently missed to contact him.

End page photo: Aerial view of Weems, Virginia, in 1998. Courtesy of Bonnie Gwathmey.

Cover photo: (From left to right) Marion Oscar Ashburn, Jr., Pat Lumpkin, and Patsy Parrish enjoy an outing on Carters Creek. *Author's Photo.*

TABLE OF CONTENTS

DEDICATION

This book is dedicated

to all the good people of Weems, Virginia,

both past and present,

whose spirit will always compliment the land about them.

FOREWORD

"If I had influence with the good fairy who is supposed to preside over the christening of all children, I should ask that her gift to each child in the world be a sense of wonder so indestructible that it would last throughout life..."

Rachel Carson

My sense of wonder was given to me in Weems, Virginia, most likely on my Christening Day at Campbell Memorial Presbyterian Church, while being held in the arms of my grandmother. It has lasted all my life making me understand and particularly appreciate Pat Rose's book, *TIDES THAT BIND.*

What is noteworthy about her book is that it is specific to a place, Weems, yet encapsulates what is universal in spirit to small villages everywhere. Pat Rose has captured a sense of place, a sense of the people, a sense of history. Her book is a marvel of research, rich in details of times of joy and hardship, an interweaving of threads with ties that bind. It is a pleasure to read about the Weems community with the fresh vision from Pat's eyes. The remarkable photographs she has collected enable us to travel through the book, identifying familiar places and people known from the past. There is a rhythm to the book as similar as walking through town to the Weems wharf, the old post office, Campbell Church, King Carters Lane, Wharton Grove, and beyond. All along the way, long forgotten memories resurface.

I first met Pat when we were children at Campbell Church. My grandmother Margaret, my Aunt Margery, and my mother Mary Meade knew then that "Patricia" was especially gifted. Having lost touch since my youth from this girl I admired with the long golden hair, it has been wonderful to reconnect with her as she has been researching and writing *TIDES THAT BIND.*

We live in a time, a period of history when all the bustling activity, all the businesses, the oyster houses, canning factories are gone. No longer is there a grocery store or even a post office. What is left in Weems are many old-fashioned homes, the church, the beauty of the natural areas, the seashore, the lapping of the creek and river, the call of the osprey and seagull, a sense of quiet and peace.

Beloved by my family for five generations, Weems is the place where my grandfather, James Oscar Dameron, came in the 1880s to establish businesses connected with steamboats. Much later, during World War II, I lived in the Dameron home with my mother, grandparents, and aunt for the first three years of my life while my father was in the Pacific. Since then, my brother Chip and I, along with families, children, and grandchildren, have returned again and again to enjoy fishing and crabbing off old worn docks, watching the brilliant sunrises and sunsets, and seeing the starlit skies at night. We have now returned to our roots, retiring recently to be beside the water on the land of our grandparents.

Weems has made an impression on succeeding generations. One granddaughter wrote:

"There is an ambiance of the region, an atmosphere of calm and tranquility...an impression of goodwill, an atmosphere of security and hospitality."

Another grandchild described Weems in this way:

"I love to sit on the porch of our old house at Weems with my grandmother and hear stories about times long ago. I hope when I grow up and have grandchildren of my own, I can sit on the same porch and tell them stories of our family and good times at Weems."

Recently, Margaret and James Oscar Dameron's great-great grandson, in his two-year-old way, when asked where he was going for the weekend, answered:

"HALLOW WEEMS!"

Our family feels he has deemed this town with a name most fitting, as it has been for generations a hallowed place for us, the true place of our hearts.

Pat Rose's *TIDES THAT BIND* will take you to this hallowed place to reawaken memories of specific people and places, to engender a sense of wonder of the graceful beauty of the area, and to celebrate the values and traditions of small communities everywhere.

Margaret Woodson Nea

On her christening day at Campbell Memorial Presbyterian Church in Weems, Virginia, Margery is proudly held by her grandmother, Margaret Dameron. *Courtesy of Margaret Nea.*

ACKNOWLEDGEMENTS

Initially, ideas are born and grow with energy when a writing project is undertaken. Sustaining that energy is the key to the story's birth to print. Coupled with their infinite research skills, Alice and Ben Winstead worked diligently to bring the story of the Weems Community to life. They continually streamed information, photographs, and stories my way often accompanied by good food when we sat around their kitchen table. Thanks, Alice and Ben, for your desire to keep our Weems story alive.

Once again a special thank you makes its way to Martine Rose for her interest, time, and patience in guiding me through the tedious editing process and computer maze. You are simply a constant...always there, full of encouragement. This is your story, too.

Key in this effort has been the skillful willingness of my granddaughter, Katie, who spent countless hours discussing the storyline, proofreading, and exercising her computer skills.

As for comfortable bed and board during the many research trips and interviews carried out around the Weems community, I give appreciation to my sister-in-law, Norma Lumpkin, for her interest and generosity in this project.

My family, Les, Graham, Andrew, their spouses and children, was always available with listening ears and relevant comments about the developing Weems story. Their sharing of the special love for the time they spent enjoying those indelible Weems moments always encouraged me to write this story.

Invaluable information about Oscar and Walton Dameron and their families literally "pieced" this story together. For this I owe Margery Woodson Nea, granddaughter of James Oscar and Margaret Dameron, sincere gratitude for her unconditional sharing of family ledgers, albums, letters, and photographs. Her warmth for this project shines throughout. I remain thankful for the renewal of our friendship.

Joining the ranks, as well, are countless people who gave of their time through interviews, telephone chats, e-mails, letters, scrapbooks, tapes, photographs and wonderful conversations about growing up in Weems. Their input and generosity will always be treasured.

Warm appreciation for their time and interest in this Weems project is extended to: Robert J. Teagle, Education Director and Curator of Christ Church; Frances S. Pollard, Vice President For Research Services Virginia Historical Society; Reverend Clay Macaulay, former pastor of Campbell Memorial Presbyterian Church; C. Diane Roche, Chief Curator of Department of Historic Resources Commonwealth of Virginia; Sarah Whiting, Society for Preservation of Virginia Antiquities; Randy Carter, Shirley Plantation; Augusta Sellew and Carroll Lee Ashburn, Kilmarnock Museum; and Anne Long McClintock, Steamboat Era Museum.

There will be unintended omissions of people and events in this book. Much understanding is asked to be extended to the author on these accounts. Every effort to verify information about people, places, and their stories to form a true picture has been diligently pursued. The result is that a large portion of the story of Weems has now been attended to in print.

A REMINISCENCE

It's true. I wasn't born in Weems, Virginia. However, I had been traveling to Weems since infancy. My paternal grandparents (Bertha and Andrew Lumpkin) lived in a white two-storied farmhouse situated upon a steep slope that tapered gracefully onto the waters of Carters Creek. A wide planked dock tethered my grandfather's boat and several skiffs alongside high wooden pilings.

Nearly seventeen acres of land encompassed several sheds that housed chickens, pigs, "Bossy" the cow, "Frank" the horse, and many active kittens. Nearby, a fertile garden plot grew an array of vegetables. Several acres bordering the garden were allotted to growing watermelon and cantaloupe. My grandfather sold them seasonally from the deck of his boat in the Baltimore Harbor. The remaining acreage was planted in corn topped with tassels that swayed beside a rutted dirt lane.

When daylight faded, my grandmother set a flickering kerosene lamp in the "sitting room" a step up from the kitchen. I'd munch on vanilla wafers and listen to my grandfather's stories about sailing on the water. Afterwards, I'd climb steep wooden steps to a tiny room with a pink wrought iron feather bed weighed down with mountains of quilts.

This setting was quite a contrast to my beginnings in the bustling city life of Baltimore, Maryland. My parents began their married life in a compact three room upstairs apartment in a brick row house. My maternal grandparents (Florence and Seldon House) lived downstairs. The city block perimeter was shared with mazes of automobile traffic and crowded shop venues. Street cars clicked and clacked on shiny steel tracks around the corner. An amusement park was only a half hour away. Motion picture marquees glittered at night. I roller skated on the sidewalk in front of our house. My school had a fenced in concrete playground.

By the end of World War II in 1945, my father left city life and factory work at Western Electric for good. His desire to return to Weems had become all consuming. We lived in the farmhouse of his birth now relocated on the main Weems road. His livelihood centered upon carpentry jobs as well as crabbing and oystering on the water. Mother learned to plant a garden, can vegetables, scrub clothes by hand, and cook country style. Our very being became immersed in a new way of life. Years later my brother, Raymond, recalled the good fortune of growing up in Weems.

Once Grandfather Lumpkin jokingly wrote his two-year old granddaughter, "If they don't treat you right up there, just come down to live on the farm." I still smile when I unfold and reread that letter. I took his invitation...literally. In the succeeding years, I passed that invitation along to my sons, and they, in turn, to their families. We often share the wonderful memories we made along the country path.

Weems...always home.

Patricia Lee Lumpkin Rose

Patricia Lee Lumpkin Rose

The Lumpkin farmhouse and surrounding land was purchased on December 8, 1911, from Annie and S. C. Thomas. The sale included three or four acres of established oyster shore. This picture was taken in 1930. *Author's photo.*

A lovely view of Carters Creek could be seen from the farmhouse. My parents, Gladys and Raymond, skated on the frozen creek when they honeymooned here in 1936. *Author's photo.*

The Lumpkin and House families became fast friends through a chance meeting of the men at the Baltimore Harbor dock. (Front row - left to right) Andrew Lumpkin, Bertha Lumpkin, Seldon House, and Florence House. (Back row - left to right) "Boots" Lumpkin, "Bunks" Lumpkin, Raymond Lumpkin, Jeannette Kirckhoff, and Louise Lumpkin. Another daughter, Bertha Lumpkin, is not pictured. *Courtesy of Edith House Becker.*

A House family portrait at their Baltimore, Maryland, home. (From left to right) Elmer, Seldon Thomas, Edward, Thomas, and Florence. My mother, Gladys Marie, stands in the background. The first child, Lillian Viola, passed in 1912. *Courtesy of Edith House Becker.*

My mother, Gladys House, visiting the Lumpkin farm in the 1920s. The large garden and animal sheds appear in the background. *Author's photo.*

Father, Mother, and I, pose in the backyard of our Baltimore home in the 1940s. *Author's photo.*

Enjoying good times together on the farm with Aunt Louise. *Author's photo.*

Aunt "Bunks" and her father pose with "Frank." *Author's photo.*

Aunt Bertha and I on the banks of Carters Creek. *Author's photo.*

Grandmother Lumpkin and I take the long walk down the lane from the farmhouse on the creek. *Author's photo.*

Aboard my grandfather's boat for a day of family fishing. My mother is on the left with my grandfather and friends in the background. *Author's photo.*

My mother, brother, and I enjoyed life in the country. *Author's photo.*

With my family in Weems on Easter Sunday in 1953. *Author's photo.*

GRANDFATHER'S LETTER TO AUTHOR
JANUARY 24, 1939
WEEMS, VIRGINIA

Addressing his two-year old grand-daughter as "Dollie Dumps," my grandfather Andrew Calvin Lumpkin, urged me to "sneak out and take the bus down here, and I will meet you in Kilmarnock."

He shared that the horse was well and ready to ride, and that Grandmaw had bought a new runt pig.

the Bus down here and
Will Will meet you in b...
the Harre, dally has got ...
and now you can dri...
next Sumer, your self gr...
mar has baught a nuther
Pig, she will haue him t...
enuf by the Sumer an...
you can ride him, Whe...
you came down, dant pa...
no atencan to what th...
Say to you up there an...
tell Luise dant let yu...
you a round, and iff y...

He continued the return to Weems urging through these words..."Tell your Mom and Dad you don't have to take no foolishings from them because Grandmaw and Grandpa wants you down here."

His closing stated: "I am about run ashore now so come as soon as you can, Grandpa."

you tell your muthe...
and dad you dant ha...
to take no foolishinge ...
them be case grand mar...
grand Pap wants you d...
here Dally you ought to ...
Raggie Wone he can ...
and Sing and bryse too...
he is caming out the Sh...
giue my law to mamy...
Pap all so to Louise and
grand mar down stare
O yease I got a little Rat...
tary Pupy he is rit b...
When you came you will ...

- xvii -

Carters Creek as seen from Weems Cove bank in 1964. Many hours were spent crabbing, fishing, water skiing, and swimming in its waters. *Author's Photo.*

PART I

TIME BEFORE US

The land makes its own statement and sets its own priorities. Its physical properties attract and to some extent mold its inhabitants to a specified way of life. Their possession is a limited sojourn. By the law of nature, the people, in due time, move on. But the land remains. What transpires in that time is the account of people, how they chose to interact with one another, and the use of the land about them. We naturally begin our quest with observations of what occurred before Weems, Virginia, came into existence.

With undefined juts, crannies, and protrusions, the four major rivers (James, York, Rappahannock, and Potomac) poured into the Chesapeake Bay yielding strong navigational routes and harbors for approaching ships. These waters and the land they bordered became a voyager's vision and a settler's dream in the 1600s. But, in fact, this land had long been utilized with care for centuries by the Native American people. Throughout the Tidewater area some two-hundred villages organized as tribes and under the vigorous leadership of Wahunsenacawh (Powhatan) embraced their forested homeland. Specifically, five villages of Cuttatawomen Indians existed on the banks of the lower half of the Corotoman River alongside Carters Creek. The well-documented altercations between the Native Americans and the English settlement inhabitants over ownership and land dominance came quickly into play. A crucial tug of war for both cultures showed evidence of widely different expectations for practical and careful use of the fertile land. One waning civilization opted for prolonged sustenance while the newer emerging peoples looked towards yield and profit.

This land that George Percy, journalist in 1607 Jamestown, wrote about as "...faire meaddowes and goodly Tall Trees...great plenty of fish of all kindes...as in the first creation without toil or labor" was also described by Captain John Smith as "...over growne with trees and weedes being a plaine wilderness as God first made it." (Both referenced in James Horn's *Adapting to a New World*.) Not to be so encouraged or even dissuaded by these descriptions, about 900 settlers took up residence in 1620 throughout the "necks" or peninsulas of the Chesapeake area growing steadily into the Tidewater and Piedmont areas. Their numbers swelled to 85,000 by the 1700s. A way of life now described as a "society" began to take hold apart from their English roots. By 1750 seventy-nine parishes could be accounted for as far as the Blue Ridge.

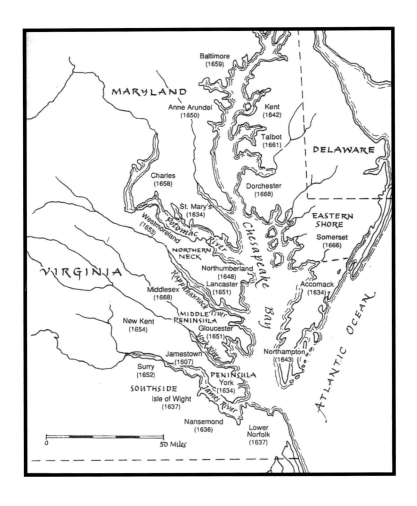

Left - A map depicting Chesapeake in the 17th century. Note Lancaster County within the Northern Neck region. Drawn by Richard Stinley. From **Adapting to a New World English Society in the Seventeenth Century Chesapeake** by James Horn. Copyright 1994 by the University of North Carolina Press. *Used by permission of the publisher www.cpress.unc.edu*

A Reverend Mr. Hugh Jones, Anglician Clergyman and author, offered, in part, this observation of his witnessing of Virginia as now a "colony" in 1724--"...about a thousand leagues (3,000 miles) from England...oriented to the anchorages of four principal rivers...most houses built near some landing-place..." (Referenced in Rhys Issac's *The Transformation of Virginia 1740-1790.*) The growth of this "colony" had positioned itself well to the land and its waters. This formed a sound connection to accommodate the regularity of the imports from and exports to England. Desirous of seeking out the best landing sites hastened this development.

Again, in *Adapting to a New World*, James Horn extends these settlement concepts to that of the importance of "political connections" and "planter opportunities." A paramount observation then surfaces of key importance to the settler's story-- that in this new world one pursued effectively "kinship and neighborliness" (as) "influencing the choice of destination." Desired patented land was thought to be that of "maximizing (ed) the possibility for contact; preferably a relative." Perhaps, unknowingly with this pronounced caveat, the die had been cast for generations to come in Virginia. It certainly proved to be a reality in Lancaster County and much later in the story of the development of the area we know today as Weems, Virginia.

In the time as early as the 1640s, despite the Jamestown Assembly's caution and fear of the Native Americans in the Northern Neck region, a Mr. John Carter had been given a sizable grant along the Rappahannock River. He was not alone. Sixty patents (exclusive grant of land by a sovereign) encompassing more than 53,000 acres had surfaced by 1650. Lancaster County was on the map by 1651, completed its patent explosion in the late 1660s and sprinted far ahead of the Lower Norfolk.

Left - Publication of John Smith's map in 1612 in England took into account some twenty trips (2,500 miles) of travels in the Chesapeake region (Virginia, Maryland, Delaware, Pennsylvania, and Washington, DC). Notice the Powhatan drawing and mention of the Susquehannock. Detailed in noting "shorelines, rivers, tributaries, bays, and islands," Smith positioned North to the right as aboard ship coming from the Atlantic. *Used with permission by the Virginia Historical Society.*

Merchants and planters on the Corotoman River listed eighty-three "tithables" (specific individuals subject to levy and payment of taxes) in 1653. Seemingly, Lancaster County had struck the right chord with settlers through its attraction of a mixture of soils perfect for productive tobacco growth. Well on his way to procured status as a planter and a merchant, John Carter's assessment listed twelve of these "tithables" as his. His claim for twenty-one slave "headrights" (transportation payment for slaves equating to 50 acres) several years later was also duly recorded as steady growth. With their laboring presence in and around the growing plantations, slave numbers swelled in three decades to about 300 accompanied with the arrival now of indentured peoples.

New cultures of non-English immigrants (Irish, Welsh, Scottish) rounded out the region's profile. The natural labor intensity of tobacco growth for profit would require any and all of their combined energy. Successful corn production would summarily offer all plantation inhabitants necessary sustenance. Laborers were in demand. Conversely, by 1705 the original peoples to the land were nearly eroded...that of the Native American. Now the land itself with

its dense forests and bountiful waters accommodated and supported a new beginning existence…Tidewater style.

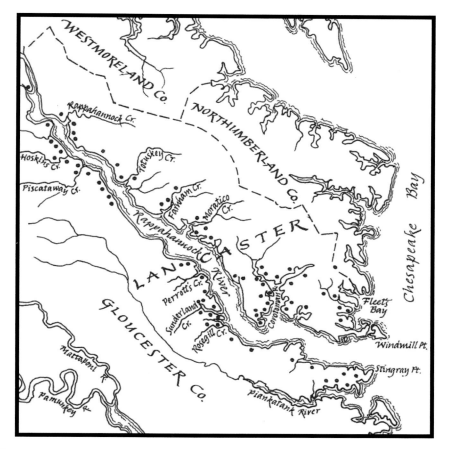

The 1653 settlement patterns in Lancaster County in Virginia. Note the
Corotoman site. Drawn by Richard Stinley. From *Adapting to a New
World English Society in the Seventeenth Century Chesapeake*
by James Horn. Copyright 1994 by the University of North Carolina
Press. *Used by permission of the publisher www.cpress.unc.edu*

JOHN CARTER OF COROTOMAN
1613-1669

No doubt the speculation of a spacious new land with un-
fathomed opportunities rushed through John Carter's mind as he
crossed the ocean aboard the "Safety." To immigrate to Virginia
in 1635 on the cusp of untold adventures was a rare opportunity
… one that had been supported by descent from a family line in

London leading to membership in a merchant group known as the Vintners Company. And look at the pay off. By twenty-nine years of age, he had patented some 6,610 acres of Lancaster County land and begun construction of a plantation home known as Corotoman. Had John Carter possessed the ability to "fast forward" into his future, he would have been further amazed to know that he would sire a son, Robert "King" Carter, who would amass 300,000 acres inclusive of Indian Town and Hills Quarters north of Corotoman, acquire 750 slaves, hold prestigious offices, and build the present day wonderfully preserved Christ Church. Undeniably, this son would become the wealthiest man in all of Virginia. Inclusive of the Robert "King" Carter family descendants would be three signers of the Declaration of Independence, eight Governors of Virginia, and two United States Presidents.

Known as Slaughter's or John's Creek, the 1,300 acres between Corotoman and Carters Creek would be home for John Carter and his sons John II and Robert. The Carter estate of Corotoman extended from the mouth of the Corotoman River and crossed over Carters Creek waterways. A current calculation would position the estate beyond the present day Kilmarnock and inclusive of the town of Irvington. Facing a vintage view and sweep of the Rappahannock River, this Carter home was perfectly positioned for successful family business and wonderfully adapted plantation living. Managing this operation would require thirty-four servants, and forty-three slaves...encompassing 2% of Virginia slave ownership in 1670.

During a planned ancestral journey to visit his great-great grandfather's estate in 1886, Robert Randolph Carter of Shirley Plantation recorded this account in his journal "...landed at Carters Creek, a rising village on the north side of the Rappahannock just below the Corotoman River...rose at daylight and roamed through the village, seeing little to admire besides the beautiful canoes that harbor in the picturesque coves of Carters Creek, a favorite resort of the oystermen and fishermen, that being the chief business of this region, famed for the size and flavor of its oysters... we breakfasted on them... were again on the board to Old Christ Church...distance two miles up the creek..." This description seems as if it could have been a current day journal entry, doesn't it?

Historical plaque J85 erected in front of Christ Church shares complementary information on the fate of the Corotoman plantation in Weems, Virginia. *Author's photo.*

If prodded, Robert Randolph Carter would probably have proudly cited verbatim the structural layout and successful vision(s) of the father (John) and later his son (Robert "King") and their shared Corotoman destiny timeline. He might recount that John Carter had received the issuance of 1,300 acres on August 15, 1642, by Sir William Berkeley, Knight Governor of the Virginia Colony, and further add that John Carter had been second in line to a Daniel Gookins patent claim of this land. Indeed, Nansemond County had been John's first settlement choice. Here he acted as a representative in the House of Burgess. Ultimately, it would be the Northern Neck that beckoned with its fertile soils and prodigious waters. John Carter further solidified his livelihood with an additional 300 acres purchased in 1653. Accompanying this "planter extraordinaire" profile was a modest man who viewed Carters Creek and the Rappahannock River from a small two-room frame dwelling with a single bricked chimney. His son, John Carter II, would follow his father's measured and frugal lead in subsequent acreage purchases and increased plantation labor force enrollment. Corotoman plantation life consistent with 17th century Virginia continued until the 1814 British raid of the Chesapeake region. With many slaves fleeing the site to join their ranks in hope of personal freedom, the demise of the plantation was inevitable.

THE SPINNING HOUSE
1680-1930s

Amazingly, a structure remained on the Corotoman estate (cited as the "colonial place of power") until the 1930s through sheer endurance. That surely must have intrigued Robert Randolph Carter during his 1886 visit. It was the framed building known as the "Spinning House" or "Spinster's House" (1680-1685) built most likely by John Carter and to the far right of his orchards. Hence, present day appropriately named Orchard Lane in Weems. Its unassuming modest two rooms were enclosed by a 21 x 32 foot wooden frame with a brick chimney and anchored with wide planked flooring supported by a brick foundation. An overhead loft was divided into two rooms and probably used as sleeping quarters. The two separate portions of the downstairs areas served as living and eating spaces as well as a sleeping chamber. A root cellar used for vegetable and fruit storage preserved the family diet. In 1979 an archaeological survey conducted by Carter L. Hudgins for the Virginia Research Center for Archaeology (VRCA) unearthed the footings of the building as well as fragmented glass artifacts. The assistant field director and laboratory supervisor, Alice Guerrant, cited if indeed documented through this "dig," this unassuming house may well have been the earliest English house in the area. Its sporadic service as an early Lancaster County Court meeting place was also noted.

Right - The Spinning House dig reveals the modest dwelling of John Carter located in what is now Weems, Virginia. *Courtesy of Virginia Department of Historic Resources.*

Another test square revealed (as conducted by the same archaeological team) an 1820 foundation wall "that constructed doubled the size of the structure (Spinning House) to give it a four room plan and two additional chimneys." Site photographs show a one and half storied wooden structure "with a dormered two-room loft over each portion." (Both referenced by Carter L. Hudgins in *Archaeology In The King's Realm.*) A porch with brick footings extended across the house to take in the sweep of the river itself. The fifth generation Carters seemingly saw the need for an expansion of living quarters though not residing there themselves. Having no connection to the actual art of spinning whatsoever, this enlarged version of the "Spinning House" may have been an overseer's residence. Excavations at the expanded house portion contained a bed and pharmaceutical supplies in support of this statement.

Left - Aerial view of ongoing excavation of Spinning House in 1979 overlooking the Rappahannock River. *Courtesy of Virginia Department of Historic Resources.*

The locust timbered "Spinning House" survived ownerships beyond the possession of the Carter family who gave up their prominent hold of the land by the mid nineteenth century. Its resilience through the Weems residents "love it or leave it" approach became legendary. Pillaging was evident. A visit to inspect the house interior by Mrs. Julia Buck Pembroke and her daughter, Mrs. J. Flexmer Chase, with a mind to perhaps preserve the house as a county library never materialized. In the end the house would be dismantled and reduced to firewood for local inhabitant's use after a 1960 bulldozing. Today the distinct outline of an historical home that once was stirs our imagination.

Most likely the last surviving structure of Robert "King" Carter's plantation, the Spinning House falls into disrepair. *Courtesy of Virginia Department of Historic Resources.*

ROBERT "KING" CARTER OF COROTOMAN
1663-1732

It is highly speculative that Robert Carter was born at Corotoman. Fatherless by the age of six, Robert's future was placed in the hands of his half-brother John Carter II. It was a perfect matchup. Under John's prescribed educational plan, Robert moved deftly between England and Virginia's shores receiving invaluable training skills he would implant in later life at Corotoman. His continued financial investments in the annuities, stocks, and government bonds with the Bank of England solidified his success. Profit became his goal. As the growth and sale of tobacco soared, the cultivation of corn, beans, fruits, wheat, hogs, and cattle production added to his coffers. Dependent upon a finely tuned labor force comprised of indentured white servants and African slaves, Robert Carter's innovative methods of slave training and well-being were nevertheless offset by strict and harsh treatments.

With storage sites and the ability to market products along the river and the bay, Robert Carter carried out his trade routes even acquiring his own vessel fleet. The Virginia Research Center for Archaeology (VRCA) 1977 findings include bale seals signifying "...payment of customs duty on merchandise." A second-time appointment as agent for the Northern Neck Proprietorship propelled Robert Carter into land sales for the king of England as well as additional income for himself through so called "quit rents." (This was one shilling per fifty acres payment to King.) This acquisition and usage of land and water before him became all-consuming and immensely profitable.

A powerful figure in 18th century Virginia, this portrait of Robert "King" Carter in later Corotoman years is suggestive of great wealth and status. His ten children born of Judith Armistead and Betty Landon inherited over 300,000 acres of land. *Courtesy of Shirley Plantation.*

Turning his eye toward the public stage, Robert Carter's list of accomplishments in Lancaster County were inclusive

Robert Carter III (1753) of Nomini Hall poses for a masquerade ball portrait by Thomas Hudson while in England. The namesake of Robert "King" Carter, he later renounced the concept of colonial society institutions. Over time he freed some 500 slaves. *Used with permission by the Virginia Historical Society.*

of vestryman of Christ Church Parish, justice of the peace, House of Burgesses (1695-1699), and member of the Governor's Council. His attention was also given to the construction of private housing as he would provide a dwelling for his family as had his father. The Virginia Research Center for Archaeology (VRCA) during their 1979 "dig" at Corotoman provide us with a time frame (between 1685 and 1690) construction to envision a brick foundation that supported stone floors and three rooms. A "builder's trench" revealed "...bone, window and wine bottle glass... fragments of Rhenish stoneware and Nevers delftware." Serving as a respite in Robert Carter's later life, the existence of the dwelling would fall into the non-use category in 1840.

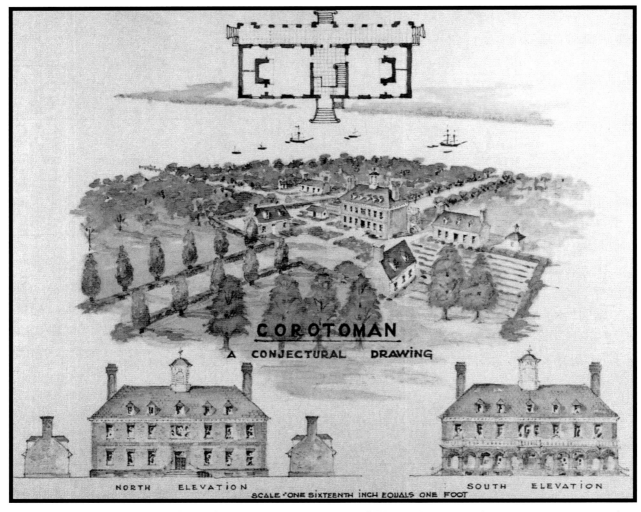

A conjectural drawing of the Corotoman Mansion and Plantation reveals an extravagant and thriving community bordered by the Rappahannock River. Drawing by Alan McCollough in 1985. *Courtesy of Foundation for Historic Christ Church, Inc.*

THE CARTER MANSION

But what of the 40 by 90 foot two and a half-storied structure overlooking the Rappahannock River that Robert "King" Carter had built in the 1720s quite close to his father's modest plantation homestead? Simplicity would be quite an understatement. Well aware as to his prominence within the Virginia community, Robert "King" Carter chose to construct a magnificent Renaissance style mansion. And he topped it off with a unique and one of a kind design in Virginia in the form of an "arcaded portico" or piazza.

Rising magnificently from the sloop landing, its bricked exterior enclosed a hall of black and white marble tiles. The effect was stunning. First floor central led the family and guests alike to two larger rooms featuring massive delft fireplaces touting lovely white tiles of floral and pastoral designs. The equally appealing stairway to the second floor yielded head turning furnishings among the study, closets, writing, and dressing areas. Expertly crafted brass, iron, and finished hardware appeared throughout the residence. Magnificent brick pilasters towered above. Crafted galleries revealed an eye catching piazza above and a working English basement level below. Glass panes enclosed within lead window casements extended the eye towards the lovely outdoor surroundings. This view was inclusive of an "ornamental vista" some ten feet wide forming a border between the mansion and the Rappahannock River. An extensive brick lined four foot arched tunnel revealed a speculated escape system but more likely an "elaborate drainage system" to Carters Creek.

Sadly, a mere four years into its life, this beautiful structure was felled by a raging fire in 1729. The heat destroyed the house contents, morphed the glass windows into shapeless phantoms, and cracked open the sturdy stones and bricks. This incident was a loss beyond repair for Robert "King" Carter. Although attempts were made to retrieve personal possessions from among the charred remains, the mansion's fate had already been determined. It would not be rebuilt nor hold a central position as the heart of the Corotoman plantation. With "King" Carter's descendants moving on to fashion their own future plantations such as Berkeley, Shirley, and Rosewell among others, the splendor of Corotoman gradually became a distant memory. "King" Carter would spend his widowed and waning years in the brick house nearby that had been built for his bride, Judith Armistead. At his death an estate inventory listed in great detail every item ranging from wig powder and a cake of casteel soap to a backgammon table, a dressing glass, and 17 black leather chairs. And books? Accounts support as many as 521 volumes lined the shelves in his private library. Robert "King" Carter had amassed a fortune in his lifetime and left an ancestral legacy second to none.

CEDARS OF COROTOMAN

Eventually any topic inclusive of Robert "King" Carter turns toward the curiosity of the rows of cedars he had planted aligning his route from Corotoman to Christ Church. Imagine an early Sunday morning resplendent with prancing horses and fine carriages transporting the Carters to worship. Dust spewed in the air as they swayed from side to side. Planted twelve feet apart with their outstretching branches providing shade as well as a defined route of natural ornamentation, the cedars were a magnificent scenic backdrop. Slaves positioned on high ladders trimmed their foliage. They were, in effect, homage to the "king." The natural progression of years upon the cedars as well as the preferences of the people in Weems would naturally take a toll. While some saw their practicability as a "fence in livestock fields" (Wilbur Haydon, Weems resident) others saw the trees as unsightly and hazardous with deep fronted water ditches. By 1954, only three cedars remained.

Virginia State Regent and Cobbs Hall Chapter Regent of the Daughters of the American Revolution (Mrs. Carl Stark and Mrs. W. E. Pheris respectively) stand beneath the remaining Corotoman cedar after the ceremony. *Courtesy of Rappahannock Record April 1975.*

Fifteen years in the making, the Cobbs Hall Chapter of the Daughters of the American Revolution (DAR) conducted an unusual dedication in Weems on April 7, 1975. They honored with a ceremony and a plaque (across the lane from the Campbell Memorial Presbyterian Church) the enormous 270 year old cedar tree as the lone survivor from the Corotoman plantation days. Henry W.

Bashore, forester spokesman for the Department of Conservation and Economic Development, shared the Eastern Red Cedar Tree measurements as 61 feet high with a 138 inch circumference. This cedar would stand for an additional 24 years until a storm through Weems brought it down.

In 1999, the last majestic Corotoman cedar was brought down by a severe windstorm, ending its 294 year old existence. *Courtesy of the Rappahannock Record April 15, 1999.*

James Wharton, Weems resident and local historian, shared these words at the ceremony. "It is a noble tree, taller than any other cedar in the country side about. It forks into a double tree with enormous ponderous branches. Its girth is 12 feet and 3 feet above the ground. It stands as a lonely sentinel standing fast after the dispersal of its fallen comrades."

CHRIST CHURCH

Subsequently, a governmental system and social order had begun to emerge within the original Lancaster counties (eight listed in 1643) and parishes in the growing communities. The former provided measures of law and order and set policies of the govern-

Completed in the 1730s by Robert "King" Carter's sons, Historic Christ Church
is recognized as the "best preserved colonial parish." *Courtesy of Margery Nea.*

ment. The latter addressed concerns and supervision of the poor,
sick, and elderly. It would be the development of the parishes that
significantly impacted the lives of area peoples. Often overlapping
with the court system, the parish vestry set their levies in support
of church maintenance and congregational welfare. Even daily life
events could be subject to commentary from the parish.

By 1669 an important development occurred when the Lancaster and Piankatank vestries formed a new singular unit--Christ
Church Parish. Owing to the importance of churches located as
central to the needs of the communities, the construction of the
original Christ Church gave way to its location on John Carter's
Corotoman Plantation. His son John Carter II would diligently complete the wooden framed church project at his father's death, thus
securing an influential presence among the vestry. Adding to that
secured legacy would be the personal quest of Robert "King" Carter
in 1730 to construct a magnificent brick church. Utilizing brick

firing kilns on site as well as wood from the land and stones imported from England, "King" Carter relished his personally funded project, but died in 1732 before its completion in 1735. Unlike the eventual demise of his beloved Corotoman mansion, this church warden would be amazed to know that Christ Church has stood the test of time. As Americans emerged

Christ Church as it appeared in 1896. Note the tombs of Robert "King" Carter and wives on the left with a horse and carriage in the foreground. *Courtesy of Foundation for Historic Christ Church, Inc.*

from the Revolutionary War with "freedom to worship," the private land and personal monies he contributed toward the Christ Church building process helped advance its independent preservation for all time.

"King" Carter selected a myriad of master carpenters and workmen from his Corotoman mansion to lend their construction talents to this new church project. A cruciform styled church emerged giving way to excellent proximity for ministerial presence among the congregation as one preached from the eastern "triple-decker" pulpit. With half a million bricks shoring a sturdy foundation, framing prominent north, south, and west entryways, and providing remarkable designs throughout, the effect was inspirational. A steep roof housed an interior of plaster ceilings, stone flooring, and painted pine woodwork that fashioned the enclosed boxed family pews and benches where people worshiped. No doubt "King" Carter was often on-site and surveyed with admiration the 12 ½ foot by 4 foot windows with their semi-circled top sashes that emitted light throughout the church. Its three classically designed ornate doors with above positioned elliptical windows beckoned the worshipers to enter into prayerful mediation and recitations from The Book of Common Prayer. Their presence was a monthly requirement subject to fine and validation.

Left - Positioning the clerk, the reader, and the priest on triple decker levels, the pulpit in Christ Church is connected to the hooded canopy by a masterful curved stairway. Photographed by John H. Whitehead III. *Courtesy of Foundation for Historic Christ Church, Inc.*

With a hope for their future, the worshiper's eyes traced the black and yellow gilt letters of the impressive canvassed tablets of the Ten Commandments, Lord's Prayer, and the Creed. The 4 ½ foot marble font adorned with four cherub heads was positioned nearby to baptize the youngest of the congregation. By foot, carriage, horseback, and waterway, the parishioners gathered to worship at Christ Church. Its status diminished in the 19th century due, in part, to a religious endeavor known as the Great Awakening. Now there was a sweep of "freedom of religion" choice for all people. Other denominations gave way to lessened interest in utilizing and maintaining a structure that would much later come to be known as a premier preserved colonial church. The growth and activity of Christ Church lay dormant for a time. Its spiritual and physical presence was spent. A long and tedious revival followed resulting in the efforts and energies of many individuals and organizations to preserve Christ Church. Today it stands a wonderful site to visit and explore and in 1961 was designated a National Historic Landmark. With a mission of "preservation and education" its ongoing research, program versatility, museum exhibits, and conferencing abilities at the Bayne Center help keep the historical significance fresh and new.

Right - Parishioners gathered early to greet friends and relatives before worship in Christ Church. Robert "King" Carter reserved a comfortable family pew on the northeast side of the church in view of the two Ten Commandment tablets. Photographed by John H. Whitehead III. *Courtesy of Foundation for Historic Christ Church, Inc.*

The builder/benefactor of Christ Church, Robert "King" Carter, has long been laid to rest beneath a marbled ornate style altar tomb quite befitting his status. Perhaps owing to years of hospitality in his Corotoman estate, Robert "King" Carter's tomb inscription cited in part... "To all whom he courteously entertained, he was neither a lavish nor a frugal host..." What a poignant reminder of a time when his plantation community and house of worship were literally central to the lifeblood of the people. Perhaps, too, that statement was a foretelling of another settlement that would embody the land years later...setting the stage for the life stories of new peoples living in Weems, Virginia.

Carved in England, this cherub closeup on Robert "King" Carter's tomb signifies immortality. *Courtesy of Foundation for Historic Christ Church, Inc.*

COROTOMAN DIG

Since 1975, the Reverend Conrad H. and Henrietta Goodwin took delight in returning to life in Weems, Virginia on the six and one-half acre Corotoman estate and their ancestral roots. History definitely had a hold on them. Retiring as an Episcopalian clergyman, Reverend Goodwin was a direct descendant of Robert "King" Carter. Land ownership by his parents had been re-established in the 1940s and spanned forty years. Together the couple granted access to John Carter's land, and pioneered the way to revisit the

Corotoman plantation archaeologically. Their gift was and still remains immeasurable.

        As resident archaeologist of the Colonial Williamsburg Foundation, Ivor Noel Hume worked in tandem with Dr. William M. Kelso, commissioner of the Virginia Research Center For Archaeology (VRCA), to survey five colonial structures through the testing and probing of grass patterns at Corotoman. Matching grants from Heritage Conservation and Recreation Service, the VRCA, and private donations bolstered the investigation with a $50,000 federal matching grant awarded to the Goodwins for the project in 1978. Some of the household artifacts that were discovered (such as the Carter family coat of arms, tobacco stems, bowls, small dressing sword, hoe blade and collar) are now displayed in the Christ Church museum within fine exhibits detailing the Corotoman story.

Henrietta Goodwin, avid researcher into the "life" of Robert "King" Carter and his Corotoman Plantation, saw its history as "...a living vibrant part of the past that is with us today." *Richmond News Leader.* November 20, 1981. *Courtesy of Margery Nea.*

Archaeological dig conducted at Corotoman in 1977 of Robert "King" Carter's mansion in Weems, Virginia. *Courtesy of Virginia Department of Historic Resources.*

        In 1999, the Corotoman acreage was purchased from the Goodwin family by the Association for Prevention of Virginia Antiquities (APVA). An easement "protected in perpetuity" is held by the Virginia Department of Historic Resources (DHR). The property is currently for sale, but "...removes the right of subdivision and restricts any future building whatsoever to areas jointly determined by the owner and the Commonwealth to be archaeologically safe." Public access at this time is limited.

The washing of the hundreds of thousands of artifacts on hand from Corotoman remains an ongoing project at the Department of Historic Resources (DHR) under the eye of chief curator, C. Diane DeRouche. Officially, the Corotoman land site was listed on the Virginia Landmarks Register on December 2, 1969. National Register of Historic Places recognition was acknowledged on September 15, 1970.

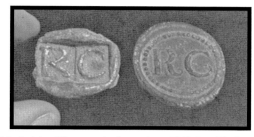

Metal bottle seals bearing RC for Robert Carter discovered at the Corotoman dig site. *Courtesy of Virginia Department of Historic Resources.*

Fragmented section of delft tile unearthed at the Corotoman site. *Courtesy of Virginia Department of Historic Resources.*

An expanded unearthed aerial view of the Corotoman dig. *Courtesy of Virginia Department of Historic Resources.*

COROTOMAN DECLINE

The Carter family eventually gave up its hold on the Corotoman plantation prior to the Civil War. Impending signs of a dwindling English trade were evident. Falling tobacco prices and freedom for the slaves had already contributed to the faltering Virginia economy. The land upon which the plantation stood was now dormant and had simply fallen out of favor. Corotoman's charred ruins became a magnet for scavengers in its ensuing years. Unfortunately, many artifacts were disturbed and removed from the site such as wine bottles, damaged china, and broken green bottles. Bricks sold at 40 cents per hundred found their way into underpinnings and flues of local homes. Reports of the sale of tons of the melted lead roof as well as the "hand chiseled flagstones" made the rounds. Rumors persisted that local watermen used the lead for net sinkers and crab pot anchorage. Void of the knowledge of the home's historical significance at that time, all seemed up for grabs.

Each successive sale of Corotoman saw a financial decline amid a succession of buyers. In 1869 George Kern an inventor from Philadelphia purchased 1,458 plus acres for $30,000. He farmed the land until his death. His wife Caroline and heirs turned to real estate agent, John Palmer of Kilmarnock, for subdivision and sales of the land. Issuing a printed booklet detailing the attractiveness of the Corotoman site, Mr. Palmer sold the first lot to Mr. Ellery Cross of New York. Caretaker Aleck Ball and family from King George County occupied the

A pitcher discovered at the Corotoman site. Notice the full mid length crack. *Courtesy of Virginia Department of Historic Resources.*

nearby "Spinning House." In 1974 the remaining six and one-half acres of the Corotoman site with its 1,000 feet facing the Rappahannock River was protected by an "open space easement." Lovely waterfront homes and cottages eventually built alongside the riverbank perimeters gave the former plantation site a large berth.

Tall grasses swayed nonchalantly above the ground upon a summer evening visit to the Corotoman dig. The outlined bricked formation detailing the perimeter of the Carter house was still visible. The official dig site had been filled in with sand and a layered soil surface for protection. Nearby the tunnel extending to the river waters had been enclosed and capped by a wooden structure. A short distance beyond the site, the Rappahannock River waters lapped and rolled against the 1,000 tons of granite placed by the English to serve as a protective breakwater. Corotoman is a serene and special place in Weems to reflect upon. People who lived well and labored long have come to rest there. Secrets and dreams remain intact, well before our time.

Top left - Glass bottle stopper used at the Carter mansion. Top right - Corotoman wine bottles with stamped RC. *Courtesy of Virginia Department of Historic Resources.*

A vista water view of the Corotoman excavation site in progress. *Courtesy of Virginia Department of Historic Resources.*

A close up of the entrance to Weems Wharf during the early 1900s.
Originally known as Sloop Landing Point, the site was named after the
Weems Steamboat Company in 1886. *Courtesy of Margery Nea.*

PART II

RENEWAL OF THE LAND

SLOOP LANDING POINT

The waters of Carters Creek lapped lazily upon the land known to folks who lived about as Sloop Landing Point. In the early to mid 1800s the point would be a fairly quiet and unassuming place destined to hold fast an historical marker. For it was here that "King" Carter had successfully run his sloops full of goods in and out of the creek to the river and beyond to England. He would be laid to rest at Christ Church some 154 years before this landing would reach out to embrace its fullness once again. At that time only a few houses dotted the landscape. The inhabitants within no doubt enjoyed the "gentle" farming aspect of their lives with accompanying seafood bounty. Yet the land was about to be roused again through a series of rapidly unfolding events beyond which they never could have imagined.

JOHN ARMISTEAD PALMER
1846-1929

On August 6, 1886 the heirs of George Kern (Corotoman Estate) sold 3 acres, more or less, of Sloop Landing Point "with the bottom of Carter's Cove" to John A. Palmer. He and the agent/attorney in this transaction, Richard C. Sydner, would actively continue to sell Kern's Corotoman lots for the next twenty years. This transfer land purchase to Mr. Palmer would "...run from Cedar Lane to Carters Cove and by water line of Loomis and Cross, south and east by the waters of Carters Creek and the mouth line of Carters Cove...."

This transaction highlighted John A. Palmer as no stranger to the virtue, value, and potential of historical land. Indeed, he had been born at "Clifton" (located "adjacent to...Lancaster County line...town limits of Kilmarnock)" on January 21, 1846, and situated within Landon Carter's (son of Robert "King" Carter) massive land inheritance in 1732. In turn, John's father had purchased "Clifton" in 1843 from Anne Carter Tomlin, Landon Carter's direct descendant. Now it was John's turn, and, at 21 years of age, he received 312 acres, more or less, of a new home known as "Upper Clifton." At age 40, he practiced law in Lancaster and Northumberland County, maintained a keen interest in farming and agriculture, and contributed significantly to "civic, community, and social affairs." He was ever on the alert for a good business deal.

Could it be that the industrious John Palmer envisioned a business perspective with potential for market growth at Sloop Landing Point? At this moment, one can merely speculate if he possessed a long term vision for the area. He began by constructing a wood framed store operated by John B. Noblett and later his son, Albert. In all probability, this venture was profitable. But how to capture a great link for the commerce and trade that was bound to blossom on this water site? This was John Palmer's dilemma. Enter the steamboat.

Officially, the steamboat and its transport abilities (1813-1937) made a pronounced effect on the lives and livelihoods of people

Left - An unidentified steamer approaches Weems Wharf in the early 1900s. *Dr. Henry J. Edmonds photo collection.*

throughout the Chesapeake Bay, Patuxent, Potomac, and Rappahannock Rivers. Delivering dry goods, livestock, produce, mail, and travel passengers, the Weems Steamboat Company had an unmistakable visibility. Its shrill whistle, puffing black coal smoke, and spewing cinders accompanied by the ringing "all ashore who's going ashore" cry, was enthusiastically welcomed by growing enterprises along the small town shorelines. How keenly profitable it would be to load your homegrown vegetables, watermelons, tomatoes, crabs, oysters, livestock, and, in time, even your mail aboard this vessel for sales and distribution in cities such as Baltimore and Norfolk. A wharf across from Carters Creek already had a steamboat stop in what is now called Irvington in working order. It seemed to be doing a healthy business. Why not create another stop? Mr. Palmer's mode of persuasion was not lost on the operative Weems Steamboat Line and its "Mason L. Weems" steamboat. If the company would consider a Sloop Landing Point stop, Palmer offered to build the wharf and name it "Weems" in honor of the line. The bargain was sealed. In 1886 "Weems Wharf" made its land name debut. It has remained so until present day.

Four years later (1890), John Palmer would sell his one-half interest from the same lot parcel ("with the bottom of Carters Cove

Weems Wharf postcard dated 1912 with predominance given to its water entrance. The beacon was situated in the Rappahannock River in 1902. Channel dredging occurred three years later. *Courtesy of Margery Nea.*

properly abreast of said lot") to W. A. and S. W. Eubank, respected and astute businessmen from Kilmarnock. The "Mason L. Weems," with its lavish staterooms and stained-glass skylights was off the circuit by 1890. Steamboats continued to play a major role at Weems Wharf for many years thereafter.

A section of Weems Wharf steamboat dockside is shown during the winter of 1908. The large mounds of oyster shells indicate a prosperous season. *Used with permission by the Mariner's Museum.*

A VISIT TO CLIFTON
2013

Summer morning sunlight flooded across the manicured grounds of "Clifton" as John Palmer's great-grandson, Eugene "Bud" Hudnall, opened the front door and invited me inside. Now a designated registered national historic landmark, meeting the criteria of a mason's mark with three prints on the brick, he purchased the house and furnishings in 2000. Restoration and livability was top priority. He spends six months out of every year enjoying the "footprint" his great-grandfather left behind.

"Clifton," home of John Armistead Palmer (1848 - 1929) is a registered national historic landmark located on the outskirts of Kilmarnock, Virginia. *Author's photo.*

We spoke about the numerous accomplishments of this gentleman who practiced as an attorney in Kilmarnock, founded the Holly Ball, became editor of Kilmarnock's first newspaper (The Chesapeake Watchmen,) and incorporated the Northern Neck Railroad and Transportation Company. Most significant to our Weems story, we speculated that John Palmer's meeting with Henry Williams (President of the Weems Steamboat Line) in 1895 was inclusive of the open water capabilities that steamboats could transport produce efficiently from Northern Neck Virginia areas to Maryland and other markets. How the ears of the four shippers of produce on the wharf must have perked up. At John Palmer's passing in 1929, Oscar Dameron (Weems Wharf retailer) was one of the seven honorary pallbearers at his funeral.

Right - Among his prolific contributions to community and civic matters, John Palmer pioneered the Holly Ball crowning Miss Cora Brent in 1895 with a sprig of holly from a tree growing in his field. The tradition continues with proceeds from the Tidewater Foundation supporting "cultural enrichment and education" in the Northern Neck/Tidewater areas. *Author's photo.*

"Bud" shared his pride in the devoted legacy of supporting Catholicism in the area with his great-grandfather's land donation (in 1885) of the present day St. Frances Catholic Chapel site in Kilmarnock. The brick church and rectory were also part of Clifton. A portion of the house tour highlighted the Palmer family's religious life with a sideboard used as an altar and a high back chair where confession was held. Levity is added with a vision of the Palmers removing folding tables and dancing in the main area alongside stacked wood and hanging sides of ham.

Totally functional, the wonderfully furnished home has five bedrooms, two baths, and a comfortable 2001 restored wing where the family spends a great deal of their time. With configurations in place, the first floor dining room is now the master bedroom, a window and closet has become a bathroom, and a utility room has morphed into a bright and airy compact kitchen. One can't help but feel the attention to detail so evident in Clifton's restoration.

"Clifton" provides an elegant warmth suggestive of years of treasured tradition. *Author's photo.*

We ended the tour in the front foyer flanked by two elegant staircases alluding to the division of female and male bedrooms above. It was here that bride, Miss Ada Katherine Kelly, walked down the stairs to marry her perspective husband, Alfred Armstead Hudnall, Sr. She was a master

teacher in the Lancaster County school system for thirty-five years molding many fortunate pupils in Kilmarnock, Weems, and surrounding areas.

Ada K. Hudnall, teacher and friend. *Author's photo.*

Impressive separate stairways lead to traditional ladies and gentlemen bedroom quarters above. *Author's photo.*

DAMERON BROTHERS
JAMES OSCAR DAMERON   WALTON A. DAMERON
1866-1949   1859-1940

With the Weems population standing at 45 in 1895 and expanding to 300 people in a 1911 census, the area seemed to be highly regarded as attractive for families to settle and work upon. Two perceptively astute brothers, Walton Alexander and James Oscar Dameron, sailing from Kinsale in search of land/business prospects in 1889, instantly sensed the potential. Their planned journey from the Potomac River to the Chesapeake Bay and into the Rappahannock River to search for a business site ended at Carters Creek. Here, they decided without a doubt, was their preferred opportunity to settle, set up a business, and eventually raise their families.

There are no written records of James and Walton's (sons of James Albert and Mary Courtney Dameron) first impressions and discussions as they surveyed Weems Wharf. However, we may be able to surmise through their "mind's eye" how the wharf site and extended land appeared at that time. Foremost, the abundant richness of the land and beauty of the water was easily evident. The drawing factor may well have been its perfect simplicity and welcoming nature. A fairly narrow landing wharf site (wide enough for two cars to pass through in later years) jutted out directly into Carters Creek and the Rappahannock River. Here goods were conducted and transfers were made. A fee known as "wharfage" was also paid. A man and his wife lived in a combination home/restaurant nearby and prepared food for the deck hands. Two retail and goods stores were built partially over the water. One was operated by John Noblett (store owned by John Palmer), and the other by Samuel C. Thomas and son George. A post office was operative within (in all probability) the Noblett store. Two canning factories, a blacksmith shop, several bar-rooms, and a railway rounded out Weems Wharf productivity.

Had they been given a seasonal report, the Dameron brothers would have nodded approvingly and studied with great interest the steady businesses operating a bit inland and to the left of Weems Wharf. In the spring, a fish packing business had materialized with the salted wares packed in 10 x 20 foot vats and shipped possibly to Baltimore. Summer warmth produced healthy tomato plants that after picking headed to the canneries in horse drawn wagons to be peeled and canned for buyers. Cold weather found oystermen utilizing their shaft tong techniques to bring in bushels of oysters to be shucked and packaged by the "locals," and later distributed to consumers. Industry was evident. Here the brothers could enter onto the "ground floor" of the heart of a new community and make an impact. They must have readily agreed to stay on.

Within the two dozen or so homes that comprised the Weems area, Walton and James surely noticed the lovely eye-catching and spacious twenty-three room hill home of Evan Owen that overlooked Carters Creek. Home ownership progression has been noted as that of Evan Owen, Charles Neuter, Oscar Ashburn, Marion Ashburn, and E. L. Webb. Owen had already established a thriving railway business as well as an oyster shucking house by 1901. A notation in the 1900 newspaper, "The Virginia Citizen," describes a #2 Marine Railway that was operative by Owen and "prepared to give prompt dispatch."   S. C. Thomas ran the tomato cannery nearby. In March of that year it was noted that a Harding Brothers mercantile business with Meredith Bonner as clerk was offering retail services. Residences were that of the families of S. C. Thomas, Peter

Eilskov (Denmark native), Lawson Winstead, and A. A. Ball among others. There may have been movement on the lot sales in Weems of the George Kerns property as well.

A 1906 view of Weems Wharf. From left to right - W. A. Dameron & Bro store, large storage house, crab house, Owen's shipyard, and Evan Owen's hilltop residence. *Postcard courtesy of Margery Nea.*

The Weems Wharf portrait was steadily brush stroked in succeeding years. An article entitled "A History of Weems" as published in The Virginia Citizen/Irvington, Virginia by "Coon" bears sharing in part "...other successful enterprises (include) a steam sectional railway, planning mills, saw mill, two blacksmith and machine shops, two canning factories, three oyster shucking houses, two carriage and horseshoe shops, one brick kiln, wood and coal yard, four large oyster buyers and shippers, four large produce shippers, post office, two churches, one public school, and several mercantile establishments...a more thriving village cannot be found." This settlement, of which Oscar and Walton steadily became a part, must have confirmed their thoughts as to the possibilities that lay before them on Weems Wharf. They immediately purchased the existing store there (built by John Palmer and operated by John B. Noblett) and began their business venture buying out W. A. Ashburn's full stock by 1902.

Again, commentary printed throughout The Virginia Citizen (first paper in Lancaster County) in the early 1900s

Built by John Palmer in 1889, the W. A. Dameron & Bro store was initially operated by John B. Noblett followed by his son Albert Noblett. The
framed house on the right was used as both a Sunday school teaching
area and an overnight pastor's dwelling. *Courtesy of Rappahannock Record.
Published in 1972.*

share interesting insights as to the growth of the Dameron retail
and wholesale business. In 1901, for example, the steamboat wharf
was being "shored up" with stronger timbers. A record steamer
shipment of over 1,000 gallons of oysters in one day was transacted
through the Dameron store only a year later. Another meaningful
statistic highlighting the harmony between the water bounty and
business ability saw the Damerons working for three days to fill a
Thanksgiving order of 3,000 gallons of oysters..."the largest shipment ever made in the lower Rappahannock." One year later The
Virginia Citizen cited 100,000 bushel of oysters were produced an-
nually from the waters. In May of 1905 the brothers built housing
on the flats to store gasoline. Weems Wharf was on the move.

In August of 1909 an advertisement for a Dameron & Brother
store clerk stated: "...a worker must be sober and industrious...one
of some experience preferred." No doubt this individual would be
selling "a selected Christmas stock" to customers that Oscar Dameron had purchased first-hand from his Baltimore visit. That same
year a new wharf replaced the old. News in 1910 related the up-to-

One of the earliest views of Weems Wharf in the 1890s. In all probability, the small building is the office/waiting room for the steamboat. Years later this point of land will be "built up" with oyster shells dramatically changing its appearance. *Courtesy of Chip Woodson.*

date new Dameron tomato canning factory. A Weems commentary section sized up the brothers most accurately. "They are progressive men and when there is anything at all 'doing', they are apt to be found doing their share." The developmental phase of Weems Wharf had been placed in good hands.

Another significant "beginning" was taking place on September 8th of 1889...the founding of Weems Campbell Memorial Presbyterian Church. It seems plausible that a short period of time elapsed between the Dameron brother's arrival and the organization of the church. It is noted that among the first congregational roster of twelve people the name of Mrs. Walton Dameron appears. Both Dameron fami-

W. A. Dameron & Bro store in 1909. Notice the store addition to the left as well as the extended wharf walkway protruding over the water. *Courtesy of Margery Nea.*

lies would become significantly involved in the spiritual life of the community through their ongoing church involvement.

On September 7, 1893, John A. Palmer and wife, Louisa Jane, sold "1/4 undivided interest in Weems Wharf at the mouth of Carter's Creek, together with appurtenances, etc." to W. A. and J. O. Dameron. Sixteen years later (January 1, 1909) W. A. and S. W. Eubank and wives sold to the brothers "…1/2 interest in same…at Weems Wharf, said to contain three acres, more or less, bounded on the north by the main road leading to Weems Wharf until some turns, thence by land of Evan Owens to Carters Creek, on east and south by Carters Creek and on west by the land owned by W. A. Dameron on which said land rest the foot of Weems Wharf, together with their interest in the wharf and all houses, stores, shops, etc.…." Within a four year span Walton and James Dameron had fulfilled, if you will, their "dream" of establishing a business base, developing family connectedness, and pursuing spiritual growth on a land of their choosing.

Walton Alexander Dameron, the eldest brother, had previously married Helena Kleefisch (1861-1927) when he joined Oscar in temporary living quarters above the general store. They later adopted a daughter named Cornella (Toddy). The emboldened sign painted on the store's water and land side, W. A. Dameron & Bro, was fast becoming a Weems Wharf landmark. Eventually, the brothers built houses directly across from one another "up the hill" from their water enclosed business ventures. With building modifications and several owners over the years, the Walton home still stands today with the original iron fence bordering the sidewalk. A mere few steps across the asphalt road, Oscar's home was beautifully restored in 2016. Serving three generations of his family, this lovely and special homestead continues to offer the pleasures of life in the Weems area.

At 81 years of age, Walton, known throughout the Northern Neck for his business and social involvement, passed away with services held at Campbell Memorial Presbyterian Church on October 1,

Dameron - "Sloop Landing Point"

R. C. Snyder, agent and attorney-in fact for
Caroline W. Kern, widow or
George P. Kern, deceased,
Bertha K. Newbold and husband,
Maria K. Simpson and husband,
Edith Kern and Charlotte Kern
to
John A. Palmer

Dated: August 6, 1886
Recorded:
Deed Book 46, page 76

Lot of land and creek bottom to-wit: Lot known as "Sloop Landing Point" with the bottom of Carters Cove, properly abreast of said lot...said lot contains 3 acres, more or less... bounded as follows:

> West by the lot sold Mrs. E. Rayner and now owned by J. W. Mitchell, north by the road laid out by John A. Palmer, Commissioner of Corrotoman Estate, running from Cedar Lane to Carters Cove and by the water line of Loomis and Cross, south and east by the waters of Carters Creek and the mouth line of Carters Cove...

John A. Palmer and
Louisa Jane, his wife
to
W. A. Eubank and S. W. Eubank,
Eubank and Bro.

Dated: August 16, 1890
Recorded:
Deed Book 47, page 339

...1/2 interest in lot of land and creek bottom known as "Sloop Landing Point: with the bottom of Carters Cove properly abreast of said lot (same description as Deed Book 46, page 76).

John A. Palmer and
Louisa Jane, his wife
to
W. A. Dameron and
J. O. Dameron

Dated: September 7, 1893
Recorded:
Deed Book 48, page 204

...1/4 undivided interest in Weems Wharf at the mouth of Carters Creek, together with appurtenances, etc., in fee simple...

Progression of "Sloop Landing Point" Deeds of Conveyance in 1886, 1890, and 1893. *Courtesy of Margery Nea.*

Walton Dameron original homesite in late 1800s. *Courtesy of Margery Nea.*

Oscar Dameron original homesite in late 1890s. *Courtesy of Margery Nea.*

The close proximity of the Dameron households in Weems promoted family togetherness.

1940. There followed in the Rappahannock Record, among other tributes, an appreciation submitted by Thomas Sanders of Weems. Mr. W. A. Dameron "...kind, possessing a loving disposition...extending a helping hand to those in need...took time to listen and advise...considerate of his employees...possessed a pleasing personality and a loving Christian heart...an emptiness in our lives and our hearts that will be hard to fill...."

After Walton passed away, Oscar continued the retail business at Weems Wharf. He fulfilled the mission for nine years working diligently to keep a "principled merchant-industrial working enterprise" servicing the Weems area and beyond. His extended activities were inclusive of Weems postmaster (1914-1940), president of the Northern Neck Mutual Fire Association of Irvington, elder and superintendent of Sunday School at Campbell Memorial Presbyterian Church, and a 50 year member of the Masonic Order. In failing health, he retreated to the comfort of the front hall parlor of the family home and with his family in attendance went to rest on the

On page 61 of the Dameron Store Day Book of cash sales an entry notes..."September 30 closed...W. A. Dameron died Sunday 8 p.m. September 29, 1940." *Courtesy of Margery Nea.*

Right - This was the Carters Creek view the Weems residents enjoyed in the early 1900s. Postcard dated January 23, 1908 reads..."Am here tonight. Terrible storm blowing and all the boats have put in the harbor for safety. This is all ice and snow now. L.H.M." *Postcard courtesy of Margery Nea.*

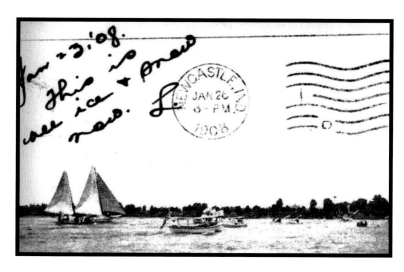

land he had loved so well. His obituary in the *Rappahannock Record* had this to record "...a gentlemen of the old school, always friendly and interested in his fellowman, made many friends in his 60 years as a merchant at Weems." The North Weems section of the paper added their condolences. "We wish to express our

Fashionable skaters enjoying a frozen Carters Creek in the 1900s. *Courtesy of Margery Nea.*

sorrow at the passing of our good friend Mr. Oscar Dameron. He was known and loved by many. It will be a long time before we forget him and his friendly manner."

In a Campbell Memorial Presbyterian Church testimony written a year later the session members (Albert C. Daniel, E. H. Webb, G. A. Pembroke, W. F. Ward, Wilbur Haydon, Leon H. Hayden, and moderator Richard Taylor with clerk Harry W. Ball) penned in part..."Whereas, his whole manner of life, both in the Church and the community in which he lived, was exemplary as a servant of the Church, father in the home, and one who was zealous in good works...he was held in highest esteem by persons in all stations of life...."

The sentiments conveyed about Walton and Oscar Dameron hold fast within the context of the development and social reminiscence of Weems. The brothers were simply an exemplary team that brought the land to life. They maintained a strong sense of the inner-workings of a community truly valuing the well being of others during their life span. They appreciated and loved the contours of the land in Weems, and they successfully fashioned their lives and the lives of their families to accommodate both.

MARGARET BOLLING JONES DAMERON
1877-1966

On June 26, 1902 the wedding of James Oscar Dameron to Margaret Bolling Jones took place at Concord Presbyterian Church in Brunswick County, Virginia. The bride's father, Reverend Thomas Thweatt Jones, who served as pastor there for thirty years, conducted the ceremony "most impressively" a news article revealed. The bride and groom would be lauded respectively as a "beautiful and accomplished daughter" and "a popular young merchant of Weems." Indeed, Margaret had already distinguished herself in a series of teaching fields--music instructor at the Chesapeake Academy in Irvington, teacher at her mother's boarding school at Sunny Side as well as a girl's boarding school in Clarksville, and private tutor of a young girl in Orange, Texas. Already prominent in business circles in Weems, James Oscar had previously been a highly regarded salesman for James Bailey & Son of Baltimore.

The story Mrs. Dameron later recounted in a Chesapeake Academy article bears repeating. "I was a student at Fredericksburg College when I was asked whether I would be interested in teaching music at Chesapeake Academy after my graduation. I was from Dinwiddie and wanted to see the Irvington area about which I had heard

Mr. and Mrs. James Oscar Dameron pose for their official wedding portrait in 1902. The bride would call Weems home for sixty-four years. *Courtesy of Margery Nea.*

so much. I accepted the offer and I am glad I did. I think it was the happiest year of my life. One evening, at a social gathering just a short walk from the Academy, I encountered and was favorably impressed by a young gentleman from nearby Weems. He and his brother were in the mercantile business. His name was J. O. Dameron, a name I was to assume later on and my permanent home on the beautiful promontory facing Carters Creek and Rappahannock River where the bay steamboats landed for many years. It was a happy place, and I will forever remember it that way."

Enveloped within a family legacy of ministers, missionaries, teachers, and doctors, Miss Margaret Bolling Jones was the 9th of 11 children born at Sunnyside, Dinwiddie County. Her mother, Margaret Ann, ran a private boarding school. Her father, Thomas Thweatt, was a country minister, circuit rider preacher in five rural Presbyterian churches, and a State Senator. All of their children received a college education, returning to teach, and in turn assisting their siblings with financial expenses. Their petite and lively daughter, Margaret, followed the family's high regard for education and service from the onset. Her formative educational path flowed through attendance at the Cincinnati College of Music and later to advanced studies at Frederick Collegiate Institute (now Mary Washington College.)

With her husband by her side, Margaret undoubtedly embraced Weems on sight and relished the water view from the comfortable two-storied frame home her husband had built at the top of the wharf hill. She set about establishing an atmosphere of nurturing and teaching coupled with extraordinary kindness. Morning and evening prayers were

Right - Miss Margaret Bolling, daughter of Dr. and Mrs. Thomas Thweatt Jones, was an accomplished young lady whose teaching abilities touched the hearts of the Weems community. *Courtesy of Margery Nea.*

faithfully carried out. Scriptures were read and studied. Everyone was truly welcome at the Dameron hearth. All who knew her returned the love she freely gave in like kind.

When early on her husband hired migrant laborers to work in the canning and oyster businesses, Margaret promptly set out teaching their children Bible stories and hymns on Sunday afternoons. Adhering to her daily Presbyterian upbringing, she worked in every facet of the Weems church inclusive of both children and adults. Teaching, leading, organizing, and helping became her desire. Impressions are lasting. I still recall the lessons Mrs. Dameron taught our small Sunday school group in the furnace room of the basement of the church as well as her guidance with the Christian Endeavor youth group. Always evident in her teaching was a measured patience and sweetness that naturally made one aware of the importance of developing a "sense of service" to family, friends, and anyone in need.

Margaret and James Dameron led their lives with extraordinary traits of kindness, generosity and consideration of others. *Courtesy of Margery Nea.*

A presentation was made to Margaret Jones Dameron by Mrs. William L. Ball and Ida Verlander in the form of an Honorary Life Membership by the Women of the Campbell Memorial Presbyterian Church for "work done in the Sunday School, church...ever since she came here in 1902 as the bride of James Oscar Dameron." The words "ever since she came here" strike a memorable chord of a young woman's continual devotion to the life of the Weems community, a rare attribute.

MARGARET FITZGERALD DAMERON EDMONDS
1909-1999
MARY MEADE DAMERON WOODSON
1912-2000

Two daughters and a son were born to Margaret and Oscar in the Weems house--Margery Fitzgerald, James Oscar, and Mary Meade. James Oscar passed away at six years of age at the homestead from complications of malaria. Early family pictures share a trio of children happily growing up in Weems. The Dameron home, shaded by trees alongside, and buffered by flowers, vegetable gardens, and crushed paths of oyster shells stood at the curved crest of the hill that led to Weems Wharf. Its expansive vista of Carters Creek and the Rappahannock River swept down to catch the activity of the people and boats below. Like an ever moving cogwheel, there was always something going on from morning to night. Midday dinner would often be prepared for business associates or for folks stopping by from the steamboat. Sunday dinners found the local minister and his family at the spacious food laden table. In and around the home for the immediate family's well being or on special occasions, Jan and Brunie prepared food and lived on the premises. Charles Henry planted and tended to the garden and the surrounding property. They were all an integral part of the Dameron family's daily existence.

Both girls were taught at home in the tradition of their mother's upbringing. Their teachers were part of the live-in household and responsible for both an academic and manner/etiquette styled curriculum. Governess Miss Fannie Hull Robinson (later organizer of Ferrum Training School now Ferrum University) instructed the girls until Irvington School became their 5-8th grade learning base. Later, Margery obtained her undergraduate degree from William & Mary in Williamsburg, Virginia, with Mary Meade graduating from Peace College in Raleigh, North Carolina. Interestingly, the sisters returned to Weems at different intervals to work for a time at their father's general store where the post office was located behind a cordoned off section in the back. After her father's passing, Mar-

Right - James Oscar, Margery, and Mary Meade Dameron in an official sibling pose in the early 1900s. *Courtesy of Margery Nea.*

Left - Mary Meade, Margery, and James Oscar Dameron (left to right) join in play on the Dameron's front porch. *Courtesy of Margery Nea.*

Right - Dameron children cuddle puppies on parent's lawn in Weems. *Courtesy of Margery Nea.*

Margery, Mary Meade, and James Oscar are photographed in front of a thick hedge row bordering the Dameron property. *Courtesy of Margery Nea.*

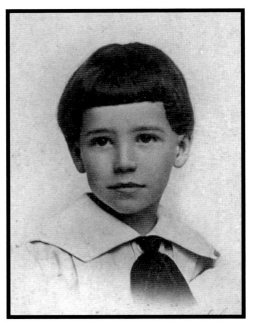

James Oscar Dameron at age six. *Courtesy of Margery Nea.*

gery acted as Postmaster until a permanent replacement could be found.

Mary Meade married Benjamin Felix Woodson on August 26, 1939, at Christ Church in Lancaster County. They had two children, Margaret Kathryn and Benjamin Meade. Mary Meade would twice make her home in Weems living at the Dameron house when her husband served in the Pacific during World War II and later in retirement. The couple built a new home on the lower slope just down from the original W. A. Dameron homestead overlooking the Rappahannock River. They eagerly joined the Weems community and participated in the Weems Presbyterian Church for the remainder of their lives. Mary Meade was a welcomed leader and teacher. Ben was both a deacon and an elder serving also in Interface Ministries and as Director of the Salvation Army.

Jan and Brunie worked for many years in the Dameron household as cook and handyman. *Courtesy of Margery Nea.*

Mary Meade and Ben Woodson pose with their daughter, Margery, in front of the Dameron homeplace. *Courtesy of Margery Nea.*

Christmas greetings from Mary Meade, Ben, Margery, and Chip Woodson. *Dr. and Mrs. Henry J. Edmonds photo collection.*

On January 18, 1947, Margery became the bride of Henry Jeter Edmonds III, a dentist and resident of Kilmarnock, Virginia. Given in marriage by her father, her sister stood by as Matron of Honor with "little Miss Margery Woodson, the bride's niece, as flower girl." Her mother-in-law, Mrs. Sarah Frances Cox Edmonds, lived with the couple until her death in 1973. Margery and Henry had one son, Henry Jeter IV, born on November 6, 1948. He lived at the family home "Chase Manor" in Kilmarnock for 66 years. During an Honorary Life Membership given to Margery by the Weems Presbyterian Women of the Church, Mrs. Rufus Rankin had this to say "...following her Mother's example Margery became a dedicated church worker. Through the years she served in almost every capacity of the church...circle chairmen, President of the Women of the Church, church school teacher, church choir director, and organist."

Miss Margery Dameron in 1942...five years before her marriage to Dr. Henry Jeter Edmonds III. *Courtesy of Margery Nea.*

A highly respected dentist in the local area, Henry J. Edmonds also served in the United States Army during World War II. *Courtesy of Dr. and Mrs. Henry J. Edmonds photo collection.*

Margery and Mary Meade maintained a special sisterly bond. As their paths began and were similarly woven in life, so did their passing enjoin at life's end. Now widows and with one sister coming to the aid of the other during illness, they lived together for a time at the Woodson house on the Weems hill. Eventually, personalized nursing care was provided for both until their relocation for a short time at Rappahannock Westminister-Canterbury. Within weeks apart, the sisters passed into the faith they had kept so well, and back to the Weems land they had loved.

A GENERATIONAL WEDDING GOWN

When Margaret Bolling said "I do" on June 26, 1902, to Oscar James Dameron at the Concord Presbyterian Church in Brunswick County, Virginia, she wore a full length embroidered Japanese silk gown interwoven over brocaded satin. It was hand sewn by her sisters. Given away by her brother, Dr. John Bolling Jones, a pearl ornament clasped the bride's veil that flowed over a shower bouquet of hand held roses. With good wishes, old shoes, and a shower of rice the newlyweds left on a north-bound train for Atlantic City.

Dr. Henry J. and Margery Edmonds and son Jete. *Courtesy of Dr. and Mrs. Henry J. Edmonds photo collection.*

Mary Meade and Margery Dameron on the front porch steps. *Courtesy of Margery Nea.*

Their future home would be in Weems, Virginia. This treasured gown was destined to be worn by a daughter, Mary Meade; a grand-daughter, Margaret Kathryn; and a great-granddaughter, Courtney Randolph. The gown has held fast through four generations.

Above left - Mary Meade Dameron Woodson - Married to Benjamin Felix Woodson on August 28, 1939, in Christ Church, Lancaster County, Virginia, Mary Meade's mother's gown was accessorized by a veil flowing with a coronet of orange blossoms that tapered to the end of a long train. She carried a Colonial bouquet of stephanotis, baby's breath, and Bride roses. Her reception was held in Weems, Virginia. Above right - Margaret Kathryn Woodson Nea - Married to George Andrew Nea, Jr., on June 13, 1964, in the Emmanuel Episcopal Church in Richmond, Virginia, Margery's grandmother's gown was accessorized by a veil of Brussels lace and a single strand of pearls. Her bouquet was of orchids, stephanotis and variegated ivy. . *Courtesy of Margery Nea.*

Above left - Courtney Randolph Nea Jones - Married to Thomas Shipley Jones on June 29, 1996, in St. Paul's Episcopal Church, Courtney's great-grandmother's gown of Japanese silk over brocaded satin was accessorized by her mother's Brussels lace veil. Above right - Anne Meade Nea Watkins - Anne Meade was married at Christ Church, Lancaster County, Virginia on August 3, 1996 to Bradley Johnson Watkins. Wearing her own gown design, she followed family tradition with a rehearsal dinner at the Dameron home in Weems. *Courtesy of Margery Nea.*

W. A DAMERON & BRO STORE
1889-1958

Renewing an acquaintanceship with the Dameron's grand-daughter, Margaret Kathryn Woodson Nea, has afforded insights of a young girl frequenting Weems as well as those of a woman who understood her grandparent's life and perspective. Her reminiscences of visiting her grandparent's home every summer and living there while her father was in the service are very genuine. She was fascinated with the opportunities to garden, crab, fish, and go boating. A great deal of Margery's childhood interests focused on the general store with its bounty of groceries (fresh and canned), meats, eggs, barrels of fish, boxes of shoes, medical items, boots, oil cloth, shirts, pants, horse collars, soap, brooms, and litters of kittens in the attic.

Margery and Grandfather Dameron in 1943. *Courtesy of Margery Nea.*

After purchasing the store in 1889, the Dameron brothers doubled its size to accommodate a growing consumer demand. A huge wood stove added warmth to the rough hewn interior. The rear portion of the store extended over the Rappahannock River water. This was the best place of all. To walk across the wide wooden creaking planks and see the water lapping against the underside seemed mystical. No useful item seemed to be overlooked in the store's huge and revolving inventory. Hanging high on nails, the watermen's display attire included a large selection of oil skins/slickers, rubber boots, waders, crab nets, buckets, and skiff scoopers. Customers could actually tie their skiffs behind the store and simply wade in to make their purchases. Two 1905 advertisements in The Virginia Citizen reminded readers that Dameron's store could improve their home roofing needs with in-stock four, five, or six inch cypress shingles. For one's indigestion

New Dameron store addition offered customers a berth for their skiff as they shopped. *Courtesy of Margery Nea.*

a bottle of Kellum's cure was available for only a dollar. One could also post and receive mail, purchase postal stamps, and send packaged goods with complete confidence. While this all-purpose country store operated an efficient supply and demand business, its proprietors also projected high standards of fairness and trustworthiness to everyone.

A 1947 view of W. A. Dameron & Bro store with an Esso gasoline pump addition. Notice the structure in the far right background that housed overnight pastors. *Courtesy of Margery Nea.*

James Oscar Dameron enjoys a stroll with Granddaughter, Margery, on Weems Wharf. *Courtesy of Margery Nea.*

The store survived two major storms. In 1933 "The Storm of August" sent the store awash with destroyed merchandise inventory and washed off food labels floating about. Yet it would be "Hurricane Hazel" that struck the east coast on October 15, 1954, with a $15 million dollar and 98 per mile wind wallop that nearly brought it down. The tide reached the top of the hill at Weems Wharf. Everyone scrambled to secure their boats. Just as the "eye" was passing over, Jack Jones (Weems youngster) rushed behind Harry Ball's property to secure the family boat. As he passed the Ball's chicken house, the hurricane force winds lifted the structure off its foundation and dropped it directly on the path he had just taken. Just ten paces forward had made the difference between life and death.

Dameron's store is hit hard with "Hurricane Hazel" tide surges in 1954. *Courtesy of Chip Woodson.*

Sadly, in 1958, a raging fire rapidly spread throughout the store one early morning despite the efforts of the local firemen. With pumps aimed at its sides and water freezing on the firemen's coats, W. A. Dameron & Bro was reduced to charred cinders. W. H. Patterson was store operator at that time and lived in the Dameron home during the winter months. Again, Jack Jones vividly re-calls the moment. "It was mid-December and the sight of those foot long icicles hanging from the electric wires with fire licking all around them is still as vivid today as it was then." A stalwart Weems landmark was gone.

The White Stone Fire Department answered the early morning call in 1958 in an attempt to save the Dameron Store. *Courtesy of the Rappahannock Record.*

Left - Remaining smoldering rem-nants of W A. Dameron & Bro store in Weems, Virginia. *Courtesy of Chip Woodson.*

Amazingly, the Dameron store ownership had spanned sixty-nine years. The Weems community keenly felt its extinction for, in addition to the convenient wares, it had also provided a wel-coming and pleasant place for friends to meet and discuss daily happenings. Time well spent. Today, two distinct original oyster housing imprints are visible on Weems Wharf. W. A. Dameron & Bro store site markings vanished many years ago.

A 1912 postcard view of W. A. Dameron & Bro store, cannery
and warehouse, Weems, Virginia. *Courtesy of Margery Nea.*

Margery will remind one that it was the "small things" that mattered so much during her Weems visits. Listening to her grandmother's stories about her youth, gathering eggs from the hen's nest, and sifting through the corn and grain bins were favorite pastimes. Years before her mother and aunt would describe their shell tea parties at the beach with clover chains hanging around their necks. In turn, Margery led her daughters, Courtney and Anne Meade, to try their hand at picking apples and raspberries, fishing, crabbing and strolling about the Weems lane. Five generations of this family have frequented Weems, and still "hold fast" to the memory of their grandparents in that place. Her brother, Chip, still docks his boat at the wharf and spends some of his time living in Weems and enjoying life on the water.

"Our home at Weems has been a touchstone all of my life. There has never been a summer that I have not been there. My brother, Chip, our children, and our grandchildren love this place. For five generations, it has been, and continues to be, the place of our heart."

Margery Woodson Nea

Left - Margery and Mary Meade Dameron pose at Rappahannock River's edge. Francis Point is in the background. Right - Margery and Mary Meade Dameron at water's edge at entrance to Carters Creek in early 1900s. *Courtesy of Margery Nea.*

"Ever since I was an infant, Weems has been in my blood. It was a place for strong family love, filled with laughter, warmth, and adventures. As an adult these same qualities draw me back to the village I have come to treasure."

Chip Woodson

"For joyful hours on Carter's Creek and the Rappahannock River...for the hundreds of years of his family's contributions to this area and his deep connection to this place... we give you thanks, O God."

Litany of Celebration for Henry J. Edmonds IV
1948-2014

Weems tree bordered road leading past Oscar Dameron's house on the far left. Carters Creek can be seen in the distance. *Courtesy of Margery Nea.*

Two lane dirt road winds down to the Weems Wharf area. *Courtesy of Margery Nea.*

View from top of Weems Wharf overlooking Carters Creek. Frame house on the right built by the Damerons was occupied for a time by family helper Charles Henry Barnett and later rented by Carroll Davis and family. *Courtesy of Margery Nea.*

Tranquil beauty of Carters Creek cove with moored workboats. *Courtesy of Margery Nea.*

Notice the various types of watercraft in this 1937 photo at the mouth of Carters Creek. This may have been a fourth of July event. *Dr. and Mrs. Henry J. Edmonds photo collection.*

A close up view of the Weems Wharf extension in 1937. The steamboat docking area is positioned to the far left end of the wharf. The stone jetty on Francis Point is seen in the background. *Dr. and Mrs. Henry J. Edmonds photo collection.*

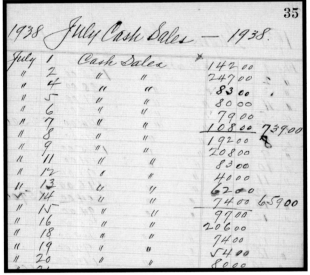

Left - The October 1937 "Order Book" listed number of oyster bushels purchased with payment made to shuckers on a monthly basis. An adding machine talley totaled each month. In some instances expenditures were noted to individuals. Above - A "Day Book" ledger of Dameron store cash sales from September of 1935 to December of 1943 shows increasing profitability. It is interesting to note every month's sales relative to productive weather permitting working months, local community activities, and seasonal/holiday times. *Courtesy of Margery Nea.*

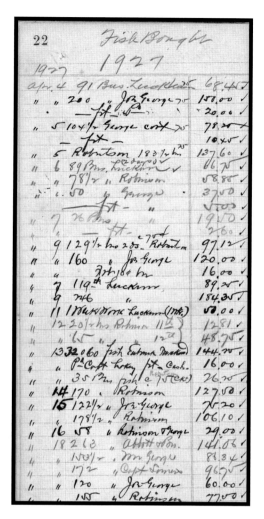

The April 27, 1927 "Fish Book" entered daily expenditures to individuals inclusive of sales and labor. Note postings of $141.06 to Abbott Brothers, $89.25 to Luckman, and $120.00 to Joe George. A study of companies involved reveals a widespread and positive business berth. *Courtesy of Margery Nea.*

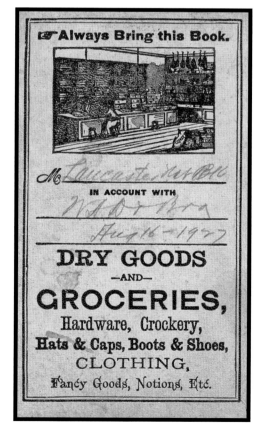

REGISTERED NO. 119

_____ Gals. Standards   _____ Gals. Selects

To _____

FROM

W. A. DAMERON & BRO.

Oyster Packers and Planters

Dealers in General Merchandise

Telephone via
Fredericksburg, Va.   **Weems, Va.**

Original Dameron store oyster packing and shipping label. *Courtesy of Margery Nea.*

Original Lancaster National Bank book for W. A. Dameron & Bro in August of 1927 noting daily deposits. *Courtesy of Margery Nea.*

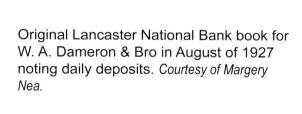

☞ **Always Bring this Book.**

IN ACCOUNT WITH

DRY GOODS

—AND—

GROCERIES,

Hardware, Crockery,

Hats & Caps, Boots & Shoes,

CLOTHING,

Fancy Goods, Notions, Etc.

TIDES THAT BIND ~ WEEMS VIRGINIA

Alice and Ben Winstead enjoy reviewing the Dameron store ledgers from 1933-1937. Itemized listings of goods purchased from the store's wide inventory are precisely hand written and posted to the customer's credit account. *Author's photo.*

Within Dameron's store a lucrative postal service accommodated the Weems community. This page from the 1937-38 record of C.O.D. parcels shows the regularity of packages received by local residents (George Abbott, Carroll H. Davis, U. Gaskins and Dr. J. W. McCrobie) from Maryland, Illinois and Ohio. *Courtesy of Margery Nea.*

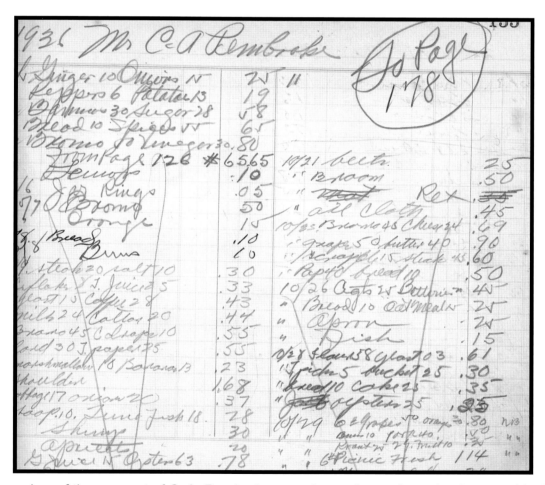

Note the dual business activities printed on this July 1939 merchandise check with J. O. Dameron's signature. *Courtesy of Margery Nea.*

A closer view of the account of C. A. Pembroke reveals goods purchased, prices, and in this case a continuance of shopping on page 178. Payment was accepted through cash, check, and even tokens from the cannery operation nearby. Purchased goods ranged from eggs, beef, corn, coffee, soap, oil cloth, chicken feed and lard to socks, stockings, brooms, putty, and nails. An entire section was devoted to watermen's gear. Groceries were delivered for a fee. *Courtesy of Margery Nea.*

With impressive Weems statistics of their own, Alice and Ben
Winstead have been residents for fifty-three years. Owing to a
chance meeting at Pouchet's Snack Bar in Kilmarnock in 1958,
they celebrated fifty-seven years of married life on June 12th.
They have been fully vested in the Weems community that they
call "wonderful." *Courtesy of Alice and Ben Winstead.*

Recently discovered in an attic, an early 1900s photograph of Dameron store workers taken at the end of Weems Wharf captures the immensity of a successful business
enterprise. Working within the framework of a compatible partnership, brothers James
Oscar and Walton A. Dameron efficiently managed the purchase and sale of Chesapeake Bay herring, hand packed tomatoes, Rappahannock River oysters (inclusive of
planting), and a full line general merchandise store. Noted for their honesty and fairness
in dealing with workers and customers as well, the Dameron brothers left a lasting legacy in the area. (In the far right front row, Walton A. Dameron appears in a three-piece
suit with a dog in front of him. James Oscar Dameron is seated to his right.) *Courtesy of
Margery Nea.*

With directions "empty contents as soon as opened," the "F.F.V." brand of Chesapeake Herring for a time was a product of W. A. Dameron & Bro in Weems, Virginia. *Courtesy of Margery Nea.*

Displaying a "F.F.V." colorful steamboat logo, tomatoes were hand packed and readily available on Weems Wharf. *Courtesy of Margery Nea.*

CHARLES HENRY BARNETT
1872-1964

It is recounted that a young man made his way from Essex County down to Lancaster County searching for work. It was 1892. After five years of farm labor, he looked to the possibilities of being hired on at Weems Wharf. He observed the W. A. Dameron & Bro business with its dual sea food plant ("about sixty shuckers") and retail store/post office operation. He stepped up and asked for a job. His first work offer was politely rejected by James Oscar Dameron, stating there just wasn't enough to do to hire him on. But the next morning the young man, identified as Charles Henry Barnett, was hoeing in the Dameron garden as if to say ...there is always work to be done. Just standing there nodding and smiling, he looked at Mr. Dameron, waiting for a second chance. He got it and stayed on for sixty-five years.

Always resourceful, Charles Henry early on helped to "catch and heave the lines" to manage the steamboat's arrival and departure at Weems Wharf. Interviewed years later in the *Richmond Times-Dispatch*, he had this to say about that moment. "This wharf used to be a lively place then. Yeah, they used to come in all hours of the day and night." Charles Henry's good nature and willingness to work quickly slotted him into a variety of jobs, oystering in the river, working on the fish boats, handling the mail, and working in the store...he seemed to be everywhere at once.

Charles Henry made his way into the heart and hearth of the Dameron families. Living in a two-storied framed building provided by them on the front edge of Walton Dameron's property, he rose early and attended to the jobs at hand.

Charles Henry used his many talents in and around the Dameron homestead. *Courtesy of Margery Nea.*

Charles Henry and Chip Woodson on front steps of Dameron's store in 1954. *Courtesy of Chip Woodson.*

He could be counted on. Being that "right hand man" in and around the home suited him perfectly. Seen often walking around the Weems village, he greeted everyone with a wave and a smile. He attended Weems Presbyterian church regularly and sat in his chosen back pew following the ser-

vice closely. As a little girl, Margery Dameron Nea recalls walking hand in hand with Charles Henry to ring the church bell. She confirmed Charles Henry loved music. He was an enthusiastic singer, ukulele player, and wash tub drum beater. Often he could be heard quite well in the stillness of many Weems village summer evenings.

Charles Henry takes a work break on Weems Wharf. *Courtesy of Chip Woodson.*

Charles Henry poses with his uke in front of his house. His singing and playing could be heard throughout the Weems community. *Courtesy of Chip Woodson.*

As he approached middle-age, Charles Henry focused more and more on his interaction with the Oscar Dameron family. Walton Dameron willed all his possessions as belonging to his adopted daughter, Cornelle, with the exception of $250.00 to assist "...Henry Barnett to do with as he absolutely please." With both Walton and Oscar gone, he spent his days handling basic chores and helping Mrs. Dameron in any way he could. She had taught him to read as a young man, welcomed him into the life of the family, and looked out for his welfare. Now he countered, in turn, living upstairs in the room above the kitchen all year long and readying her private living quarters for summer visits. Without central heat, Mrs. Dameron spent winters with her daughter, Mary Meade, and in April returned to the Weems community life. Charles Henry, always there, provided a reliable presence. At age 92, he passed away at a facility outside of Kilmarnock and was buried in the Dameron family plot. He had lived through two generations of the Dameron family.

"The history of life is what helps you," Charles Henry would say in that early interview. "Remembrance is a long time. 'Taint what you read. Plenty of people know more than I do. And I ain't going to let nothin' worry me. Just so I had a suit of clothes and something to eat, and lived honest with everybody. That's all I ever need." His friend, Albert Daniel reflected "…he is rich in a contented mind." Indeed, he was.

Always remembered and acknowledged by the Weems community, Charles Henry rests in the Campbell Memorial Church Dameron family burial plot. *Courtesy of Chip Woodson.*

CAMPBELL MEMORIAL PRESBYTERIAN CHURCH
FOUNDED 1889

Life was most satisfying for Evan Owen, a gentleman of Welsh descent, whose sectional marine railway was successfully operative early on at Carters Creek near present day Irvington. As a natural consequence of a strict Presbyterian upbringing, he knew that a hand mightier than his was guiding the progress. A strong spiritual need grew to provide a means to worship for himself and his family.

With his Weems neighbors in agreement, Mr. Owen's "call" for a preacher on October of 1886 was answered by Dr. William Addison Campbell, an evangelist, from the East Hanover Presbytery. Already serving Methodists and Baptists in Union Chapel on Carters Creek Irvington side for as long as a week at a time, Dr. Campbell eventually added a monthly Weems gathering. He preached there in the most imaginative of places…the tomato canning factory and the Weems Wharf black-smith shop sharing the word over top an anvil pulpit. Weems store owners also obliged and cleared out small corner spaces for worship. The small Weems community gatherings began to grow with an earnest desire to sing, pray, and read scripture from the Bible. The regularity of these meetings foretold that a more definitive means of a worship site was necessary and desirable. Mr. Owen conferred with Dr. Campbell. He was delighted with the outcome. A church of their own was about to unfold.

Dr. William Addison Campbell provided inspirational organization for the local Weems church founded in 1889. Named in his memory, Campbell Memorial Presbyterian Church opened its doors to a community of worshipers. *Courtesy of Campbell Memorial Presbyterian Church Centennial book written by Donald Lane Miller.*

To be "called" to preach and administer spiritual nourishment to the people in Weems required a marathon transport plan in 1886. The land in and around Carters Creek was simply inaccessible for most individuals to reach within a reasonable amount of time. A day and a half by train, overnight aboard a steamer or side-wheeler, and a pick up at the dock was the standard drill. And, of course, having completed such a journey one "stayed a spell." Dr. Campbell had made a big commitment, and often was welcomed to the warmth of Weems homes. Later, a small cottage was built behind Walton Dameron's home near Weems Wharf to serve as a preacher respite.

In July of 1889, Dr. Campbell preached passionately implanting a definitive and purposeful message to the Weems worshipers. Before the final prayer ended, he had organized a Sunday School and inspired the congregation to begin to plan and build a church by fall. He would return to review their progress. It is amazing no one felt this challenge insurmountable. There would be twelve individuals (six men and six women) who came forward on September 8, 1889 to strike the sounding chord for the founding of a community church. It is the wonder of that moment inside a temporary lumber shed that captures our attention. With little to go on except a fervently desired church vision, it must have been a most exciting and satisfying meeting of the hearts and minds of these men and women. Was their vision also inclusive of the sincere hope that

- IN MEMORIAM -
EVAN OWEN
BORN 1833 — DIED 1912
Elder of this Church
1889 — 1912
He walketh with God

Early on Evan Owen acted upon a spiritual need for guidance in the life of the Weems community. This plaque still exists in the church in his memory. *Author's photo.*

an exceptional life in this compact Weems community be fostered by the church? Although we do not have a mission statement or notes/minutes from this time, one has to feel a surge of "yeas." Notably, there is a cornerstone on the left side of the present day church which bears the engraving "Weems Church 1891" to mark the intent for the "life" of a church to begin. Entering into church membership either by "certificates from other churches or profession of faith," these twelve individuals were administered communion. Elected as the first elder was Evan Owen.

But how to go about accomplishing such a task must have been monumental. On what land would the church be built? How would the funds be raised for such a project? Could service be sustained and effectively meet the needs of the people? Of course, all their questions would be answered. The establishment of the church was accomplished with timely interventions and creative endeavors. Stepping forward again would be John Palmer, a Roman Catholic by faith, who owned land adjacent to the church. With permission from Caroline W. Kerns and other heirs of the George P. Kerns Corotoman estate (conveyed from R. D. Carter and wife to George P. Kerns in 1863), he negotiated the transfer of ½ acre of land in Weems to the Trustees of the Presbyterian Church recorded by deed on November 29, 1890. Trustees of the transfer were Evan Owen, W. A. Dameron, and Peter Eilskov. The land that had once served as a passage for "King" Carter and his opulent carriage processional to Christ Church would now house a sanctuary for the fledging Weems community.

A mere three years later, work began on a small white framed building. Its front steps led to a single entrance door built within an imposing high storied rectangular frame topped by a bell tower. How wonderful the most appropriate Thanksgiving Day Dedication on November 24, 1892 must have been. One can only imagine the scene as the tolling of the bell welcomed the streams of people who came from Weems Wharf and the surrounding area to hear Reverend Robert P. Kerr preach and listen to Dr. Campbell's complimentary remarks. That the church be named in honor of Dr. William Addison Campbell through a motion and vote was not surprising. After all, they must have reasoned, he was the diligent pastor who had answered the "call" and successfully raised the walls. Campbell Memorial Presbyterian Church it would be. In addition, a merger with the Milden Presbyterian Church at Sharps (in development on/about the same time frame) would link the churches together in pastorate services until 1952. But now service to the spiritual needs of the Weems community family consisting of farmers, waterman, and businessmen had begun in earnest "at the juncture of two roads known then as King Carter's Cedar Lane and Palmer Avenue."

Left - Progress on the first framed church building in 1892 notes the construction of the bell tower. Right - Dedicated on November 24, 1892, the familiar tolling of the bell called the community to worship. *Courtesy of Ben Winstead.*

The simplicity of the interior church design revealed two rows of benches lining opposing walls of an open room. Two wood stoves provided warmth. Preaching services as well as Sunday School lessons were held in the same area with classes breaking up into smaller groups for the Bible study. The structure of this first church had followed the traditional architectural style trend of a century ago. Mr. McDonald Lee from Irvington was its surveyor and

The relocation of the bell in the newly designed church building in 1938 can be viewed today on the front lawn. *Author's photo.*

the first superintendent. Numerous fund raisers had provided for the building of this modest structure. Strawberry festivals, oyster roasts, entertainments, suppers, rummage sales, and following the Weems tradition with a pie or two for sale along the way. This grass roots method of "ways and means" has followed suit throughout the ensuing years in the Weems community.

A most recent and wonderful "find" of a 1901-02 Superintendent's Condensed Record book of Campbell Memorial Presbyterian

On the 125th church anniversary, Dr. Clay Macaulay, John Hunt, and BHB Hubbard enjoy the recreation of the strawberry strum festival at Campbell Memorial Presbyterian Church. *Courtesy of the Rappahannock Record.*

Church (CMPC) bears the names of officers, founders, and class members with their attendance days regularly recorded month after month. So precise was their Sunday meetings that hymn numbers, prayer givers, titled lessons, collection amounts, visitors, and even weather conditions were penciled in. The members were, as Mr. Owen would confirm, worshiping and managing together "by the book." It is obvious that the faithful did not waver in their church obligations concerning record keeping. Although a fiscal accounting form was not provided for in the record book, church individual and class contributions were penciled in as well as expenditures. Cash on hand on October 1, 1901, was $26.44. Expenditures listed throughout eight ensuing months posted: stamps 6 cents, library expenses $1.00, firewood $1.50, ice for dinner picnic at Christ Church $2.15, Bible 75 cents, sugar and lemon

The first elected officers appear in this original record book of 1901-1902. Listed are: Superintendent, H. E. Owen; Assistant-Superintendent, Peter Eilskov; Secretary, Henry Daniel; Treasurer, W. A. Dameron; Librarian, Julia Buck and M. F. Owen. *Author's property and photo.*

flavoring $4.65, and $1.50 for Children's Day, to name a few. These amounts offer us a glimpse into the life of its members, and the activities of a working and forward going church since its inception.

Sermons during this time strictly adhered to the lessons from the Bible with topics such as "The Call of Moses," "The Lame Man Healed" and "The Disciples Scattered." The November 17, 1901, entry makes a practical commentary..." on account of cold and no stove, no further service here today and week." A total of 56 people had posted their collection of $1.32 and made their way home. Interestingly, on Easter Sunday in March of 1902 recitations and songs were presented by the scholars and the lesson was termed a "Review." Nine classes were listed with teachers and scholars numbering at roughly 94 church goers. Already the newly formed two year old church was seemingly making a pronounced impact on and taking a central role in the Weems community.

In 1893, as part of East Hanover, a merger between Campbell Memorial and Milden Church in Sharps occurred placing them in the Norfolk Presbytery for a time. With the dedication of Wesley Chapel on Taylors Creek in 1921, a shared pastorate was now inclusive of these three churches. In 1959 and 1988 respectively, the Milden and Wesley Churches (within East Hanover) separated.

Class number one is listed above with attendance markings. There were nine enrollment classes with the following teachers: Evan Owen, Sr., Mrs. W. K. Owen, Mrs. N. Eilskov, Mrs. H. V. Thomas, Mrs. H. Dameron, Miss Edith Buck, Peter Eilskov and J. O. Dameron. *Author's property and photo.*

Notations on early 1900s church activities reveal a movement for sidewalks in Weems. A drama entitled "Who Stole My Oysters?" was acted out by the men of the church to raise funds. Corotoman Point was the site for the 1903 annual picnic that included a tub and sack race for the children, and a baseball game for the adults. The gentlemen conceded to play left-handed. Team names are quite interesting as Captain Deggs, Swamp Angels, Captain Dan Jones, and Wharf Rats took to the field. That same Thanksgiving an oyster supper was held with crab cakes, bananas, oranges, lemonade, and ice cream on the menu. No doubt some of the monies funded the "planting of shade trees" in the spring on Thomas' Hill (up a way from Weems Wharf) to aid the project of the Ladies' Guild. And in accordance with church custom, Santa arrived in December with "good things distributed to all children." A large log cabin had been constructed on the pulpit where the jolly man appeared and disappeared with a great jingling of bells.

The late 1920s found members enjoying suppers at Mr. Dameron's tomato canning factory to raise money for the preacher's salary and other church expenses. Bible School was held in workshops conducted in various buildings at nearby Wharton Grove... the intriguing established evangelistic setting for worship during a period of ten days each summer in Weems. The ending picnic was an unforgettable "good time" for the church youth. In later years, the Daily Vacation Bible School would be held at Campbell Memorial Presbyterian Church with student teachers from the Presbyterian School at the Seminary to lead the classes. Well into the 1970s my own sons looked forward to visiting Grandmom, Gladys Lumpkin, joining in the Bible School lessons and craft making activities such as ceramics and kite making.

By 1936 the congregation was flourishing and took up a new issue... that of a larger worship sanctuary and the need for additional Sunday school rooms. The expansive bricked building design, now void of the bell tower, held to a colonial style of architecture. As Walter N. Macomber, architect of Mount Vernon drafted the blueprints, he envisioned relocating the bell that had rung for years in the Weems community. He positioned it in a brick framed structure in front of the church. It remains there today. Completed in 1940, this 56 by 36 foot

Ceramic plaque made by Raymond Lumpkin in Bible School. Mrs. Katherine Jones was the art instructor. *Courtesy of Norma Lumpkin. Author's photo.*

bricked church building was dedicated in 1947 with much community pride. With four hundred people in attendance, the keys to the building, held by contractor L. A. Jones, were passed to the chairman of the building committee, Frank C. Hatch, Jr., who presented them to the pastor, Rev. Harvey A. McBath. A full morning and evening of consecration witnessed musical selections from the Woman's Club of Lancaster, appreciation of various organizations, as well as gifts of silver vases, the pulpit, and the communion table.

But there are always stories behind the story. The "pennies for bricks" idea to aid in the cost of the 1936 church was adopted out of the Worker's Council. This organization was comprised of church officers and teachers who formed "to study the needs and problems of our Sunday school and to carry on the work in a more efficient manner." As a boy of 7 or 8, Ben Winstead recalled canvassing the Weems neighborhood asking for a donation of one to three cents to buy a church brick.

Attendance in the 1930s Bible School pose on front church steps. *Courtesy of Campbell Memorial Presbyterian Church. Centennial book written by Donald Lane Miller.*

Many other children joined in. June Ward Mason collected her coins in a small handmade sock. Along with suppers, dances at the Community Hall, taking advantage of merchant discounts, as well as special contributions a new church construction began. Again, Ben's words add credence to the resurfacing of the founding spirit of the church community many years later. "This was right after the great depression. I try to imagine the faith in God that these members of Campbell Church must have had to take on such a project at that time."

Left - Now built in the colonial brick style, Campbell Memorial was completed in 1947. *Courtesy of Ben Winstead.* Right - Congregtion gathers during the 1947 church dedication. *Courtesy of Margery Nea.*

The minutes from the 1930s and 1940s Worker's Council projected a church profile placing great emphasis upon individual and family attendance, Bible memory work, extended youth involvement, creative and advanced classroom teaching techniques, and an enhanced music program. Monies were also set aside to aid in special-

Another view after church dedication ceremony. *Courtesy of Ben Winstead.*

ized church causes. It was a time of incentives as well. Pins, bars, and rotating class banners were given for good attendance. Vera Mae Ward Winegar still holds her twelve years of perfect attendance pins very dear. After memorizing her catechism, she joined CMPC at 9 years of age. Compact editions of the Old or New Testament were presented to youth or new church members. From the onset this was an ongoing practice in the church. Records from 1903 reveal prizes for perfect attendance given to adults who achieved this goal. Mrs. Peter Eilskov received a year's subscription for "Ladies' Home Journal" while Albert Daniel, Freddie E, Alexander Ball, and John and Bertha Norris added "handsome books" to their library. Henry C. Daniel was awarded a "Creeden's Concordance."

Job descriptions within the church in the 1930s were numerous, and it was recorded that Mrs. John Ashburn, Miss Edith Buck, and Leon Hayden decorated the church for Christmas. A committee of three girls prepared the bags of Sunday school treats... Florimond Hayden, Estelle Harding, and Genevieve Webb. Mary Meade Dameron provided leadership for the music committee. A beginning church Worship Program was planned by Mrs. Herbert George, Mary Meade Dameron, Jeanette Sickle, and Pastor Mc-Bath. Two young boys of the church, J. P. Franz and Lawrence Winstead, served as good role models guiding others standing outside the church to a "timely" appearance inside as the service began.

Serving as organist and assistant organist were the talented musical team of Leon Hayden and Miss Inez George. Officers guiding the Worker's Council are listed as: Mr. Crawford, Chairman; Mr. Daniel, Vice-Chairman; and Jeannette Sickel, Secretary and Treasurer. Working tirelessly, these individuals and many, many more laid the groundwork for the growth of their Weems Presbyterian church.

A strong young people's organization emerged with meetings on Sunday nights. They fashioned their own program emphasizing helping the sick or supporting church venues through an offering. Visits to different houses for refreshments followed

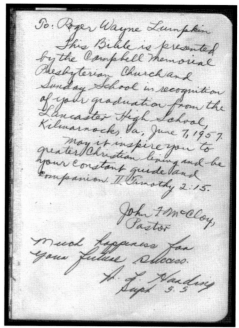

Customarily through the years, Campbell Memorial presented Bibles to its youthful members. Roger Wayne Lumpkin's Bible was presented in 1957 in recognition of his high shool graduation. Superintendent was A. L. Harding. *Courtesy of Roger W. Lumpkin. Author's photo.*

Following graduation from Kilmarnock High School, Roger enlisted in the United States Navy and served four years as a Quartermaster in Navigation. His tour of duty took him from Norfolk to North Africa, Greece, Italy, Sicily, and Spain aboard the U.S.S. Cambria. *Courtesy of Roger W. Lumpkin.*

Roger and Pat Lumpkin (cousins) pose in Weems before his naval tour begins. Upon returning to the states, Roger relocated to Richmond, Virginia, attended Smithfield Massey, and retired from Capital City Iron Works after thirty-seven years. He enjoyed many hours fishing and boating on the Rappahannock River. *Courtesy of Roger W. Lumpkin. Author's photo.*

Siblings (left to right) Elaine, Ida Louise, and Roger were born in Weems, Virginia, to Luther "Boots" and Ida Lumpkin. *Courtesy of Roger W. Lumpkin.*

and was accompanied by music and singing. Later, in the 1940s, monthly gatherings were held at the Weems Community Hall with Mrs. Leon Hayden and Mr. and Mrs. Welford Hudson acting as chaperones. Recognizing the need for fulfilling significant tasks in a "good will" fashion became the unspoken practice of this church population.

In due time, an Educational Wing (1953), Narthex (1957), and Ministries Building (1986) were completed at Campbell Memorial Presbyterian Church. The educational section provided more class rooms, choir rehearsal space, and conference rooms. The Ministries Building stood upon land that had been "gifted" by Mr. and Mrs. Samuel C. Thomas with memory recognition from their families. Several land gifts beside and across the road in front of the church had been given by Margaret and James Dameron (in 1925), and Mrs. Dameron and her daughters, Mrs. Henry Edmonds and Mrs. Ben Woodson in (1952). In 1957 Mary and Joseph Childs provided for a church septic tank field with a land easement "in perpetuity" across Cedar Lane. A manse was eventually built across the street from the church, bordered on one side by the parking lot. In 1968 a manse renovation took place. Now a new sanctuary front entrance has been added with a handicap ramp. A friendship garden was dedicated on August 23, 2009. The estate of Milton Andrew Cross gave a substantial sum for the good of the church in 1988. Today these gifts and additions still define the property of the church combined with the original conveyance of one-half acre situated on the corner of Weems Road.

Anniversary dates have given way to celebratory programs for and about the life of this resilient church. Activities in its 90th year consisted of sporting events, games, family-style dinner, and a youth folk musical, "Sam." An acknowledgement of Daisy Hodges, the oldest member of the congregation, was made as she cut the church birthday cake. With five former pastors in attendance (Reverend Dr. James Clark, Reverend Dr. Richard Taylor, Reverend James Wilson, Reverend Dr. John Lown, Reverend Richard Forbes),

An 1989 view of Campbell Memorial shows the extended Fellowship Hall addition to the left where many community events are held. *Courtesy of Campbell Memorial Presbyterian Church scrapbook.*

a dedication of the expanded sanctuary inclusive of memorials and gifts took place.

It has remained for the people over the years who spoke from the heart as to the comforting and spiritual impact Campbell Memorial has had upon the Weems community. We return gratefully to some of those recorded memories.

"The love and fellowship we shared are still indelible." Louise G. George

"There was always Christmas at Campbell with Santa, Christmas carols, and candy and apples for the children." Emma Hodges Robertson

"What a happy memory listening to the lovely music played by Margery Edmonds and June Mason on organ and piano before each Sunday morning service." Genevieve Webb Cockrell

"Growing up in the church, there were many highlights... our church picnic to White Stone Beach, boat rides to Sharps, eating and socializing on the lawn at the hotel of Milton and Thelma Cross." June Ward Mason

"Mrs. Bertha James always made the Women of the Church a lovely sheet cake for their May birthday celebration. It had lots of butter and eggs. Delicious!"

Left and below - Contrasting interiors of Campbell Memorial Presbyterian Church in 1978 and 2012. *Courtesy of Campbell Memorial Presbyterian Church scrapbook and author's photo.*

Ladies fellowship gathering includes Lois Hudson, Effie Davis, and Herthel Conley (left to right). *Courtesy of Campbell Memorial Presbyterian Church scrapbook.*

With Gladys Lumpkin and Genevieve Cookrell to the forefront other members gather for outdoor church picnic. *Courtesy of Campbell Memorial Presbyterian Church scrapbook.*

Jr. Choir on church steps in 1958. (Bottom row left to right.) Peggy Harding, Theresa George, Donna George and Jane Haydon. (Middle row left to right.) Judy Gregg, Mary Ida Verlander and Margaret Kent. (Top row left to right.) Charles Haydon and Johnny Sheppard. *Courtesy of Patricia Hinton.*

Ladies Circle cooking meeting in 1951. (Left to right.)
Miss Winnie, Mrs. Olds, Mildred James, June Mason,
Effie Davis, Joyce Winstead, Bertha Winstead, and
Clara Verlander. *Courtesy of Campbell Memorial Presbyterian Church scrapbook.*

The Amigos program for adults over fifty meet in the educational building of the church in 1973. Imogen Daniel, Hilda Ward, Bertha Lumpkin, and Daisy Hodges are among the group. *Courtesy of the Rappahannock Record.*

Ladies circle meeting held at Mrs. Dameron's home. Some of the ladies present were Clara Verlander, Lena Diller, and Irma Ashburn. *Courtesy of Margery Nea.*

"We both had grown up in a rural church. We returned to a warm and welcoming Christian community like the one we remembered from our childhood." Rosa Lou and Mandley Ray Johnston

"At age 14 I was inducted into the choir. Every Christmas I sang 'O Holy Night'. I'm still reminded of this every year." Vera Mae Ward Winegar

"We didn't have telephones, so we would go from house to house to beg for pies, canned goods, potatoes or money to buy turkeys. We used the money to pay the expenses of the church as far as it would go." Mildred Warwick James

CAMPBELL MEMORIAL PRESBYTERIAN CHURCH
125th ANNIVERSARY CELEBRATION

On September 6th and 7th in 2014, members and friends of Campbell Memorial Presbyterian Church welcomed everyone in celebration of its growth and endurance to "glorify God through worship and service; and to nurture all as we grow in relationship with Christ." With a stirring musical concert and bonding unity service encasing the words of Reverend Dr. James K. Wilson, Jr. (pastor 1960-67), the congregation worshipped through "cherishing of the past, celebrating the present, and charting the future."

Campbell Memorial Presbyterian Church truly holds a central spot as the "heart" of the Weems Community now for 125 years. It stands in tribute to its founders and early members who sought spiritual fulfillment and constantly strove to complete missions of love, understanding, and helpfulness. We, and generations beyond, are all the better for their foundational journey.

Left - Emma Robertson
(oldest church member)
and Norma Lumpkin
enjoy the fellowship
time together. Below
- Weems stories are
happily shared by Alice
Winstead and Donnie
Self. *Author's photos.*

Left - Gathering at the 125th anniversary of
Campbell Memorial Presbyterian Church are
left to right (front row): June Mason, Emma
Robertson, and Pat Rose. (second row):
Sheila Newman, Patrick Newman, Margery
Nea, Delores Carnes, and Carroll Davis, Jr.
Courtesy of Norma Lumpkin.

CAMPBELL MEMORIAL PRESBYTERIAN CHURCH
CHARTER MEMBERS OF 1889

Mr. Evan Owen, Sr.
Mrs. Gwen Owen
Mrs. Winnie K. Owen
Mrs. Lizzie O. Hamilton
Mrs. A. A. Ball
Mr. A. A. Ball
Mrs. W. A. Ball
Mr. Peter Eilskov
Mr. Walton Dameron
Mrs. Lawson Winstead
Mr. Lawson Winstead
Mr. Griffin Ashburn

LATER MEMBERS
Mr. G. L. Ball
Mr. Henry Daniel
Mr. Albert Noblett
Mr. W. A. Ball
Mrs. W. A. Dameron
Mr. Evan Owen, Jr.

WEEMS STEAMBOAT LINE OF BALTIMORE CITY
1819-1905

GEORGE WEEMS
1784-1853

Once the success of the family owned store of W. A. Dameron & Bro was noted alongside the river shoreline, other individuals with start-up businesses began to steadily make an appearance on the wharf. They moved forward to invest in the rich resources about them. It would be an adventuresome experience that lasted for many years. Interestingly, it would fall to another family owned business in another state to set its eye upon this fledging business site...the Weems Steamboat Line of Baltimore City. They, too, would have their day.

The Weems Steamboat Line was a two-generational family steam-boating journey. All told, the ten impressive white steam packets it produced would span 120 years of plying the Patuxent,

Potomac, and Rappahannock Rivers respectively. Along with fellow steamers, its role in the development of the Tidewater area was crucial in providing an economic lift bonding planters and merchants to a new and profitable market world. Even after the steamboat era officially ended, the "Weems Line" provided excursions. And for a time beginning in 1886 it spent glorious times "tapping" into the energy of a new community with a wharf that would adopt the steamboat owner's name...WEEMS.

In 1816 the nicely appointed steamboat, Surprise, had been making successful "runs" on the Chesapeake Bay. Fitted with an inventive rotary engine (built by George Stiles and Son) it cruised along at 5 miles per hour. It caught the eye of George Weems. At age 26, Weems, having already turned a profit as a ship owner/shipmaster/adventurer, desperately desired to establish a steamboat worthy of his great ambition. His over-the-top enthusiasm for Surprise matched his restless and jubilant persona despite his brother's (Gustavus) reluctance to enter into a $20,000 bond to register George as its shipmaster. But they did. Breaking down repeatedly and requiring extensive repairs from workers unfamiliar with the rotary engine, Surprise nearly bankrupted the company and strained the brother's bond. Steamboat service was terminated for a time on the Patuxent River. This was not the type of beginning the brothers had in mind.

It was 1827 when the Weems steamer, Patuxent, made its debut in the Weems Steamboat Line history setting a standard for exceptional service and fine dining. With an eye toward the unsecured market on the Rappahannock, George Weems advertised one day excursions featuring "oyster, fish, and every luxury the season could afford." For two dollars extra he offered dinner and music as well. Competitiveness was the order of the steamboat day and time. Even though George Weems made a bold move to revamp the Patuxent to manage more efficiently the irregularity of water depth, fluctuating tides, and challenging river inlets of the Rappahannock, the outcome was disappointing. He refused to see his steamboat venture as a mere profit and loss statement. Undoubtedly, his per-

A detailed look at the 1930s Weems steamboat wharf. The high wooden pilings provided a sturdy wooden enclosure as the steamboat churned the waters and pulled alongside to dock. A family waits passage after purchasing tickets in the small station to the left. *Dr. Henry J. Edmonds photo collection.*

severance thorough the 1820s and 1830s was notable. It would fall to his son to embrace the Tidewater area and recognize its business potential.

Indeed, the "timing" was just not right to persuade farmers/planters to disband their tried and true method of transporting goods. The small single mast sloop with a fore and aft rig slipped in and out of the maze of waterways just perfectly giving way later to

Dameron siblings await their steamboat departure in front of the WEEMS sign on Weems Wharf. *Courtesy of Margery Nea.*

the larger twin mast schooners. Individualized landings had been built to provide these sailing crafts a welcoming berth. What could be better? Decades of successful location transportion openly negated the offerings of a steamboat vessel transport that had not yet proven its capability.

Retiring in 1838, George Weems gratefully witnessed the emergence of his eldest son Mason Locke's (1814-1874) steamboat skill set. He would see to it that his father's legacy materialized in an elegant "palace boat" appropriately named "George Weems." At Civil War's end in 1865, he sailed the steamboat Matilda from Baltimore to Fredericksburg and stopped at the Rappahannock wharves. His father had longed to have this area become a part of the steamboat line. Now the "timing" was perfect.

With the passing of Mason L. Weems, the company came under the direction of Henry Williams (1840-1916) attorney/agent husband of Georgenna Weems. His adroit management would eventually mold the steamboat company into "one of the oldest and most respected companies in the United States." Ever confident and diplomatic, he journeyed down the Patuxent and Rappahannock Rivers, turning his ear to the problems of watermen, farm-

Aerial view of "Steamboat Wharf and Village of Weems, Virginia" in 1936. Weems homes can be seen in the background. *Dr. Henry J. Edmonds photo collection.*

ers, and merchants in the quest for refined steamboat services. On December 14, 1891, the Weems Steamboat Company of Baltimore City with Henry Williams as president and general manager was officially acknowledged. A new house flag (blue with a centered red ball) and a bold W appeared on the steamboat smoke stack. After contentious negotiations in 1895 Charles R. Lewis, general manager of the Maryland and Virginia Steamboat Company, sold its line to Williams. Now with a firm foothold in the packet line, Williams stood proudly at the helm of a Weems steamboat line that seemed indestructible.

From the 1890s through the 1900s lingering Civil War economics, distrust toward the line's rates, and the establishment of Farmers' Alliance groups confronted the Weems Steamboat Company. Its steady progression was also hampered by fires, collisions, groundings, and the wrath of Mother Nature. Hurricanes, storms, and even ice gorges laid damage and destruction to helpless vessels. A 1904 Baltimore fire lit up the Pratt and Light Street financial district. Although the Weems Line piers were just scorched, the offices of commissioners and the merchant master planners of the steamboat where scheduling and planning was reduced to cinders. Then the hurricane of 1933 whipped up high tides and a gale so severe in the Northern Neck area only ten of the twenty-seven steamboat wharves were partially standing. Flattened beyond usefulness were crops and buildings. Business could not be conducted for a long time.

If the steamboat business took a long, long breath so too did Henry Williams. New challenges appeared on the horizon. With rising sales of automobiles gracing miles and miles of newly paved concrete roads and inlaid iron railroad tracks curving throughout the United States, the steamers' continuance seemed to be eroding. Williams reluctantly resigned on January 3, 1905, accepting a package from the Pennsylvania Railroad (PPR) bound to the Queen Anne's Railroad and Chester River Steamboat Company. It was all but over.

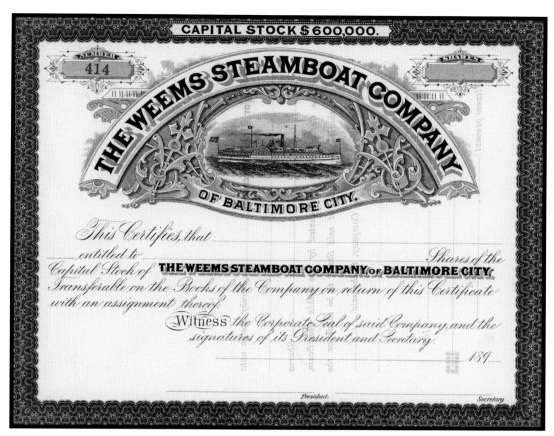

Stock Certificate #414 is imprinted on The Weems Steamboat Company of Baltimore City share. *Author's photo and property.*

Through the efforts of William's son, Mason Locke Weems Williams, the operation of the Baltimore and Carolina Steamship Company (B & C) commenced for nearly twenty-five more years. Prospering again under the old Weems flag logo, it coastally traded and brought stellar service and luxury furnishings to its customers. The fleet sold in 1931. It fell to the Anne Arundel and Captain John D. Davis on September 14, 1937, to make a farewell run for all the white packets. Clearing the wharf at Pier 3 on Light Street with selected friends aboard, she majestically steamed slowly for two days past her old haunts. Her whistle blew loud and long in an appropriate goodbye.

The highest accolades still remain for the Weems Steamboat Company Line. Its presence aided in the booming economic, social, and cultural progress of the citizens of Tidewater. Standing quietly atop the hill at Weems Wharf, one can almost envision the pag-

STEAMER CALVERT at Weems, V.

Steamer Calvert makes its docking appearance at Weems Wharf. Leaving Pier 2 at Light Street wharf in Baltimore, Maryland, daily, the steamers "called" at Weems and Irvington on Saturday and Monday only. *Dr. Henry J. Edmonds photo collection.*

eantry of phantom steamboats-on-parade. Sailing through sun and storm, they brought individuals to the comfort of a shore hearth full of welcoming family and friends. Perhaps for this reason alone the historical footprint of the Weems Steamboat Line will long be appreciated and remembered.

STEAMBOAT ADVERTISEMENTS

In the late 1800s, mindful of its prowess, the Weems Steamboat Company printed an advertising booklet of "Summer Homes and Historical Points" along its routes. Its contents lured the reader to indulge in a summer respite. Within the Weems area, one could make selective stops in the tidewater area yet to be "transformed by modern enterprise and so-called improvements." For a nominal fee serenity and seafood seemed to be the order of the day. Just take your pick.

Courtesy of the Virginia Historical Society.

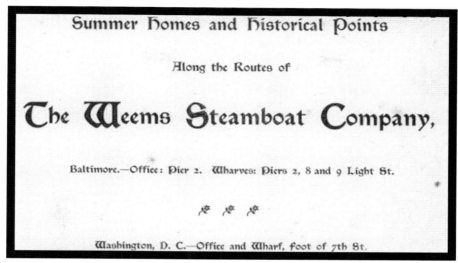

Summer booklet of the Weems Steamboat Company provided handy descriptions of onshore accommodations for their clients. *Courtesy of the Virginia Historical Society.*

CARTERS CREEK

"Delightfully situated on the River Front at Weems Wharf. Healthy climate, good bathing, boating and fishing...post office at the Wharf. Rates, $16.00 per month."

Mrs. H. M. Crittenden, Weems Post Office, Va.

WHARTON GROVE CAMPGROUND

"Beautifully situated on the lower Rappahannock, near Weems Wharf. Camp opens the Saturday preceding the third Sunday in July. Ample hotel and cottage accommodations. Rates, board, 10 days, $5.00; room in hotel, holding four people, 10 days, $5.00."

Rev. F. W. Claybrook, Kilmarnock, Va; Rev. H. M. Wharton, Baltimore, Md.

WEEMS

"A few summer boarders can be accommodated at a country home on the Rappahannock River, a short distance from Weems Wharf and post office...one mile from Wharton's Camp Grounds.

Mail three times a day...healthy location and good table...$4.00 per week."

Mrs. E. C. Cross, Weems, Lancaster County

(These advertisements are compliments of the Virginia Historical Society. "Summer homes and historical points along route of the Weems Steamboat Company." Baltimore, Williams & Wilkins Company Press.)

CAPTAIN ARCHIBALD MITCHELL LONG
1867-1948

What a unique position to be in...atop the pilot house of a beautifully appointed steamboat surveying miles and miles of every natural land and water amenity the Northern Neck had to offer. Somebody had to do it, and that somebody was Captain Archie Long of Weems. For twenty-six plus years, he expertly sailed from Baltimore to Norfolk and up and down the Chesapeake Bay. A dapper and polite gentlemen, Captain Arch greeted steamboat passengers walking up the gangplank with a handshake, a wide smile, and often a hug, for well-groomed ladies turned out in their loveliest gown and hat creations. He made the initial impression that their choice of unforgettable steamboat travel was in the very best of hands...HIS. Welcome aboard!

Born on October 4, 1867, on a farm in Trappe, Maryland, Archie was in all probability enamored with his father's stories of involvement in island trading through ownership of commercial schooners. With his schooling complete, he moved to Baltimore and began to pursue an apprenticeship with various Captains to study and learn the waterways. Hours of practical experience as a mate under master teachers steadily increased his knowledge. The dedicated work ethic paid off. He sailed proudly out of Baltimore Harbor as one of the youngest Captains to grace the waterways. In 1905 he joined a distinctive Captain list as "one of the finest" of the Weems Steamboat line. He was thirty-one years old.

Upon marrying Ella Belle Griffin of Easton, Maryland, he moved his bride from Baltimore to Weems, Virginia. In 1905 a home was built overlooking the water on Orchard Point. Here Captain Arch raised two sons and became a well-respected figure in the Weems community. Young people gathering for socialization and dancing in the Long home more often than not listened to his steamboat stories told with an adventurous flair. Captain Arch's ability as a genial host had successfully bridged the gap between home and life aboard the steamboat.

Moving toward career's end, he served as relief captain on the Essex, the Westmoreland and the Calvert. The Piankatank and the Lexington would remain under his guidance. As steamboat useful-

ness began to wane, he joined in to captain the Mohawk and the Robert E. Lee from Washington to the Potomac River. But it would fall to his longest relationship as Master Captain of the Potomac (1906-1908; 1911-1932) that would heighten his reputation and secure his legacy through contemporary times.

As one story goes, during a difficult docking situation in severe weather Captain Arch was at the helm. Everyone seemed on edge. A nervous passenger queried, "Does the fog bother you much?" "Nope," Captain Arch replied, "Not much." "Well," the gentlemen pointed out, "There's no fog up ahead." "We're not going that-a-way," the Captain re-

Captain Arch Long aboard the Steamer *Anne Arundel* at Irvington Wharf in 1939. *Jack Long photo collection.*

sponded, slipping the steamer into the dock with razor sharp precision. Today Captain Archie Long and his steamboat prowess still draws us to an intriguing era.

STEAMBOAT POTOMAC

In 1894 the Potomac, built by Neafie and Levy, was purchased by the Weems Steamboat Company for $150,000 the following year. Moderately sized this propeller driven steamer was 176 feet in length with a 41 foot beam. Complimenting the glass windows allowing light and scenic views to flow into the main deck dining room, the artful saloon led to thirty-seven tastefully decorated state-rooms. Piloted by Captain Archie Long on the Rappahannock run, she proved to be a stable form of steamboat travel for many years.

However, a string of mishaps became a part of the Potomac's history. The first occurred in 1895. While docked at Pier 8, Light Street in Baltimore, four of her berths were destroyed by mattress fires. That same winter found her iced in the Bay with the crew involved in ice hockey play for diversion. Nevertheless, the Potomac battled her way through twelve inch ice. Heading to Baltimore two years later, she severed the Three Brothers only to be severely damaged on the starboard side by her fellow steamer Essex. Groundings were also common and the Potomac had her share. Losing her rudder in a shallow creek, a long pole on board provided the crew the makeshift capability to keep on course.

Although hanging by a thread as one of the final four Weems steamboats, the Potomac watched the Anne Arundel bid its farewell in 1932. Together they had kept a series of $9.00 overnighters (Baltimore, Rappahannock landings, Tappahannock, Chesapeake Bay) going for vacationing passengers. Freight transport had become nearly non-existent. Time was short. On February 22, 1936, the Potomac, wedged in ice, was a sitting target when the freighter Jean rammed her side.

Shown above are Captain Long's possessions: traveling United States Guide, binoculars, pocket watch, glasses and directional compass. *Author's photo. Courtesy of Steamboat Era Museum.*

Sold to Chesapeake Corporation in West Point, she performed barge duty hauling pulpwood to the paper plant. Her ship's pilot house and officers' quarters were salvaged and barged to Taft Beach in White Stone. There Captain Ben Colona used the structure as personal cottage living space. Numerous ownerships and years of shuttling from museum to museum (Mariners Museum/Newport News; Colonial Beach) left the Potomac pilothouse in need of a permanent home. It found welcoming arms at the Steamboat Era Museum in Irvington. Presently, the pilothouse awaits restoration as the main artifact of the "last surviving deck of a Chesapeake Bay steamboat" with a 2018 opening at the museum. Wouldn't Captain Arch be tremendously proud to know it would fall to his granddaughter, Anne Long McClintock, to stand at the helm to restore his beloved Potomac? What a happy ending.

Anne Long McClintock points to her grandfather, Captain Archie Long, waving from the steamboat "Potomac." *Author's photo. Courtesy of Steamboat Era Museum.*

The Long family (from left to right)) Ella Mae, Jack, Anne, and Mother Ida pose aboard the Potomac. *Courtesy of Anne Long McClintock.*

Steamboat Potomac proved her worth for 42 years sailing tributaries, rivers, and the Chesapeake Bay. *Dr. Henry J. Edmonds photo collection.*

Sidling up to Weems Wharf, the Potomac is majestically framed in Carters Creek. *Postcard courtesy of Debbie Morgan.*

The pilot house of the steamboat Potomac was once utilized as a summer cottege. *Courtesy of Anne Long McClintock.*

ABOARD THE POTOMAC
GLADYS MARIE HOUSE LUMPKIN
1907-2005

As a young girl living in Baltimore, Maryland, my mother Gladys strolled with her father (Seldon T. House) nearly every Sunday down to the Pratt and Light Street wharves to inspect schooners laden with vegetables and fresh fruit from the Northern Neck. They were fascinated by the activity of swirls of people bantering with the skippers and their customers. Her father eventually made contact with Captain Andrew Calvin Lumpkin from Weems, Virginia. Within a few years both families formed a very close friendship. Although relocation to Irvington by the House family for several years wasn't successful, the die had been cast. Mother married a Lumpkin son, Raymond, in 1936 and returned to live in Weems in 1945. She fully credited the steamboat Potomac for early on bringing her to Carters Creek and Weems to form rare friendships in a place she called "home" for sixty-two years.

The story became sweeter with each retelling. With her brother, Edward, she first boarded the Potomac in the early 1920s. A week's vacation at the Irvington Beach Hotel with friends and a visit to the Lumpkin family farm was planned. What a scene she described at the Baltimore steamboat dock full of piled high carts, frantic livestock, stacks of freight, and people waving good-bye. The Potomac sailed "weather permitting" every Tuesday and Thursday at 4:30, and advertised itself as a vessel of safety and style. It had well-appointed staterooms and would assuredly lull one to sleep at a steady thirteen miles per hour. Smoothing out the dresses her mother (Florence Gay House) had fashioned for every occasion, Mother enjoyed every ambiance the steamboat had to offer. She often spoke of the breathtaking water views and the greenery of small towns. The steamboat cuisine was a particularly favorite topic. All in all, a young girl's dream vacation had come true.

Gladys Marie House, age 16, stands on Irvington wharf during her first vacation trip aboard the Potomac to visit friends. *Author's photo.*

When the Potomac pilothouse resurfaced beside the Steamboat Era Museum in 2003, Mother was very excited. She shared that its role in her life was that of an important "memory store keeper." Finally, she happily noted, it was being valued and harbored for everyone to enjoy. She inspected every part of its weathered siding carefully. Her eyes moved to the enclosed pilothouse. Pointing upward Mother simply turned to me and said, "I was right there." As we left, I felt she may have had a vague notion to "climb aboard" one more time.

During its initial berth on the grounds of the Steamboat Era Museum in Irvington, the Potomac's pilot house awaited restoration as Gladys recalled her early steamboating days. In 2009 it was moved , shrink wrapped, and has become the museum's central focus for restoration with an on-going campaign. *Author's photo.*

Holding fast friendships and family throughout her lifetime, Gladys House enjoyed her visits to Irvington, White Stone, and Weems. To her left, Leah Burke. Second row left to right: Muriel King, Ed House, and friend Dorothy. Others unidentified. *Author's photo.*

A full view of Weems Wharf shows a vibrant workplace of retail and oyster enterprises. Dameron's store (far right) and the steamboat landing (far left) frame fishing buyer boats and local workboats. Albert Luckham's boat, "Pat," appears in the foreground at dock's end. *Dr. Henry J. Edmonds photo collection.*

Gladys and Raymond Lumpkin during their 1936 January honeymoon in Weems, Virginia. Taken in front of Ball's Service Station in Johns Neck. *Author's photo.*

PART III

WE EMERGE

The growth of the Weems inland area was at hand. Diligent peoples strove to place their energies into creating homesteads, businesses, as well as religious and educational opportunities. Over a significant period of time, they enjoyed and sustained an environment compatible with the needs of their community. Some of the landmarks are still visible today.

WEEMS POST OFFICE
1886

Coincidentally, the U. S. Postal system and steamboat companies had a working relationship by 1811 through the replacement of rowboats, rafts, and packets to carry the mail. Conditions were most specific stating steamboat mail delivery had to occur within three hours of daylight docking or two hours after sunrise the following day.   By the late 1820s the postal department had issued over 200 contracts to steamboat lines. The steamboat as a major mail carrier peaked in 1853 due to the advent of the railroad. By 1923 this system declared "waterways to be past roads."

A 2012 photograph of Weems Post Office. This endearing postal service was officially suspended in 2016. *Author's photo.*

Established on October 11, 1886, the Weems post office was probably operating out of John Noblett's store on Weems Wharf. With the arrival of the Dameron brothers in 1889, the older brother Walton would assume the postmaster duties from Julius W. Mitchell (documented first Postmaster) and hold the position for eight years. In 1914 James Oscar Dameron operated out of the W. A. Dameron & Bro store as a full service postal facility for 26 years. Customers could purchase stamps, buy money orders, mail packages, pay insurance premiums, and receive items brought to the wharf by the Weems steamboat line. As a rural carrier for seven years (1910-1917), Peter Bittner kept the mail lines operative by horseback on a twenty-four mile route inclusive of Weems, Howeth's, Johns Neck, Morans, Dunhow, Tombs, and back to Weems. He alternated two horses every other day losing six during his mail carrier tenure. With no loose coins acceptable, the customer utilized a postal coin holder to purchase stamps through the carrier. Even as late as the 1950s, rural automobile carriers would accept pennies placed in the mailbox to ensure the letter would be later stamped and on its way. What enduring personal service.

Upon Mr. Dameron's retirement in 1940, a small white clapboard structure was built mid-Weems. Imogen Ellis Daniel, who lived next door, leased the property to the U. S. Government postal system. She served for 25 years as postmaster. With a clear view of the Rappahannock River (and the present Robert O. Norris bridge) from its rear entryway, this building consisted of a consumer space with a large open framed window for postal transactions. Rows of metal mail receptacles were positioned to the

Mary Ellen Haydon on her first day as Postmaster of Weems Post Office in 1979. She retired in 2006. *Courtesy of Charles Haydon.*

right. Everyone paused to exchange the latest community happenings or to wave to the worker sorting the mail in the back. Here one could post a letter containing important bits of family news, re-

Interior mailbox display in the Weems Post Office.
Author's photo.

ceive an abbreviated greeting on a picture postcard, or tuck underarm the coveted Sears Roebuck "Wish Book" catalog. Virginia Lee Ashburn Simpson recalls the delightful "peep, peep, peep" experience of waiting at the post office for a tray full of furry yellow chicks to be picked up and raised on the Ashburn property.

Mail transactions were simply a highlight of every day in Weems. Whether you walked to the post office to pick up your mail or waited beside the mailbox for the carrier to appear, you were provided a daily opportunity to "keep in touch" with family and friends. Records show that over twenty postmasters have faithfully served the Weems community. Poignantly, on August 23, 2016, after 130 years of unparalleled community service, the Weems Post Office lowered the American flag and closed its doors for a final farewell.

The final flag ceremony was conducted on the Weems Post Office lawn with the "Patriot Walkers" observing their last salute together. From left to right: Crystal Duvall, Brittany Diggs, John Hunt, B. H. Hubbard, and the Reverend Clay Macaulay. *Courtesy of the Rappahannock Record.*

WEEMS SCHOOL
1892-1967/68

It was a long and extraordinary run for the little school in Weems "that could" and did. For seventy-five years, the wooden framed and shuttered building that later upgraded to a brick and gabled tin roof structure (about 1916), nurtured and educated the children of the Weems area. All accomplished with little or no snow days either. When the elongated doors with side windows and a transom above closed at the end of the 1967-68 school session...it did not go quietly.

Communities into their growth spurt invariably turn toward the direction of providing solid educational venues for its youth. Recognition that an "educated citizenry is a progressive citizenry" (Richard E. Brann, County Superintendent) has always been a goal. Some families in the Weems area had been providing live-in tutors for their children's growth as well as visiting instructors. Also, in Irvington, the private Chesapeake Academy (1889-1907) with William McDonald Lee as its director flourished for eighteen years. Children were welcomed as day students and boarders as well. But another thought was in the making. On August 15, 1892, the Lancaster County Deed Book revealed that William A. Ball and Annie E. Ball "sold one half an acre of land on the main road leading into Weems to the school trustees of White Stone District in the county of Lancaster and State of Virginia for the amount of $50.00." A land foundation for public education in Weems had begun.

A one-room framed building (16 x 28 feet) greeted its fledging pupils with Mary T. Carter as their first teacher. By 1916 a bricked building emerged from the ashes of the original school onto an additional one and a half acres again procured from the Ball family for $156.25. Now a front hall led into two classrooms complete with an auditorium and stage. Three pot-bellied stoves provided warmth with a wood assist (stacked under the school for dryness) from students coming in from recess. A kitchen would later replace

The former Weems School is privately owned and stands in its original building site just off Weems Road. *Author's photo.*

the stage area and with the addition of restrooms and oil heaters, Weems School would enter its modern phase. Privately owned, the school building still stands upon the original site "just a way up the road from Weems Wharf."

The names of earlier teachers were listed from time to time in The Virginia Citizen along with a comment or two about their dedication, expertise, and desire for their return the next school session. We recall the talents of Misses Emma Haynie (1903), Ella Cutter (1904), and Sally Fitchett (1909) who boarded with the Oscar Dameron family. Edith Buck (1915) taught as well with Miss Barnes as principal. The voices of many Weems children fondly recalling their school days always seem to begin with their teachers. Miss Ruth

With his school bus "change out" at Christ Church, Cosby Dunaway had time to play pranks on his walk home. A waterman, builder, and businessman, he figured out his "own future destination" from Weems beginnings. Left to right - Cosby Dunaway and Pat Lumpkin. *Author's photo.*

Coppedge, Principal and teacher of first and second grades, taught from the 1920s to the 1940s before retiring. As Cosby Dunaway (Weems resident) recalled, the third and fourth grade teachers during this time were Elizabeth Marsh and Marian Farley. Cosby walked several miles to school and back home every day. Always ready to help out, he toted water when needed and stacked fire-

Mr. and Mrs. Tinsley J. Dunaway
Photo by E. McCrc

Irene and Tinsley Dunaway (Cosby's parents) were our first neighbors in Weems and wonderfully helpful friends. They met at Wharton Grove Campground and married in 1927. Here they celebrate their 50th wedding anniversary. *Courtesy of the Rappahannock Record.*

wood. He remembered the classrooms to the left of a hall intersection with lunch served in the stage area. Mrs. Jayne Jackson, teacher-principal, during the 1950s and 1960s was the last Weems School educator. She completed her teaching career in White Stone.

Memories accumulated through the years from individuals certainly accentuate rural school experiences. My Aunt Bunks, Ila Lumpkin Hindman, attended first through third grade at the Weems site. "I lived in a farmhouse on Carters Creek, and walked about a mile to the main road to have my teacher, Miss Coppedge, pick me up. At least once a week I cried because I didn't want to go, but my parents were very insistent. One morning I hid behind a haystack and watched Miss Coppedge drive by. My story of the teacher not showing up didn't go so well. I was reprimanded and had to apologize to her the very next day." This was not an unusual parental reaction. The teacher, as always, was right. Her school progression would be to White Stone School and later graduation at Kilmarnock High School. Early on her brother and sister, Raymond and Bertha, with lunch pails containing butter and biscuits crossed Carters Creek in a skiff and walked through a wooded area to attend the Irvington School. One day Raymond dropped his primer on the way home and didn't bother to retrieve it. The story he related to his parents was that "the pig on the neighbor's farm ate my school book." Another apology followed. A writer in the Communication column of the Virginia Citizen in 1910 would receive the editor's rebuke for criticizing the School Board for not providing a ferry across the creek to accommodate the children's steady school attendance. He specifically stated that "Weems children are the most neglected of all children in the Northern Neck...

Top left - Weems School class photo taken in 1913. *Photo by Adams and Wilbert, Irvington, Va.* Center right - Weems School class photo taken in 1915. In the center is Maggie Thomas Webb wearing the white sweater. Edith Buck was the teacher. Bottom center - Weems School class photo in front of new brick building in 1916. *Genevieve Cockrell photo collection.*

coming home wet to the skin...owing to 6 or 7 boys dropping out of school." The lack of funds and low school population blocked such a move the Editor declared. There would be no ferry. All in all, the students seemed to embrace the "getting to school" adventure quite well.

The 1930s and 1940s school days still found the Weems children on their walk-a-thon...rain or shine. The perks were many. Picking berries, eating fox grapes, and gathering wild asparagus was the standard practice with pick-up games played along the way. Automobiles were rarities. However, Ben Winstead recalled that on some rainy days Ida Long would pull up in her car and motion everyone to pile in. "What fun we would have all jammed in together going to school. Miss Coppedge would be waiting, teaching all three elementary classes at the same time. She must have been a magician and had the best nerves ever. She had control of that classroom every hour we were there."

From the 1930s through the 1960s Weems School prevailed. But not just on educational word alone. Carroll Davis, Jr. and Lois Hudson also shared memories of the wonderful home cooked lunches that tempted them. Provided by a succession of ladies (Mrs. Blanche Dameron and Mrs. Elizabeth Clarke being the first and last cook), they recalled the delicious kitchen aromas. Often my brother, Raymond, revealed that it was the buttered homemade rolls that kept him coming back to school every day. Donnie Self noted the delights of mac and cheese baked by Mrs. James. He attended the school through fourth grade with Miss Coppedge and Mrs. Winstead as his teachers, studied at Kilmarnock School, and graduated from Lancaster High School. Donnie had been upgraded

Miss Ruth Coppedge spent her teaching career at Weems School and is remembered for her resourcefulness and dedication. *Courtesy of Harold B. Coppedge, Jr. and Betsy Helt Coppedge.*

Donnie Self lived with his mother and grandparents in the Franz House, circa 1915. From watching the boating activity on Carters Creek to exploring King Carter's home site and the Wharton Grove campsite, he reveled in every Weems moment. He spent many years in retirement there. *Courtesy of Donnie Self.*

to a school bus experience. "I stood with the other neighborhood kids at the store on the corner waiting to be picked up. Mrs. Bessie Winstead drove the bus. There would already be Johns Neck students aboard. All in all it was a great school experience." Playing baseball, tug games, dodge ball, and participating in show nights are part of Jack Jones' recollections. With parents in the audience, he drew a picture of Scottish bluebells blooming on the hills while Nan Ball played the "Bluebells of Scotland" on her trumpet. They finished in unison. Togetherness also extended in a variety of after school activities. Jack further shared. "I remember our getting together after school. We would play baseball on the ridge tilled field across from Roger Lumpkin's house...basketball and touch football as well. With clothes lines and poles to avoid it was tricky. One night

Center - Donnie and Mother, Vernie Self. Above - Standing beside his grandfather's 1947 Frazier automobile. Donnie later restored the vehicle purchased from Ozment Motor Sales. *Courtesy of Donnie Self.*

playing hide and seek, I did a complete swing around the line when I ran into it heading back to home base."

Model of Weems School made by Mr. Charles Shreve and given to Mrs. Jayne Jackson. *Courtesy of Jayne Jackson.*

In the late 1960s enrollment at the Weems School had dropped drastically. Mrs. Jayne Jackson, teacher/principal, provided a wonderful peek inside the world of its eighteen first and second graders at that time. Within the small auditorium, the day began

with the Pledge of Allegiance followed by
music until 10:30. Fully energized from
the early morning physical activity on
the gym equipment, the students divided
into appropriate grade levels to read from
Scott Foresman's "Basic Reader." They
subsequently studied math, science,
writing, and spelling. The afternoons
consisted of a variety of hands-on activities. Possibly a short walk to Mr. Ashburn's farm to learn about the animals
or to Mr. Headley's house to study about
the environment. Attention was given to
the holidays complete with Thanksgiving
Tee-Pees poles donated by Mr. Jackson or

Narrative style report card from
Weems School. *Courtesy of Jayne
Jackson.*

"The Night Before Christmas" re-enacted around a decorated tree
and red-bricked chimney. At school year's end, everyone enjoyed
a wonderful celebratory trip to the beach happily riding in a school
bus driven by Mrs. Lois Hudson. Mrs. Jackson's recollections are
very telling for they are describing a school with stalwart community support. These were all people who cared, supported, and expressed pride in the accomplishments of their sons and daughters,
and these were people who did not want to see it come to an end.

When, in truth, Weems School had hit a solid road block.
From a practical and economic standpoint, the School Board eyed
the situation as one of necessary adjustment. White Stone Elementary School, only ten miles away, stood in the wings to provide the
students with a more expansive curriculum. Weems School was
simply too costly to operate; particularly inclusive of its lunchroom
program offerings. The parents took up the cry of the benefits of
strong instruction provided on a one-to-one basis, the dedication of
the teacher in providing special experiences, and the pride the community had in the school's lifespan. Furthermore, they responded,
the "mothers would see that the children are properly fed." No
doubt about that. Food would always be a catalyst in Weems. Mrs.

Weems School 1967-68 class. Top row - Beth Wilson, Tammy Shreve, Charles Jones, Tenna Robertson, Jimmy Wilson, Trudi Blake, Mark Brent, Dennis Abbott, Mrs. Jayne Jackson, Teacher. Second row - Mary Keyser, Stony Kellum, William Ridgell, Jeffrey Verlander, Judy Benson, Carolyn Gaines, Tommy Hudson, Gail Abbott, Robin Syrett. Melvin Dawson. Seated - Jimmy Keyser, Billy Hudson. *Courtesy of Jayne Jackson.*

Weems first and second class Christmas party in 1966. This was Jayne Jackson's first class at the Weems School. *Courtesy of Jayne Jackson.*

Weems School Day is celebrated at a beach party given by their teacher, Mrs. Jayne Jackson. Lois Hudson drove the school bus for the fun event. *Courtesy of Jayne Jackson.*

Weems School wooden student desk. *Courtesy of Jayne Jackson.*

Richard H. Verlander penned these words to the Editor of the *Richmond News Leader* in part "...they (children) are taught, not merely pushed on a treadmill...the excellent preparation and individual attention they receive enabled them to lead their classes when transferred...hail to the one-room school." However, the "sole surviving one-teacher school in the existing Virginia area" had completed its educational journey. Its doors reluctantly closed but not the hearts of its students and their families.

WHARTON GROVE CAMPGROUND
1893-1927
DR. HENRY MARVIN WHARTON
1848-1927

The flat woodland area bound by the shores of the Rappahannock and Corotoman Rivers was perfect...just perfect. Standing upon the long planked wharf looking head on, one could truly feel the quiet "pull" of the land from an expansive view. Even so, an inviting stillness prevailed save the lapping of the water upon the shore. What better spot was there to mediate, reflect, and simply enjoy nature? And could there possibly be others of the same mindset that could envision the sharing of this land? As far as John Palmer was concerned there was. Only in his mind, with careful land development, that enjoyment could reach a high number count. He was, after all, a highly skilled businessman.

Campground revival meetings had grown by leaps and bounds in popularity on the east coast in the 1800s. People were experiencing a religious revival based upon the need to explore their own spirituality in a community style natural outdoor setting. Virginia's exposure would be summarily noted from 1890 to 1930 through the camp meeting grounds of Kirkland Grove (Heathsville/now a designated 1992 National Historic Site), Marvin Grove (Rainswood), and the subject of our interest Wharton Grove (Weems). All would have their specialized attraction, but the "drawing card" for Wharton Grove would be as the premier accessible campground by way

WHARTON GROVE CAMP, AUGUST, 1907

Hundreds of people walked across the Wharton Grove
Camp dock to attend services. *Courtesy of Kilmarnock Museum.*

of water. Only about a mile around the bend from Weems Wharf, this encampment eventually attracted thousands of people arriving by sailboats, gasoline boats, sail yachts, and, most importantly, the steamboat. A 1909 advertisement stated in part: "Excursions to Wharton Grove...my gasoline boat will be leaving Old Orchard Point Landing and Merry Point Landing...both Sundays on Wharton Grove Camp...25 cents...Captain G. B. Hazzard, Moran, VA."

THE GROVES WERE GOD'S FIRST TEMPLES - "WHARTON GROVE"
NEAR WEEMS, LANCASTER CO. VIRGINIA.   A. D. DART, PUBLISHER.

Wharton Grove Campgrounds situated among a lovely grove of trees drew worshipers to a grand experience. The tabernacle is on the left with cottages on the right in this postcard. *Courtesy of Kilmarnock Museum.*

For ten glorious summer days in July/August friends, families, guests, and visitors gathered in the most unique of circumstances to listen to evangelists preach their themes of salvation and redemption. It fell to reason that sociability among these participants would also become of paramount importance. Perhaps more of a key element of success than anyone realized at the time. Established four years after the founding of Campbell Memorial Presbyterian Church, many Weems residents joined in the picnic style atmosphere of the Wharton Grove camp grounds.

I remember well my grandmother, Bertha Lumpkin, recalling how the family of seven would anticipate the gatherings...packing over-sized picnic lunches, selecting their best dress Sunday clothes, and driving down the road with horse and wagon to join in for the day. She spoke of the sheer happiness of meeting relatives and friends for a day of food and worship almost in the sense of a vacation at home. Some families in Weems, James Oscar Dameron and Oscar Ashburn, had built their own permanent cottages and stayed over for the entire revival. Often, my Grandmother would allow her girls, Bertha, Louise, and Bunks to spend the night with Aunt Minnie and Uncle Oscar Ashburn in their framed cottage on the property. What stories of food abundance and fun in singing and craft making they brought back to the farm! With the attitude of how one could sleep in a corner for a night if necessary, the girls didn't seem to mind the cramped quarters with their relatives. Also, my Grandmother added... "They never tired of talking about Aunt Minnie's fancy and elaborate hats."

Yet how did this religious campground concept develop? Who would promote its message? And what would be its impact and source of longevity? It seems Mr. Palmer had set off a chain reaction through setting up a meeting with Kilmarnock Baptist clergyman, F. W. Claybrook, to talk about a grand scale campground meeting site. In turn, Reverend Claybrook garnered the attention of an engaging Southern evangelist, Dr. Henry Marvin Wharton.

A January 17, 1892, advertisement announced nightly sermons of Dr. Henry Wharton. *Courtesy of Richmond Times-Dispatch.*

Born at "Western View," Culpepper County, Virginia on September 11, 1848, this gentleman had strong credentials. The youngest of eight siblings, his education was founded in the "home school" concept. His life had taken many twists and turns from an army experience (enlisted in the Confederate Army under Robert E. Lee at the age of 15), to becoming a promising lawyer practicing at Amherst Courthouse, VA. After struggling through a drinking addiction, he studied at the Southern Baptist Theological Seminary for the ministry. His success in this field ultimately led him to establishing the Brantly Memorial Church in Baltimore all the while traveling about embracing his love of evangelistic preaching. Although he preached mainly in the south, he traveled throughout the United States and Canada. In 1881 his desirable lectures were extended to listeners in Europe. The term all used to describe him was "magnetic." Many followed him from place to place to hear the word again and again.

In "Messages of Mercy" (published in 1927 as a collection of Dr. Wharton's favorite sermons), the Reverend George W. McDaniel, D.D., pastor of the First Baptist Church in Richmond commended Dr. Wharton's combined gifts of oration and interaction with the audience. In the book's introduction Dr. McDaniel wrote of an enduring personality "...God made him a preacher and endowed him with as fine vocal chords as ever spoke or sang...his heart is as big as 'all outdoors'...he is unsurpassed as a master of assemblies." With these notable credentials nurtured by a mounting revival surge, Dr. Wharton undoubtedly sensed a successful Weems camp could easily materialize. Although popularity had brought him back to preach in some churches

Both rented and independently owned riverfront cottages began to spring up at Wharton Grove. *Courtesy of Kilmarnock Museum.*

"for seven consecutive years," this opportunity gave him a permanent home base to develop Wharton style. The deal was sealed with the purchase of 21 acres from the George Kern estate in Weems.

Investors lined up quickly and the Wharton Grove, Camp Ground Company, Incorporated, was formed with sixty shares sold at $50 apiece. Again, the names of Dameron and Ashburn appear as initial stockholders. Restrictions would be placed upon the lots (sixty were originally parceled out) where the cottages (earlier rendition known as "tents") could be built and used strictly for campground meeting occupancy during the revival. They could be rented or sold but were exclusive of land ownership. As such, each individual owner erected their two-storied wooden cottages (porches inclusive) with an individualized designer flair. Not easily architecturally categorized, these buildings boosted scallops, gingerbread

A postcard shows the unique cottages at Wharton Grove Camp in Weems, Virginia. *Courtesy of Kilmarnock Museum.*

Right - Dressed in their finery, Wharton Grove guests enjoy the evening from their cottage porch. *Dr. Henry J. Edmonds photo collection.*

Left - The tabernacle at Wharton Grove located in Weems, Virginia was the central gathering place for the worshipers. *Courtesy of Anne Long McClintock.*

trimmings, and all forms of colorfully designed geometric shapes. Topped by shingled roofs and with white painted siding, they were one of a kind. That these cottages were flanked by a ninety-foot squared "tabernacle" with openly exposed supportive massive beams, as well as two huge bench laden dining halls, plus a hotel was extraordinary. Numerous outsource style buildings (ice house, cookhouse, servants' quarters, etc.) formed the perimeter. The entire effect resembled that of a pop-up village.

Whether one traveled as far away as Norfolk, Richmond, Washington, and Baltimore or as close as the Northern Neck, the desire of people to join spiritually in a tabernacle style of outdoor worship was strong. Word spread. So they came...by the thousands. They streamed off the steamboat with parcels and suitcases and jam packed the 1,500 foot wharf leading up the incline to the main site to pay the 5 cent entrance fee. They shifted their prepared food and cots underarm to make way to the whitewashed cottages and stepped upon the porch to peer inside for bed space. No mind that the experience was to be void of screens, running water, sanitation means, or secure coverage from extreme elements, they good naturedly arrived at the campgrounds summer after summer. Refreshing themselves in the salt waters enclosed by a net to keep the nettles away, the Wharton Grove guests continued at nightfall to enjoy cottage house parties. There's no doubt the fashionably dressed ladies stepped gingerly over the raked sawdust grounds with skirts held aloft mindful of bugs and snakes. Or that the gentlemen paused to clean any shoe imperfections along their stroll. Spirits obviously soared to the ringing of the "tabernacle" bell throughout the day. Children and adults alike were treated to a genial study and worship experience. So they came with their Bibles held tightly to embrace the Lord.

Businesses naturally emerged on the camp grounds for crowd gathering convenience and comfort. A confectionary stand greeted the camp guests as they emerged from the water's edge. Two additional confectionary stands were built on either side of the camp entrance both operated by Eubank & Son, Eustace Brent, and Albert Noblett of Kilmarnock. Lemonade, ice cream, and the popular "Cracker Jacks" were top pleasers. In 1905 J. B. Cralle listed his confectionary store for rent with "...1/2 interest at Wharton Grove this summer...a splendid opportunity...for a paying business." W. T. Bassett declared that his horse lot and stage line "...will cater to the public in every way to please."

A close up view of a flagstone walkway to Wharton Grove retrieved from King Carter's Corotoman. *Postcard courtesy of Leigh Merrick.*

R. W. Foster, Kilmarnock tailor, was quick to advertise his ability to press your suit(s) to enhance your appearance at Wharton Grove camp. Even eye treatment was given by Dr. Newlin America (Quaker), eye specialist, optometrist, and optician. His headquarters at one point was the Oscar Ashburn "tent" cottage. The Reverend F. W. Claybrook reminded those interested that bids for horse lots and photography privileges would be reviewed through appointment prior to the camp's opening day.

In fact, very little was left to chance in preparation to make the annual Wharton Grove meeting memorable. Prior experience alerted the planning committee to expect "sell out /standing room only" crowds. From the careful selection of preachers, speakers, and singers to the physical improvements made to the promenade style wharf and the "tent" cottages, everything was geared to a glorious aesthetic experience. Sunday school workers flocked to listen to Reverend Joseph T. Watts expound upon "how to accomplish the most good out of the work." Lemonade and cake were served to the children every Thursday with special appropriate activities. Every gender and age group was thoroughly accommodated.

So successful was the Wharton Grove Camp that area churches closed on Sundays deferring to the stirring sermons of Dr. Wharton, Reverend Hugh H. Owen, Reverend C. L. Jackson, and F. W.

Entered into a Lancaster County Historical Society fund raiser, this oil painting of "1893 Wharton Grove Camp Ground" by David Jett features an American Flag...a gift of Hardesty Candy Corporation in Baltimore, Maryland and property of the Steamboat Era Museum. *Courtesy of David Jett.*

Claybrook to name a few. One Sunday 3,200 wharf tickets were counted with 5,000 to 6,000 people in attendance. The closing night of this 1909 statistic was upped to 7,000 participants. Even now this is an amazing gathering upon Weems soil. They came to hear Miss Clara V. Wilder, organist and choir leader, perform with "sweet volunteer singers." They came to enjoy bountiful food with relatives and friends, and to follow their hearts with a special someone. They stayed to become a part of an evangelistic historical movement that continues to mesmerize us all even today.

But after 34 years, the impact of change gripped Wharton Grove. True, in 1920 there had been another "revival" of sorts with Dr. Wharton purchasing, in entirety, Wharton Grove for reconstruction and renewal. With friends in support, he refurbished the cottages, tapped into power and water, and offered preaching with a more international theme. World War I had intervened

Dr. Henry Marvin Wharton posed for his portrait in his book, "Pulpit, Pew, and Platform," published in 1891.

and interest in religious campground meetings had waned. Its time had come and with Dr. Wharton's death in 1927 an extraordinary era of religious fervor and rare social interaction was simply over.

THE GROVE
JAMES WHARTON
1900-1992

Upon his father's death, James Wharton returned to and made his home upon the land in Weems, Virginia where his father had been a larger-than-life figure singing and preaching on the evangelistic trail. James' early life had been one of traveling about the east, taking on various job descriptions, and enjoying his fellowman along the way. That came naturally. After all, his father had set the tone. After a Johns Hopkins University (philosophy major) sojourn, James worked in proofreading for the *Baltimore Sun* newspaper and later became a reporter in New Orleans. This experience sharpened "his love for words" and gave a basis for his prolific writings in the history of the area upon which researchers have come to rely. Volumes of books stretched from floor to ceiling at his Wharton Grove cottage home. He genially followed the path of a "word smith," and like a pied piper crisscrossed over subject lines that caught his curiosity and maintained his interest. That songbooks and song posters were stacked alongside in his home gave credence to the fact that musical sounds could be heard in the dusk of evening at The Grove. As John Wilson pointed out in a 1992 news tribute to James Wharton, "his interest in people and his very presence...are the characteristics for which he is most remembered."

Now the gatherings at The Grove would take on a meaning of bringing people together for "stimulation and fun." The Grove guest orientation was aimed to provide a casual but unique experience that tapped into one's artistic senses. The agenda was refreshing. Join in the singing, writing of plays, and dancing. Appreciate the delicate taste of a diamondback terrapin from a gourmet "in cottage" recipe. Be lured into action with a tennis match on the nearby clay tennis court or bat the badminton birdie a time or two. Feel refreshed in the netted off swimming area. Take in an early evening movie projected against a white cottage wall. Gather up the youngest guests for playground activities on the banks of the grounds. Enjoy the ongoing chapter style bedtime stories. The centerpiece of The Grove was always a personal reservation spot on that famously lengthy wharf for one to sit, mediate, and reflect upon the sheer beauty of the surroundings that brought them there in the first place. The Grove proprietor would later himself reflect. "Think of all those hymns offered up in these trees."

Continuing the "spirit" of the Grove became more and more difficult. The enterprise began to fade in the 1950s. The increasing upkeep demands, shopping for fresh food, preparing gourmet dishes, and keeping the pulse of the guests to the forefront was all consuming. Although there was a quiet reopening in 1960, The Grove eventually slipped back into itself and retreated to its lovely woodland setting.

A RETURN TO THE GROVE
JULY 2013

What a pleasure to meet with Jean Nelson and set foot upon the Wharton Grove site. She is the caretaker of the remaining cottages and lives slightly behind their position facing the Rappahannock River. The "Sunburst" and "Cottingham" cottages are original. They were sold in the 1970s to the present day owners. She spoke of James Wharton playing the piano at the meeting house and organizing picnic style meals at sunset. In keeping with the Wharton Grove tradition, Jean's family has enjoyed reunions there during the Christmas season. They appreciate the time to unwind and share what's going on in their lives. They agree there's a special beauty about winter on the water at The Grove. One can feel that, too, standing on the wooden wharf overlooking the site. The valued entity of peoples and activities of many years ago still remain.

Pier leading off Wharton Grove over the Corotoman River as it appears today. *Author's photo.*

Remaining Wharton Grove cottages offer time to unwind, enjoy the water, and reflect upon the history of the area. *Author's photo.*

WEEMS TOMATO CANNERY
SAMUEL CHARLES THOMAS 1882-1942
IRA WEBB   1890-1955

A goodly amount of the success of the tomato canneries in the Northern Neck was owed to the services of the steamboat freight prowess. It's as if a sign stating "Get Your Fresh Produce Here" was painted in bold letters on the sides of the steamers. The concept was simple in nature--exchange fruits for goods. The process was a bit more complicated. However, the means for Samuel C. Thomas to eventually operate a tomato cannery near the "F. F. V." tomato brand of W. A. Dameron & Bro on Weems Wharf had been in the making for some time...in his kitchen.

It began, most predictably, with Samuel and his wife boiling and stirring tomatoes in a huge stove pot at home. Born in Shepardstown, West Virginia, Samuel's early life experiences had placed him working aboard a canal boat. He made his way to Baltimore and took notice of the operation of a fine-tuned canning factory. Fascinated by the process, he

Original Thomas homestead on the banks of the Rappahannock River. *Courtesy of Chase Webb Basilio.*

quickly learned the operational techniques. After marriage to Annie Bittner, he relocated to Rehoboth Church, VA, and began to can his own tomatoes. Upon the urging of John Palmer to relocate to Weems and operate a tomato cannery on the wharf, he took up the challenge with scant money resources to go upon. Once situated, he set diligently to work honing his canning abilities through processing berries, corn, pumpkin, and even sweet potatoes. With faith in this fledging enterprise, John and Joe Cralle (Weems retailers) respectively sold Mr. Thomas land as well as financed the factory and his private home entirely "on time." No one would be disappointed. Residing in what is now the "Peck" Humphreys home site, Samuel settled in and began operating his cannery on Weems Wharf with full access to the steamboat docking. Within a short amount of time, the Thomas Cannery was in full operational mode.

Bumper to bumper flatbed trucks stacked with tomatoes in wooden peck baskets lined the dirt road leading to the wharf. Unloading would become as precise as the 5 a.m. elongated cannery whistle's shrill and piercing call to workers that the boiler had been stoked and processing was at the ready.

Long and steamy summer days were spent inside the cannery readying for mar-

S. C. Thomas became a very successful businessman in Weems. *Courtesy of Chase Webb Basilio.*

ket. The procedure began as hot water loosened the tomato skins, and skillful hands removed the outer skins and inner cores. Next the fruit was placed in large buckets that were hand carried to a long packing table. Now placed in cans, the tomatoes awaited juices to be added and then topped with lids as a conveyor moved the wares along. Situated in a cooker within a cage like container, the tomatoes were then processed.

Tomato Cannery (about 1920) located on what is now Weems Road. *Walter Lee Harding photo collection.*

A cooling period preceded the labeling, boxing, and shipping by steamboats and later trucks. The "Redskin Brand" label that enclosed the tin can said it all. "The People's Choice...Packed Where Grown...Hermetically Sealed...S. C. Thomas at Weems, Lancaster Co., VA." In addition to the cannery, Mr. Thomas prospered as well with the operation of a herring roe fish factory situated for a short time on Weems Wharf. Packed by hand, with a printed recipe for Roe Cakes on the label, he used his ingenuity here as well to process foods that afforded his wife and family of eight children a comfortable life.

Tomato peelers and pickers received tokens as a form of currency for their labor in the early Thomas cannery years. Representative of upwards to 4 or 5 cents per peeled tomato basket, the tokens could be redeemed at the S. C. Thomas merchandise store. They could also be turned in for cash value. Hourly rates were paid to the packers and processors. As their income was derived from a short summer season, everyone kept up a fast and labor intensive pace.

By the 1920s the tomato was well on its way toward becoming the area's leading crop. Its significance spiraled upward in 1931 with 86 canneries reported in Northern Neck alone. Relocated on the main Weems road, the cannery was now operated by Ira Webb after Mr. Thomas' passing. Married to Mr. Thomas' daughter, Nettie, he involved nearly two-thirds of the Weems community in its successful production for thirteen years. Anyone and everyone in Weems who owned at least an acre of land raised the lucrative crop. For many years early steamy summer mornings revealed individuals picking the ripe fruit and gently placing them in buckets and baskets for pick up by a cannery worker in horse and wagon. Cosby Dunaway remembered working alongside Mortimer Brown and Ulysses Gaskins until the sun rose a bit smelling the distinctive odor of the tomato vines and wiping away stains that accumulated on their overhauls. Ten cents a peck was the going rate when I, along with my mother, Aunt Ida, and cousin Roger, spent early morning hours picking tomatoes and mentally calculating our earnings.

In later years many Weems residents worked before and after their day job carrying tomatoes to the cannery in early morning or in the evening dusk. To aid in the process Mr. Webb often hauled the picked tomatoes in a six-wheeler truck for a nominal fee. People in the community had a genuine affection for the landmark cannery. Walking about in the evening, the sound of "POP, POP, POP!" could be distinctly heard as the tomato cans cooled down cannery style. No doubt it was music to the ears of all those making a good living out of

The Lumpkins always had fun doing activities together. (From left to right) Ida, Roger, Gladys and Pat Lumpkin. *Author's photo.*

the crop. Years later Walter Lee Harding still displayed a snapshot of the tomato cannery in his home. His job plain and simple was to add the juice to every tomato can. He considered it a good and plentiful day's work. With a war on the horizon and less land bearing the fruit, the tomato cannery eventually ceased its operation in Weems in 1955.

Original Redskin label from the Weems Tomato Cannery. *Genevieve Cockrell photo collection.*

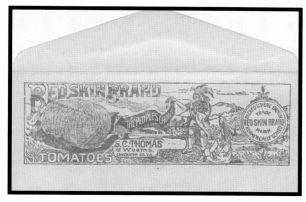

Original Herring Roe label from S. C. Thomas factory. *Genevieve Cockrell photo collection.*

Envelope with Redskin tomato logo. *Genevieve Cockrell photo collection.*

Workers preparing to haul tomatoes to a cannery. *Courtesy of Anne Long McClintock and Steamboat Era Museum.*

Samuel C. Thomas poses in front of his general merchant store located on Weems Wharf. *Courtesy of Debbie Morgan.*

Mr. Thomas poses in a field of home grown Weems tomatoes. *Courtesy of Chase Webb Basilio.*

Original tomato cannery sodering can. *Courtesy of Anne Long McClintock and Steamboat Era Museum. Author's photo.*

The original Weems cannery whistle that signaled the workers to begin their day. *Courtesy of Chase Webb Basilio.*

Tomato cannery scalding basket. *Courtesy of Anne Long McClintock and Steamboat Era Museum. Author's photo.*

Tomato peelers off the waterfront. *Courtesy of Anne Long McClintock and Steamboat Era Museum. Author's photo.*

View inside Thomas herring roe operative in Weems. *Courtesy of Chase Webb Basilio.*

A group of cannery workers pose in front of the original Thomas tomato factory in Weems. *Courtesy of Jean Winstead Robertson.*

LEVIN THOMAS BUCK
1861-1930
LEVIN T. BUCK & COMPANY
1896-1942

What ended as an enchanting neighborhood play space of crumbling mortared uneven bricked towers and secretive arched tunneled hiding spaces began with Levin Buck's medical prescription... leave Baltimore city and seek fresher air. A former contractor/engineer, he chose to take his Doctor's advice and settled in the country environment of Weems, Virginia. Hard working and industrious in nature, Levin Buck surveyed his initial seven acre purchase with a bent toward enjoying the lovely outdoor environment. He established a business locally referred to as "The Brickyard."

Advertisement of Levin T. Buck as manufacturers and shippers of bricks made in Weems, Virginia. Later notices would cite availability on short notice due to the "latest improved machines." *Courtesy of Virginia Citizen, January 1900.*

The discovery of a spacious clay pit (located behind the stretch of Weems land on what is now James Lane) prompted Mr. Buck to round up mules and a scoop and begin the excavation for his enterprise. Sturdy sets of metal rails fashioned much like a mini roller coaster supported square carts. They stood ready to transport the clay to the impressive kiln site located in an embankment near the head waters of Carters Creek. There the clay was molded into bricks and shoved into the recess of the fiery brick kilns. "Buck's Bricks" was soon open for local sales.

Within a mere four years, Mr. Buck registered a patent certificate for a new style kiln furnace grate with a combined forced draft to promote brick making efficiency. A fifty thousand pressed brick

Another advertisement of Levin T. Buck's business. *Courtesy of Virginia Citizen.*

order from The National Bank of Irvington was reported in the 1900 issue of The Virginia Citizen. A May 1919 Commonwealth of Virginia certificate of registration revealed that a "Lancaster Brand Fish Mixture" was also eligible for purchase. In addition, the growing business advertised "Fine Burnt Shell Lime" produced from oyster shells baked in the kiln as available for shipment. The business life span (operated and leased to various individuals until the 1940s) of "The Brickyard" was a down home story promoting pride in business workmanship and bolstering community spirit. Its brick product would be utilized years hence in the bygone Kilmarnock Hotel on Church Street, the Kilmarnock Drug Store, and the building housing The Pedestal Interior Designs on Main Street. The Christ Church School bell tower and dormitory, Weems Campbell Memorial Presbyterian Church as well as many local homes contain "Buck's Bricks." Once the clay pit had been dug to water level and business ceased to operate, a small pond emerged upon which Weems residents spent many hours ice skating during harsh winters.

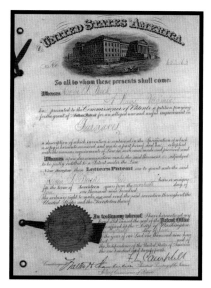

A copy of the patent certificate registered to Levin T. Buck for a furnace grate. *Courtesy of Page Pembroke Rudolph.*

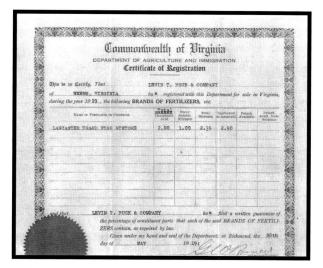

Copy of Certificate of Registration for fish fertilizer. *Courtesy of Page Pembroke Rudolph.*

The Brickyard Pond as it appears today in a park-like setting. *Author's photo.*

BACK TO THE BRICKYARD

It's no wonder that a meeting with Page Pembroke Rudolph (Great-Great Grandaughter of Levin T. Buck) one brilliantly sunny day in 2014 lent itself to the recapturing of the spirit that "The Brickyard" seemed to still hold fast. We walked the extensive property of rolling contoured gently mowed land. Protected by tall trees and varying shades of greenery, we admired the intriguing sculptures created by her father, "Sonny." The brick cart rails had long been removed and found their way as part of the Carters Creek boat railway. Several large ponds had emerged as a result of her father's creative landscaping efforts with one surrounding his sculpture cited as "The Levin T. Buck Memorial Sculpture." She shared the rigors of brick making as "dirty hard work" and confirmed that the workers wore wooden shoes overtop

Fashioned from iron rail ties original to the business, Graham Pembroke's Levin T. Buck Memorial Sculpture occupies a prominent spot on the property. *Author's photo.*

their regular footwear to shield them from the ash wafting from the furnaces. We walked to the creek's edge where the "bugeyes" had docked to unload coal for the kiln and conjured up the movement and activity of the brick making time. Pulling aside a determined tangled growth of vines revealed the remains of the brick kilns now overlooking a serene meditative style landing.

Page's ongoing account of times past reveals a true Weems extended Buck/Pembroke/Rudolph "family affair." She has happily returned to Weems living next door to the enduring James homestead. Making her way to the main house where her Father lived until his passing in 2010, one can easily detect her affection for the grounds as well as the community. The 1876 Ball family property purchased from the Oden family, her Father had added acreage from a lot owned by Paige Ball and Sam Watson. We took a nostalgic look around the main house where her Father's decorations and artwork were carefully placed for full enjoyment. The view from the upstairs nautically designed room is breath taking. One also learned her Father bought

Remnants of the brickyard kiln lie underneath heavy vine growth. *Author's photo.*

A close up view of the oval bricked firing oven. *Author's photo.*

and restored Allie and Irene Harding's home at one point. His main and ongoing project; however, was to rescue the clay pit from community garbage and restore the area to a bucolic style park setting. He succeeded. Page has added a stable for her horses on the property with the flooring set, of course, with "Buck's Bricks."

Our conversation moved to her grandfather, Graham Pembroke, who grew up in Weems and eventually retired to Dymer Creek after an outstanding 36 year career at the Standard Oil/Esso Company. At age fourteen his adventure aboard a North Sea freighter was abruptly terminated. Grandmother

Stable flooring is comprised of "Buck's Bricks." *Author's photo.*

Julia lured him back to Weems with a dual offer of a new car and an opportunity to help his grandfather, Claude, in the brick business. When his grandfather passed away, he quit the business simply stating, "I knew HOW to make the brick but I couldn't sell them." His love of sailing never left him on dry land for long. Graham's first skiff was handmade and later rigged with a sail. Often he and a friend would brave the Rappahannock River waters when the mail boat from Urbanna couldn't cross. Walton Dameron (entrepreneur of Weems Wharf) shared with Graham that more than once with the boat dipping and disappearing among the waves, he feared the youths had met their demise. Though his boyhood desire for sailing around the world eventually materialized, Graham would often "strike up a meaningful conversation" aboard his 43 foot Alden designed schooner moored at Milton Cross' dock in Weems. Foremost, the desire to help people succeed became the "things that made his life worthwhile."

During his tenure with Esso Standard Oil Company, Graham Pembroke traveled extensively but considered Weems, Virginia, a top priority. *Richmond News Leader Staff photo.*

Graham Pembroke's boat berthed at Milton Cross dock in Weems, Virginia. *Dr. Henry J. Edmonds photo collection.*

A final reminder of this Weems family's legacy still stands today; the three-storied 1897 "Pembroke House" built by Levin T. Buck as a family residence. Page recalls with joy the many hours spent in Weems as a youngster. It crosses my mind how fortunate she is to experience that part of her life all over again.

A view of Carters Creek through Graham Pembroke's iron sculpture. *Author's photo.*

(From left to right.) Edith Buck, Julia and Claude Pembroke pose in front of an early view of the Weems brickyard kiln. Carl and Bessie Dunn and family lived on the brickyard premises at one time. Carl kept the fires burning to aid in the brick making process. *Courtesy of Jack Long.*

Remaining brickyard structure as it appeared in
1966. *Author's photo.*

WEEMS COMMUNITY HALL
1931-1975

It was destined to become the most centralized of all meeting places simply referred to as the "Community Hall." And it was used year 'round. The rectangular 30 foot by 60 foot white wooden planked building with its small porch style entryway stood on one acre of land around the corner from the church. Lawson Winstead donated the land and willingly turned it over to the Weems community. It could not have been placed in better hands. Paid for and maintained by them for forty-four years this building housed and brought to life important social aspects of their lives.

The large hall interior flanked by numerous windows contained two wood stoves, a piano, and a storage area for church chairs. The open space concept perfectly lent itself to the creativity of the Weems folks. The unencumbered wide beamed wooden floors were perfect for gathering to enjoy Ed Long and the Ashburn gentlemen playing guitars and singing the evening away. Friday night teen dances became a staple. Glenn Miller records provided the musical backdrop for refreshments of cookies, cake, and lemonade. Babs and Wellford Hudson, along with Florimond and Leon Hayden, proved to be popular chaperones. With admission for weekend dances providing "upkeep" for the hall, Gippy Smith, Sunshine Sue, and the Old Dominion Barn Dance drew large crowds.

Central to the social life of Weems residents, the Community Hall as it appeared in 1933. *Courtesy of Ben Winstead.*

The annual Halloween Costume competition topped the seasonal activity list. Both children and adults draped in mysterious homemade disguises danced, maneuvered in a circled "Cake Walk", ate local goodies, and waited for the "Best/Spookiest" costume of the night to be announced. Jack Jones remembers his misinterpreted "Charlie Chaplin" moustache costume and walk as mistaken for "Adolph Hitler." No prize that year for him. However, his choices of a devil paper mache mask and later an open-mouth panther complete with big teeth and gloves were standouts. He and Mary Gates (as a witch) trick or treated throughout Weems gathering massive amounts of goodies.

However, nothing surpassed "The Fellowship Suppers." It was well known that in the long run the Weems community supported any cause through good eating. And could they sell tickets! Long wooden tables atop sawhorses with benches alongside were arranged to accommodate 100 people with two to three settings in mind. Fresh oysters, crabs, ham, turkey, chicken, and vegetables with homemade cakes and pies were the norm. The Dameron, Pearson, and Thomas Weems storekeepers donated goods as well. Tables laden with Irma Ashburn's coleslaw mixed in a washtub also held the talents of cooks like Daisy Hodges, Hilda Ward, Bessie Winstead, Mildred Bradshaw, Melissa Hutchens, and many women throughout the hall's tenure. As people from Weems and surrounding areas stood in line chatting and awaiting their turn, fellowship reached an all-time high.

Romances were not immune to the charms of the Community Hall. Emma Robertson recalls the evening the United States sailors aboard ship in the Rappahannock River followed the music to its doors for a great evening. Louise George as well as her sister Ione both met and married their dance partners. Norma Lumpkin recalls having her first date with my brother, Raymond, during the Halloween Party. The versatile hall hosted birthday parties, wedding receptions, showers, smaller church dinners, and even became a voting precinct.

With a sole street light casting its shadows across the road, the hall stood

In February of 1960 Weems residents gave Pat Lumpkin a bridal shower at the Community Hall. *Author's photo.*

witness to the fun and laughter of many outdoor roller skating parties. A pool table even found its way into the hall. Well into the 1960s youngsters looked forward to hall socials on Saturday night to enjoy hot dogs and hamburger treats cooked by Fran and Norman Blake. Merely moments away from their homes the youth of Weems logged in hours of fun and gamesmanship.

After 1975, no longer useful in terms of bringing people together within its social eaves, the Community Hall stood silently deteriorating for twenty-one years. Its purpose had been eclipsed by modern styled community needs. A church Fellowship Hall now hosted the suppers. Proximity to transportation and social media such as the automobile, telephone, and television had evolved. A younger generation had surfaced eager to embrace a new style of recreational activities.

In 1996 the Community Hall's caved roof, crumbling walls, and broken windows stood stubbornly amid the flames of a controlled fire. A few neighbors gathered silently to say good-bye. To the end it remained a testament to a time of rare Weems togetherness.

Top left - Community members (Belva McCrobie, Leon Hayden, Texie Atkins, Effie Davis, Betty Sharon Beatley, Thelma Cross, Agnes Hudson, Welford Hudson, Imogen Daniel, Harry Paul Treakle, and Russell Winstead) participate in the annual Halloween party at the hall. *Courtesy of Patricia Davis Hinton.* Top right - Patricia Davis enjoys her birthday party at the Weems Community Hall. Guests included (from left to right) Vernie Self, Jean Jordan, Virginia Lee Ashburn, Imogen Daniel, Mary Gates, Freddie Gates, Pat Davis, Bobby Wynn, Donnie Self, Peggy Harding and Wayne Harding. *Courtesy of Patricia Davis Hinton.*

Left - By 2001 the building had deteriorated badly; Right - Community Hall stands amid flames during controlled fire by the White Stone Fire Department. *Author's photos.*

LUTTRELL FARMHOUSE
WEEMS LANDMARK ENTRANCE

Defining the entrance to Weems had unofficially been recognized by its residents for many years upon passing a stately two story farmhouse offset on the curve of the road. That the lovely grounds it sat upon was once part of Robert "King" Carter's "Corotoman" gave it an historical aura. Research showed that in the mid-1800s during a Carter family parcel "sell off," Griffin J. Ashburn purchased some fifty acres. Three children, Griffin T., George Riley, and Martha were born of his marriage to Olivia in 1857. In Lancaster County courthouse records, it is revealed that the farmhouse became the home place of Griffin T. and his wife Emma E. Haydon. He entered Weems community life as a farmer and a waterman, and was active as an Elder in the Campbell Memorial Presbyterian Church. Upon his passing in 1930, six of their children (Franklin, Eleanor, Evelyn, Alonzo, Ernest and Milton) conveyed the property to their brother, Otis Newbill Ashburn. Several siblings continued to live on site. One of these siblings, Eleanor, had a daughter, Jeanette, who eventually received the property from her Uncle Otis in 1959. Married to Jimmy Luttrell, local real estate agent, Jeanette remained there until her passing in 2003. The following year Leigh Merrick purchased the farmhouse and with extensive remodels enjoyed its ambiance for eleven years. Since October of 2015 the property is currently under private ownership with the River Village development situated on the Rappahannock River serving as its backdrop. Leigh continues to live in Weems in the restored home of Ila and Dewey Jordon, and remains avidly interested in the history of the community.

Originally the Griffin J. Ashburn family homestead, the farmhouse has become a landmark entrance to Weems.
Courtesy of Leigh Merrick.

Alonzo Ashburn, wife and family pose in front of the original Ashburn homestead. The pallbearers at his funeral serve as partial listing of Weems and North Weems community members in the 1930s. (W. A. Dameron, S. C. Thomas, B. G. Dogget, Peter Bittner, C. B. Smither, Robert Bryant, Herbert George, Clifford Currell, Virgil Jones, Earl Winstead, Fred Ward, John W. Ashburn, Norman Ball, Harry Ball, Wilbur Haydon, Calvin Barrack, Milton Rose, George Hutchings, Oscar Ashburn, Emmett Franz, Robert Guthrie, Marion Ashburn, and Arthur Poor.) *Courtesy of Leigh Merrick.*

In May 1997, the culmination of Neill Shultz' Eagle Scout community service project was the installation and landscaping of the 3 by 5 foot "Welcome to the Village of Weems" sign. Creative Design, with Sandra Matthews offering advice and computer facilities, aided in the project. *Courtesy of Ben Winstead.*

At the mouth of Carters Creek in Weems, Virginia, Weems Wharf played a prominent role in the lives of the members of its community. *Courtesy of Margery Nea.*

PART IV

OUR WIDENING PATHS

A cliff-like peak invited one further into the continuance of Carters Creek. The extended land leveled off as it bordered the lovely curvy shallow water inlets. Here individuals built their homes near the water's edge just across the creek from Weems Wharf. It remains to speculation as to the origin of the name the site was given...Johns Neck. The term is indeed strikingly similar to the references made in early settlement papers as to the "necks of land." That leads us directly to the extensiveness of John Carter's land holdings. The people who eventually established homes and businesses in Johns Neck no doubt reveled in the richness of the land, but it would be the abundant crab and oyster yield that would define their lives. They formed a community within a community owing to the many relatives living primarily alongside the single entry road way. Eventually, creek home residences emerged most often with business access. Linking their lives to those conducting business on Weems Wharf, the people of Johns Neck forged cohe-

sive friendships and shared dependencies. Often my Grandmother Lumpkin would relate how neighbors "shouted pleasantries across the creek" while attending to outdoor chores.

Johns Neck developed as a residential and business waterfront community with access to the creek, river, and bay amenities. *Author's photo.*

- 149 -

Today Johns Neck is a quiet residential area. Through the courtesy of Lois and Curtis Kellum, an afternoon drive for me recalled a lifetime there. Down the asphalt road curving only at what could be noted as a once busy intersection, identification of people and places suitably began. Kellum's and Grisby's general merchandise stores stood on the right and left respectively. Straight ahead the gated fencing cordoned off the W. Ellery Kellum Seafood business and Ampro Shipyard (formerly Humphreys Railways) practically adjacent to one another. To the land side of Kellum Seafood was the Abbott Brothers business now Carters Creek Marina and the Russell Kellum Seafood building. Continuing toward the elevated land abutting Carters Creek, Curtis recalled the thriving oyster houses of Doggett, Morgan, and Warwick & Ashburn (established 1936). The Abbott brothers also operated The Northside Crab Company (1950s and 1960s) in a building now converted to a cottage. It's easy to detect the pride Curtis has in this area that has been "good to and good for" him.

Above left - Kellum's all purpose store was operated by Ellery Kellum, William Irving Kellum, and J. J. Kellum until his passing in 2015. Above right - Original store office for Humphreys Railways with Kellum's Seafood entrance to the far right. Right - Surviving property of Morgan Seafood Company on Johns Neck Point. *Author's photos.*

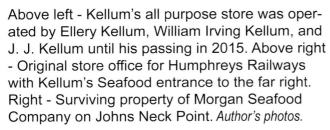

Originally Warwick and Ashburn Seafood, this current vacant facility faces Carters Creek. *Author's photo.*

This building once housed the Abbott Brother's Northside Crab Company. *Author's photo.*

Aboard a workboat the Kellum family (left to right) Curtis, Bertie Mae, J.J., Mother Rubinette, Dorothy, Jimmy, and Hathaway enjoyed exciting times on Carters Creek. *Courtesy of Curtis Kellum.*

A dedicated collector of waterman era memorabilia, Curtis Kellum
has amassed hundreds of items displayed in a building near his
home. *Author's photo.*

CLAYBROOK BAPTIST CHURCH
ESTABLISHED FEBRUARY 25, 1912

With an ever increasing interest to meet locally for Baptist
fellowship, many individuals in the Johns Neck area called for a
Prayer Meeting at the framed Weems School building in 1897. A list
of some thirty-three individuals has been verified as in attendance.
It stands as remarkable that this gathering swept up in gestures
of friendship and belief in God would provide the foundation for
what stands one hundred and four years later as Claybrook Baptist
Church. If the Irvington Baptist Pastor, the Reverend Frederick W.
Claybrook, who gave early on of his talents and services for its rise,

could deliver a rousing sermon from its pulpit today; it would undoubtedly be entitled, "A Church of Endearing Endurance."

Following the initial prayer meeting, momentum began to build. In quick succession, Robert L. Bryant opened his home to further the discussion of a need for a permanent house of worship in Johns Neck inclusive of religious instruction for the youth of the community. The idea was lofty. With ever growing families having membership in Irvington Baptist, the distance and inconvenience for travel had become a viable factor. Additionally, the pattern of alternating Sunday School in the morning and attending services in Irvington in the afternoon had become wearing. They looked toward Reverend Fred Claybrook for encouragement and promise of occasional preaching in Johns Neck. Although serving as pastor of Irvington, Morattico, and White Stone Baptist Churches, he willingly reached out with an open heart.

Reverend Frederick W. Claybrook was founder of Claybrook Baptist Church, and a tireless worker for the ongoing success of the spiritual needs of the Johns Neck community. *Courtesy of Claybrook Baptist Church Archives.*

So, too, did Captain B. G. Doggett offering the use of an unoccupied farmhouse on his land for the ever growing gatherings. Located across the road from where Sauers Service Station once stood, this site is recognized as the birthplace of "Weems Chapel," later re-dedicated as "Claybrook Baptist Church." For a time Sunday School was held there with Allen Ashburn serving as the first Superintendent. Prayer Meetings on Tuesday nights grew steadily and Reverend Claybrook often joined in with an inspired message. Families continued alternating worship in Irvington and Johns Neck as well during this time.

In 1900 Elzie Currell offered a land gift as a church site. Fund raising began in earnest. A small one-storied frame building was eventually raised. The organization of an "Aid Society" by the women of the church would continue to garner support to work toward completion. Flickering coal lamps greeted the families as they walked through the front door. Their images cast shadows upon the unfinished walls. Home crafted pine benches offered a sit down. They did so with great anticipation leaning forward to hear the message. With a final "amen," their desire for a church home had finally become a reality.

A granite marker installed as an Eagle Scout Project is situated on the original church site. The 1912 church design shows the prominance of the church steeple. *Courtesy of Norma Lumpkin.*

This modest beginning grew to accommodate jam packed revivals and witness multiple conversions. With Reverend Claybrook at the helm, the first Baptist Youth People's Union (B.Y.P.U) surfaced in Lancaster County. Officers and deacons formed in place and on February 25, 1912, the church was officially established with ninety-nine members. True to the belief in community togetherness, non church members came forward to help. Lemuel Ashburn, father of Oscar Ashburn, contributed financially. George Packett and family lent their resources as well. Mr. and Mrs. Collin B. Smithers were benefactors. Mrs. Smithers served as a Sunday School teacher, and C. B. Smithers was assistant Sunday School Superintendent in 1906. Mr. and Mrs. M. M. Haydon participated in church work as well.

With years of growth noted, by the early 1950s Claybrook membership accepted a new building lot from Clifford and Emory Currell. J. A. Lawson was awarded the contract for a spacious brick church. On May 23, 1954, a cornerstone marked its completion. In 1961 a new pastorium set in motion the invitation for a full time ministry in Johns Neck. Up until that time seventeen pastors inclusive of Claybrook, Goodwin, Hardcastle, Estall, Cosby, Alley, Pitts, Hart, and Wright had served Claybrook. Now Richard T. Bray answered the call, and became its first full time pastor with full acknowledgement of the many shared talents of the mother church in Irvington.

Above left - Claybrook Baptist Church as it appears today with additions; Above right - Closeup of church bell relocated to the side of the front entrance. *Courtesy of Norma Lumpkin.*

From the first prayer meeting to present day, the people of Johns Neck and the surrounding community are grateful for the love and devotion given by many individuals who served to see Claybrook grow and mature. They have indeed endured. For many it's the presence of the church bell permanently housed on the left front church lawn that catches and leads their eyes skyward toward the grand steeple. That's the beauty of the legacy of Claybrook Baptist Church.

The present day sanctuary of Claybrook Baptist Church is most inviting. Attendance and hymns are still posted on either side of the altar. *Courtesy of Norma Lumpkin.*

A "Golden Anniveresary Home Coming Day" was held in 1950 to celebrate "the building of the first Baptist Church in Weems." Here the congregation poses in front of the framed church that would see the cornerstone laid for a brick church in 1954. *Courtesy of Claybrook Baptist Church Archives.*

PRAYER MEETING PARTICIPANTS IN 1897

C. L. Marsh

George Packett

Henry Crittendon

L. E. Ashburn, Sr.

J. Robert Sadler

Allen Ashburn

E. A. Ashburn

Lemuel Ashburn

Joseph Kellum

S. B. Haydon, Sr.

Robert L. Bryant

W. T. Gaines

Captain B. G. Doggett

Rolden Gaines

Hattie Ashburn

Wessie Ashburn

Gertie Blake

Belle Marsh Benson

Jeter Benson

Eva Marsh Gaines

Lee Kellum

Bessie Ketnor

Lottie Lumpkin

Bertha Lumpkin

Lizzie Luttrell

Alice Marsh

Clara Sadler

Mrs. Edwin Ashburn

Lurline Sanders

Ruby Ashburn Bane

Mable Grogg Williams

Dolly Stevens

Lelia Gaines

INDIANTOWN FARM

Among the original tracts of land from the Carter estate was a sector bordering the Corotoman River known as Indiantown. Within this area the Smither's farm was established in the 1900s and consisted of 1,627 acres of farmland. Today one can head down the long lane past the Claybrook Baptist Church and drive past present day Currell's Field. The Weems airstrip is still in use. Passing the vacated family home, one can immediately feel the presence of the past. Houses dot the contour of the river bank as it comes into view and winds toward the spectacular beauty of Corotoman Point.

Collin Smither owns a thirty acre parcel of land there. His home, backed by a water inlet and marsh land, compliments the uniqueness of the property. A twenty year fish spotter for Kellum Brothers, AMPRO, and Omega, Collin has had the rare opportu-

Before and during World War II, Civil Air Patrol planes landed at Currell's Airfield in Indiantown Farm originally known as Indiantown Plantation. *Courtesy of Alice Winstead.*

nity to view the beauty of this land and its rivers from a different perspective. Living in Kilmarnock and attending school there, he relocated to Weems in 1986. He grew up appreciating the yield of the vegetable gardens and the resources of the water. Stories are recalled of his grandfather and Captain Archie Long hunting quail there, and his grandmother selling turkeys for Christmas. Rural life was simplistic and appealing. He has remained to savor it all.

The Smither family (left to right) Emma Smither, Clyde Smither (in lap), Joseph Emory Currell (in back), Collin E. Smither (in front), Collin B. Smither, and Clifford Currell. *Courtesy of Collin M. Smither.*

Emergency landing of the first airplane on Indiantown Farm. Collin Smither and pilot became friends and quail hunted often on the property. From left to right - Marvin Smither, Elzie Currell, Emma Smither, Pearl Currell, mechanic unknown, and Clifford Currell. *Courtesy of Collin B. Smither.*

HUMPHREYS RAILWAYS, INC. 1913-1988
STANDARD PRODUCTS COMPANY, INC. 1928-1988

The huge boats and menhaden ships shimmered in the daytime as a cascade of airy colors bounced off their hulls, decks, and masts. At night they became semi-illuminated with scores of twinkling lights. As a young girl, I often visited the Humphreys Railways site with my father watching the seasonal transformation of vessel repairs. There they sat. Perched high on dry dock and supported by giant rusty roller rails held fast by equally stalwart spikes. Repaired by skillful hands, they awaited a new journey as they slipped effortlessly into the waters of Carters Creek.

The 1883 inception of the Bellows and Squires Co. set in motion some twenty-seven years later the emergence of the Rappahannock Marine Railway in 1910. Working on site at that time with remarkable skills directed in the area of fish processing, H. R. Humphreys joined his father-in-law Joseph F. Bellows in purchas-

Framed by Carters Creek Marina gas station in 1968, Humphreys Railways berths ships in for repair. *Author's photo.*

ing the common shares from Henry Brusstars' railway heirs. The end result would become a stellar railway in Weems that repaired freight boats, sailing vessels, power boats, and commercial fishing vessels. Ultimately, other types of pleasure boats and yachts were

"The Maury," flagship of the state police fleet and the official state yacht, hauled up at Brusstars Railway (later Humphreys) for hull painting in 1908. *Courtesy of Lynn Kellum.*

included in the repair roster. As many as ten boats were built at this railway under Humphreys' exclusive eye and direction.

Humphreys' ability to gather a team of men to work in a zone of freedom with a creative bend toward problem solving was no doubt fostered early on.

His mother held a degree in civil engineering from the University of Dublin and encouraged him to read technical engineering material. After graduating from high school, he eventually became a construction engineer for the Chesapeake and Ohio Railway. His interest in the menhaden fishery heightened at the Weems railway that would be recognized as "one of the largest and one with long experience with the menhaden fleets." With the existing ability to engage boats up to 125 tons, Humphreys set about making changes in "standard boat designs" and built vessels one hundred feet plus in length such as the "Martin and Lancaster," "Richmond," "Swanson," "Annie Dow," and the "H. R. Humphreys."

A little over a decade after the formation of Humphreys Railways, Standard Products, Inc. based in White Stone, Virginia, and Moss Point, Mississippi, materialized. Development of the latter location had been in response to the lucrative menhaden activity in the Gulf

At Humphreys Railways, "The Atlantic Mist" is converted from a mine sweeper to a fishing boat with two Cat D 398 engines. *Humphreys advertisement.*

of Mexico. Joined now by a newly partnered son called "Peck," the White Stone plant was equipped with modern machinery driven by electric motors from a newly purchased power company. By 1949 a fish soluble plant was operative as well reclaiming fish soluble from pressed water with 100 percent of the fish usable. A fish scrap grinder emerged with fish meal "packed in 100-pound paper or burlap bags." Now able to utilize this soluble in poultry and livestock formulas the fish oils could also be processed in paints, cosmetics, and linoleums.

With "Peck" managing the Chesapeake Bay fishing and the plant on Dymer's Creek, the capabilities of the Weems railway and

Standard Products fully merged. Added to its merits in 1946 the patenting, manufacturing, and selling of a triple-action piston and unloading pump that transported fish effortlessly from the fishing boat to the factory box was designed by Humphreys, Sr. Built at the railway by his son, William Lorenzo, the invention replaced the need for "hands on" in the fishing industry. A "flexible stuffing box" was also patented fulfilling a need for menhaden fish boats and tug-boats.

When his father passed away in 1952, "Peck" became president, treasurer, and general manager of Standard Products. He took the company into the North Carolina fishery business purchasing a plant near Beaufort in the late 1970s.

Official plaque of the Humphreys Triple Unit Fish Pump designed and patented by H. R. Humphreys, Sr., in 1946. *Courtesy of Lynn Kellum.*

A windfall seventeen million fish were caught the first fall season. The honed business acumen he had procured under his father's leadership led to corporate shaping in the acquisition of various companies and fleets. The beginnings of a small plant and two charter boats had now become an "all in house" business establishing menhaden repair, boat and building repair, and patent(s) issuance.

A glance back at the ongoing growth and capabilities of Humphreys Railways could be read in a magazine advertisement. In addition to the existing sail and steam capabilities,

Railway view of Peck's Fleet on Carters Creek waters. *Courtesy of Lynn Kellum.*

Menhaden ships align for repair at Humphreys Railways.
Author's photo.

diesel service was available in the 1920s and steel boats emerged in the 1940s. The 1950s gave way to aluminum workability with the 1960s and 1970s creating a one-stop yacht/marine repair site. Inclusive of long time employed master craftsmen and skilled mechanics, the business had become "one of the largest shipyards between Baltimore and Norfolk." The railway's motto as "everything you need to put out to sea" was not a mere boast.

Left to right - A Humphreys Railways sales brochure featured Ed Bryant as master ship's carpenter for 40 years. Milton Davis was employed as a master machinist for 50 years. *Courtesy of Curtis Kellum.*

In 1988 Standard Products sold its holdings to Ampro, Inc. In turn, Omega Protein purchased Ampro's holdings exclusive of the Weems shipyard. The former railway site remains operative today as a "working boat yard." Fully staffed with repair, welding, and boat/truck construction, Ampro looks to Lynn Kellum to maintain a smooth operation. She does not disappoint. From lab tester, purchasing agent, diesel shop manager, and shipyard manager, Lynn's eighteen years of experience is immeasurable. Dedicated to keeping the history as well as the current operations of the Weems railway to the forefront, she photographs step-by-step boat restorations and longs for a time when the railway returns to full service.

GRISBY'S STORE

The two story wooden structure general merchandise store that stood on the corner in Johns Neck was originated by Monroe Haydon between 1910 and 1920. Upstairs was a barber shop and living quarters for a Mr. Northern. In 1942 widowed Nell Jones married Wilbur Grisby who began to expand the business. A route Coke salesman for 14 years, he used his skills in retailing well. A cinder block structure (private residence today) was built in 1949. General merchandise such as full groceries, hardware, fish hooks, twine, etc. serviced the area. Deliveries from Richmond sites were even available. A 1950 Ford pickup painted with R. N. Grisby on both sides was a familiar sight as it provided full customer pickup

and delivery. Open from 8 am to 8 pm, local men sat around the pot bellied coal stove nightly swapping oyster, crab, and fish stories.

Mr. Grisby operated on open book credit. A large

Wilbur Grisby poses inside his general merchandise store in Johns Neck in 1969. *Courtesy of Maurice Jones.*

Left to right - Maurice Jones, Rosa Nell Jones Grisby and Wilbur Grisby recall Grisby's store as a gathering place for friends and neighbors. *Courtesy of Maurice Jones.*

gray ledger held the individual credit limit accounts with businesses such as W. F. Morgan & Sons receiving up to $20. Some customers often utilized both Grisby and Kellum's store to alternate credit and payment amounts. Even so, Mr. Grisby wrote off only $300 after 40 years in business. The store was a family affair with help from live in Mrs. Annie Sable for 45 years. Mildred Warrick worked there for several summers proudly saving enough to purchase a wrist watch. With Mr. Grisby's health issues looming, the store was rented to an electrical contractor until 1985. That same year the property, house, and store were sold to Humphreys in Kilmarnock.

W. ELLERY KELLUM SEAFOOD
ESTABLISHED IN 1948

Making an effort to upgrade their earnings, often friends and relatives in the Weems and Johns Neck areas combined their resources and talents to operate a seafood business. It was not a shoo-in. Long hours, hard labor, weather dependency, employee management, and a strong "sense" of business expertise factored in. The gray cinder blocked structures of the early years housed oyster holding bins, shucker stalls, and a skimming/packing area from which the oysters were processed, iced, and shipped. Their location was often built upon family land sloping downward to Carters Creek.

Little did he know that while buying oysters in his 38 foot workboat for Booth Seafood in Burgess at Glebe Point, Ellery Kellum would later stand at the helm of a fourth generational seafood business. From the beginning the venture was a family affair. His oldest son, Curtis, helped to salvage scrap metal to obtain money needed to purchase cinder blocks and other materials to build the oyster facility. His wife, Rubinette, packed oysters and performed bookkeeping duties in the early years. With a thriving business the wheel barrowed shell oysters (purchased from local watermen) were shucked by eight workers. By 1974 a modernized over head monorail carried the shell oysters to the now forty shuckers. From five gallon packed oyster cans to gallons, pints, and half pints, the seafood company extended their product to oyster peddlers who, in turn, trucked them to the Virginia mountains. Increased demand extended this family business as they began purchasing five gallon oysters from other businesses. They incorporated in 1967. Ellery Kellum remained company president until his passing in 1978.

Above left - W. Ellery Kellum opened a one room oyster shucking business in Johns Neck in 1948. Above right - Kellum on workboat on Carters Creek. *Courtesy of Kellum Seafood.*

Today Kellum Seafood defies statistics. It is the only oyster shucking house in business out of the original 12 on Carters Creek and one of Northern Necks "two or three remaining oyster houses."

The present 10,000 square foot complex, with a complete cold storage facility "grows, harvests, shucks, packs and ships oysters." The product is obtained from leased water bottom in Virginia as well as oysters caught from public oyster rocks by commercial watermen in six states. Selling primarily to retailers, restaurants, and food service distributors, Kellum Seafood is managed by Joe (Ellery's son) working with Tommy, Jeff, and Brandon (Ellery's grandsons). Their oyster brand can be purchased in 32 states under a Kroger contract. Expansion is offered in "live shell products as well as fresh and frozen shucked oysters." The menu of oysters, soft crabs, scallops, and Chesapeake Bay fin fish is a tempting one-stop fresh seafood delight.

An aerial view of Kellum Seafood Company shows the expansiveness of present-day oyster operations. The mid-section is the main oyster house. Below is the original parental home. Near the water's edge are situated dock, boathouse, cooler freezer shed, and storage. To the right of these buildings is Carters Creek Marina. To the far left Humphreys Railways and Ampro can been seen. *Courtesy of Kellum Seafood.*

Owing to the industry's growth in recent years, Kellum Seafood has expanded and recently acquired a new vessel. Monthly inspections from on-site U. S. Department of Commerce occur. Working with Virginia Marine Resources Commission (VMRC), the company cites "sustainability" as the core of their business as they practice sound conservation and the "propagation of oysters for ecology." One such method occurs on their private oyster beds and protected sanctuary reefs where "spats" (hatchery spawned oyster larvae) are placed for later harvesting. A three year rotational system mirroring that of farmer's crops is strictly adhered to at the Drumming Grounds, Temple Bay, and Broad Creek zones. This policy has increased oyster harvest and produced healthier oysters. Serving on the VMRC's "Shellfish Replenishment Committee" for many years, Kellum Seafood recognizes the necessity of balancing oyster harvest and sanctuary areas towards producing healthy oyster populations. Recycled shells are provided to VMRC as well to aid in the restoration of the beds.

Above - Joe and Bill Kellum tend to daily oyster operations. *Author's photo.* Below - The small Kellum built barge offers harvesting of oysters in shallow water. *Courtesy of Kellum Seafood.*

Above - Accumulated shells from the 24 hour business operation replenish oyster larvae and provide ecological benefits. *Courtesy of Kellum Seafood.* Below - The "Captain Ellery" is docked awaiting transport of seed oysters. *Author's photo.*

Company boats driven by Jeff Kellum ("High Hopes") and Will Kellum ("Easy Rider") race across local waters. *Courtesy of Lynn Kellum.*

Visiting the office of Joe and Bill Kellum and talking over old times is genuine and comfortable. Both men share a sense of satisfaction in a legacy that has now become a year round operation. Pride in commitment to "quality and customer satisfaction" is evident. They agree that a natural resource customer based business has many challenges to manage and overcome. But they are willing to explore every possibility to move forward efficiently. Wheel barrel transport has long been replaced by an "electric eye monitor" that ensures the oyster flow from "chilled storage into stainless steel bins" that matches the shuckers' rhythmic tempo. It's one of many rational and modern day approaches they constantly seek. Living on their oyster ground and learning how to manage and improve their business is a passion. One senses their father, Ellery, would have approved.

Dispensed from seed beds to the W. Ellery Kellum boat, oysters are transported as "shell" stock into the plant storage area by a Bobcat. Bill Kellum points to the hopper style entryway that funnels the oysters into the conveyor receptacle. *Author's photo.*

The automatic conveyor system allows each worker to receive the "shell" stock parallel to their stalls in a timed sequence. Freshly shucked oysters are sized from large to small counts. *Author's photo.*

Shucked oysters are dumped into large vats and thoroughly stirred with long paddles. Quality oysters are procured from company owned beds in the Northern Neck, the Middle Peninsula, and the Chesapeake Bay. *Author's photo.*

An automated metal grill conveyor allows for shelled oyster separation. Approximately three inches in shell is the market size. The "shell" stock area is seen in the background. *Author's photo.*

Courtney expertly maneuvers the packing machine for boxed oyster shipment. *Author's photo.*

The attractive green, white, and clear logo containers says it all..."From Kellum With Pride." *Author's photo.*

KELLUM MARITIME, L.L.C.

With a need to diversify from the oyster business and obtain quality crab bait from the menhaden fish source, a company was formed and operated by Charlie Pittman, Stanley O'Bier, Curtis and Jimmy Kellum. Known as Ocean Bait, Inc., one of the vessels "The Bay Lady" had been purchased from the Kellum Brothers who had been fishing as early as 1979. It's an operation still in full swing.

In 2008 Jimmy Kellum formed Kellum Maritime, L.L.C., with two fishing vessels carrying 575,000 fish count each. With a crew of seven men (Captain, pilot, 5 workmen), each vessel carries one purse boat called a single seine, or snapper rig. Wielding a 1200 foot net the daily menhaden catch is unloaded from May until November. Two hours before sunrise will find the crew utilizing an ICOM radio system to communicate with the airborne fish spotter. Forty percent of their catch is used as bait for crabs, lobsters, and crawfish as processed by Pride of Virginia Seafood. The remaining sixty percent materializes as fish meal after sale to Omega Protein, Inc., in Reedville.

Menhaden fishing vessels "Carters Creek" and "Indian Creek" docked in Carters Creek. *Courtesy of Jimmy Kellum.*

Purse with seine net "sets up" for fish catch. *Courtesy of Jimmy Kellum.*

In an effort to better improve upon the purse boat by providing self-bailing cockpit capabilities, increased speed, prolonged safety, and roominess, Jimmy stepped into uncharted territory in 2013. Working from his shop in Weems, he procured two used purse boats from Omega Protein, cut them apart, and built an innovative 40 by 18 foot In-seine aluminum boat. Now fully documented by the Coast Guard, this vessel has proven its worth with large menhaden catches. The initial trade-off engines and excess scrap metal deal with Omega Protein has been most successful with ongoing adjustments. Hard work combined with ingenuity produced the In-seine with a lot of community business togetherness thrown in.

MENHADEN FISH SPOTTER
HENRY E. DIXON, JR.

Henry Dixon is a generational fish spotter who has never tired of the sunrises and sunsets that greet him as he banks his single-engine high-wing Cessna 172 Skyhawk to and from Indiantown Farm in Weems. Currell Airfield has been a second home to Henry Dixon. From this site he has accumulated about 40,000 hours of flight time over bay and ocean waters searching for the ever elusive menhaden fish. Radioing boat captains below, he uses an effective form of communication that has evolved from crow's nest spotting, notes dropped in bottles, wireless relays, and hand held spotter pilot "walkie-talkies" in the early 1950s. Once communicated upon open radio waves, other vessels will race to the area in what can be a most dangerous situation both in the air and on the water. Safety is always a top priority. Involvement in search and rescue operations and relaying distress calls to boat captains has been this spotter's duty as well.

Henry understands that fish spotting is part one of a process that also requires him to extend confirmation to the captain below that there is a guaranteed "catch." His experience with and knowledge of weather, wind, tide, and water conditions come into play in this highly competitive industry. An early account of spotting as told in "The Men All Singing" relates "whips" (splashes of the tails of the bunkers) and "color" (denoting age, size, and number) as being a critical measuring stick. Henry relates that "...sometimes you can see them and sometimes it's like trying to tell the difference between black and navy socks in a dark room." With forty years of fish surveillance to his credit, one senses he will continue to soar over the land a good while longer.

Currell Airfield site in Weems, Virginia, offers secure take-offs and landings for pilot Henry Dixon. *Courtesy of Henry Dixon.*

Menhaden fish spotter, Henry Dixon, has spotted menhaden fish for over forty years to and from Indiantown Farm in Weems. *Courtesy of Henry Dixon.*

SAUER'S TEXACO SERVICE
1951-1977

Formerly operated by Harry W. Ball and later purchased from T. Coulborne Treakle, the Texaco Station standing at the juncture of Weems and Johns Neck road served a dual purpose. It provided full automobile service for its customers, and became a gathering place for the youth of the area.

Owner and operator, Wendell Sauer, in 1950 moved with his wife and four children (Ruth, Lois, Stanley, Dale) to Weems from Baltimore, Maryland. Sensing a community need for automotive attention, he specialized in used and retread tires, small engine repair, and installation of seat covers. Neatly attired in his green Texaco uniform, Wendell efficiently pumped gasoline, checked water in the radiator, measured oil levels, and verified tire pressure. A flawless wipe of the windshield and back glass completed the process.

Wendell Sauer worked at his Texaco Service Station on the corner of Weems and Johns Neck Road. *Courtesy of Lois Kellum.*

Elsie Sauer (left), owner of Historyland Antiques, poses with longtime friend, Gladys Lumpkin. *Author's photo.*

Inside the newly renovated station, residents could select from a small line of groceries and pick up snacks. Often his wife, Elsie, would pitch in with a smile and ready wit. The successful self-service station concept led to Wendell's retirement in 1977. He then turned to the repairing and refinishing of furniture pieces. Elsie owned and operated Historyland Antiques in Kilmarnock for twenty years. Inviting customers to come and browse through her store became her trademark. She was also an expert chair caner. The couple worked in tandem for many years.

WEEMS CALAVARY PENTECOSTAL TABERNACLE

In 1972 a cottage prayer meeting was held in the home of Clarence and Thelma Jones of Weems. With a growing membership of over forty individuals, the need for a larger gathering place led to the rental of a home style building from Blanch Hudson on Johns Neck Road. Within five years the church had purchased the building with services alternately conducted by ministers and musicians from Callao, Virginia. Licensed as a minister in 1974, Thelma Jones became ordained by the Calvary Pentecostal Church in Ashland, Virginia, some twenty-five years later. Respected within the community, she continued to share the message from the church podium and through radio broadcasts.

The Weems Calvary Pentecostal Tabernacle had its beginning in 1972.
Courtesy of Clarence Jones.

With a need for Sunday school rooms, restrooms, and parking space, church expansion was again prompted with the purchase of a two-story building owned by William and Karen George in 1981. Eventually this facility would be razed with a replacement church building accommodating Sunday and Wednesday evening attendees. Reverend Thelma Jones, with the continued support of her husband, Clarence, continued pastorship until 1985. Reverends Marconi, Suttler, and Smith would serve until 1994. Reverend Jones returned to serve until her passing in 2010. With momentum interrupted, the church began to dwindle in membership. Its doors remain open presently on Sundays and Wednesday evenings with Clarence Jones in the leadership speaker position.

WESLEY PRESBYTERIAN CHURCH
TAYLORS CREEK

On the eastern side of the Corotoman River (beyond Corotoman Point) the bordering farmland had begun to develop with a slowly increasing population. Specifically, the Taylors Creek and Moran Creek areas provided lovely woodland settings for home dwellers. In 1918, families utilizing the land and water for income had often gathered together at Josh Talbott's home to pray, study the Bible, and share their faith. Soon other families (Bob Rose, Light Conklin, Elzie Harcum, Mamie Davis, Henry Cramer, and Upher Harman) followed suit. Wednesday nights extended the praise and singing at Sam Meredith's home on a regular basis. From these sessions developed the planning of the first church with each person offering 50 cents a week that would eventually fund the "little white church by the side of the road."

Loading lumber (purchased from a saw mill on the Eastern Branch of the Corotoman) on an old scow and hauling it up the steep terrain at Bob Rose's landing on Taylor's Creek, church ground was broken in 1920. The 25 by 40 foot building was constructed from the rough lumber and planed by hand. A cast iron stove heated the sanctuary with oil burning reflector-backed lamps providing low light. With $295.48 on hand the hard working individuals made every penny count, and within a year the church became operative. The Reverend Thomas D. Wesley accepted the call as its first minister and on May 8, 1921, he, along with Weems Elders P. Eilskov and James Oscar Dameron, received the new members. Already preaching at the Campbell Memorial Presbyterian Church in Weems and Milden Church in Sharps, he traveled by steamboat that docked at James Oscar Dameron's store on Weems Wharf. Shortly thereafter, Dr. Wesley organized a Sunday school comprised of 63 members led in song by Richard Rose and John Talbott. Mrs. Oscar Dameron's donation of a pump organ complimented the sanctuary pulpit stand built by Norman Cook and Roy Conklin.

Wesley Presbyterian Church in Taylors Creek established in 1921 continues to serve the community. *Author's photo.*

Wesley's steady growth became a cornerstone for the needs of its community. Taking place among the large oaks shading a hillside on the Rappahannock River, the annual church picnics at the Harcum's, Conklin's, and Lackert's drew them closer together. The mid 1970s showcased the newly renovated Fellowship Hall housing Halloween parties, Santa visits, birthday gatherings, and wedding and anniversary receptions. Classrooms were constructed to aid in the growth of the youth. A Women's Auxiliary oversaw many of the needs of the church as well.

Throughout the years the Wesley Church has relied upon "in house" membership to provide for its needs through building, painting, cleaning, and maintaining grounds and cemetery lots. Side by side they have experienced rare moments of fun, faith, and fellowship. Teaming with excellent pastoral guidance and leadership over the years, their commitment stands as a model today for people who continue to care for those about them.

JOHN WILLIAM McCROBIE
1868-1945
McCROBIE'S STORE
1935-1950s

Winnie McCrobie is enthusiastic and appreciative of his family heritage. He described his Grandfather, John William McCrobie, as a "jack-of-all-trades" with the ability to adapt to life's circumstances. He shared that his grandfather's seven member family naturally fell into supportive roles of the family unit. Although he never personally experienced the active environment of McCrobie's store, Winnie was intrigued by its stories and service to the Weems community. As happenstance, this store location was my first bus stop en route to third grade at Kilmarnock High School.

Oakland, Maryland, west of Cumberland, was the 1868 birthplace of John McCrobie. As a young man, he took the advice of his father, Wade Hampton, and decided to "seek his fortune" elsewhere in the aftermath of the Civil War. By train and steamboat he made his way to White Stone, Virginia. Finding the area to his liking, he opened a cobbler shop. Briefly returning to Maryland to marry the widowed Sarah Dollie Elizabeth Smith (Lizzie), he moved into the Richard E. Lee Hotel in Kilmarnock. It was here that John focused his entrepreneurial business eye, and what an eye he had!

Surveying early on the service needs of the town of Kilmarnock, he made his first move by taking a mail order course in optometry. Always keenly in touch with his talents, he became adept as a jeweler and watch repairman. John was also a photographer and throughout the years created postcards of the area.

Mac and Edgar McCrobie stand in front of John McCrobie's homeplace in Oakland, MD in 1947. *Courtesy of Winnie McCrobie.*

He worked at the corner of what is now Main and West Church Street in Kilmarnock in the Mumford bank space that became the Old Farmers and Merchants Bank. Due to destructive fires in Kilmarnock, he relocated three more times. The former Cockrell's Super Market and Crowther Auto spaces suited his needs with the next location close to Tri-Star and Dr. Gravatt's Medical Center. With a growing family accompanying his success, John purchased a story and a half home on nine acres of land behind the Seventh Days Adventist Church in 1912 for $900. His business flourished for 29 years.

By the 1930s Kilmarnock's growth had expanded and with it a need to install water and sewer lines. It was mandatory that all citizens comply. Even with his younger brother Bliss as town engineer, John refused to do so. It was time, he reasoned, to find accommodations to ease a generational illness producing the aches and pains of working on crutches. So he sold out. Another enterprise was on his mind. McCrobie general merchandise store in Weems was on the horizon.

At the corner of Main Street and East Church Street in Kilmarnock, Virginia, around 1900. On the right is the Old Eubank Hotel, Mrs. Turner's home, the Acree home, and the McCrobie home. *Courtesy of Winnie McCrobie.*

John moved his family into a framed white structure that housed a kitchen, living quarters, and bath area in an annex behind a generous store front space. The second floor contained three bedrooms and a standup attic. Sitting approximately on nine to ten acres, the building purchased from John Ashburn, directly fronted Weems Road. Customers could conveniently shop while the McCrobie family lived privately in the back and above the store. As a young girl living on the nearby Lumpkin farm, my Aunt Bunks often ran across the back fields to purchase store items. She remembers gingerly balancing eggs in

John W. McCrobie opened a general merchandise store in Weems that also provided living quarters for the family. *Courtesy of Winnie McCrobie.*

a basket her mother had sent in exchange for sewing cotton. She also enjoyed being invited to grab a bite to eat with the McCrobie family if she happened to come at their mealtime. A double delight... bartering of local goods accepted for store merchandise with a hot meal cooked by Mrs. Lizzie on the side.

The two large glass store front windows bordered double framed screen doors. The interior was heated in winter by a pot bellied stove. Showcases of goods and barrels of fish and pickles lured customers inside. With oil cloth rolls, cotton material bolts, boots, shoes, horse collars, canned goods, flour, small selection of meats, and candy on display, John McCrobie opened for business. Living just across the road from the store, as a youngster, Cosby Dunaway had a mental image of Mr. Mc-Crobie sitting on a high stool next to a counter working intently on repairing a watch. Every now and then he'd look up and smile as if to say... "let me know when you decide what you want."

J. W. and Sarah (Lizzie) McCrobie attended to their designated duties within the store as well as their family homestead. *Courtesy of Winnie McCrobie.*

Supportive of her husband's ambitious choices, Lizzie took to the garden while John tended the store. She raised vegetables, canned, tended to the dairy cows and pigs, and cooked for the family with the help of the girls. A large gray store ledger contained names of weekly credit customer with no in-

Packaged fragile optical supplies shipped to J. W. McCrobie at Weems in 1943. The other two items were a small leather change and paper money purses probably sent as a salesmen gift from the companies. *Courtesy of Winnie McCrobie.*

terest charged. Winnie recalled his Dad's (Shorty) involvement pulling customer's groceries in a red wagon from the store to the skiff or boat that was tied at the wharf a ways behind Claybrook Baptist Church. After working long hours, local farmers and watermen lingered under the single outdoor store light talking about the days' activities finally going inside to smoke tobacco

Lizzie McCrobie in Weems garden behind the store. *Courtesy of Winnie McCrobie.*

and challenge one another at checkers. The doors closed when the last person left usually about 10 or 11 pm. In the 1970s, Mr. Mc-Crobie's youngest son, Edgar, became a photographer and journalist for the Rappahannock Record and reminisced in his "Bits and Pieces" column about the store environment. "The number of regular participants was fairly constant, and each evening about 7 pm, they would gather around the stove (a huge wood burner) and begin the evening's activities. From my feed sack perch beneath the wooden counters, I observed, through a knothole, the time honored charade beginning with the casual and benign evening's greeting to the explosive ferment that threatened to topple the building."

With the passing of Mr. and Mrs. Mc-Crobie, a daughter, Edith McCrobie Northern, used her long time experience as a clerk in retail work in Kilmarnock to keep the store doors open until the 1950s. Facing a waning business with more people shopping in Kilmarnock, the advent of automobiles, and a merchandise store in Weems (Carroll Davis) now capturing local markets, McCrobie's store ceased to exist. Several family members continued to live there with their spous-

Edgar McCrobie, youngest son, after serving in the Navy returned to the area as a photographer and journalist for the *Rappahannock Record*. *Courtesy of Winnie McCrobie.*

es while pursuing careers of their own. In the 1960s a fire originating from a King heater gutted the annexed living quarters. The remaining structure would stand vacant until E. A. Stephens from Tides Inn purchased the land and the store from the McCrobie siblings. Tennis courts for clientele were constructed in its place.

Driving past scattered homes now bordered by the Tides Inn golf greens, I remember the evenings I walked from McCrobie's store at dusk toting a gallon galvanized can full of kerosene back to our farmhouse. There would be a couple of penny candies in my pocket to sweeten the chore. Kicking pebbles along the way, I would eventually skip up the back wooden kitchen steps into the inviting aromas of Mom's cooking. Perhaps this was exactly the atmosphere John McCrobie had desired in his remaining 15 years for himself and his family. Happily, he had acquired a personal standard of living quite in sync with the community contentment he found in Weems.

"Shorty" McCrobie on Kilmarnock High School graduation day in front of the family store. *Courtesy of Winnie McCrobie.*

Early McCrobie family picture (from left to right) Rhoda, Lizzie, J. W., Sr., Dosie, Edith, Texie, and Wade Hampton. *Courtesy of Winnie McCrobie.*

In later years, Lizzie and J. W., Sr., pose with W. H. "Shorty," Sr. and J. W., Jr. Mc-Crobie.*Courtesy of Winnie McCrobie.*

CHURCHFIELD/GREENTOWN
SHARON BAPTIST CHURCH
ESTABLISHED 1898

In all probability during the mid 1800s, a close knit community of relatives, friends, and neighbors settled into the Weems areas bordering Christ Church (Churchfield), present day Lancaster County School Board office land (Up the Hill), and a goodly amount of homesteads in Taylors Creek (Eastern Branch). Owing to the fertile land and bountiful creek and river water resources, they worked hard and flourished under a mainstay of helpfulness and caring. Their religious foundational heritage had been set before them.

Organized in 1778 during the American Revolution, the Morattico Baptist Church of the Northern Neck (under the pastorship of Addison Hall from 1836 to 1867) was instrumental in baptizing a large number of black worshipers. Morattico Baptist membership at this time was 319 white and 304 black. By 1863 Mount Vernon Baptist Church, located in White Stone, opened its doors. Black members requested permission to build the Old Saint John Baptist Church in 1867. These events held a light of promise for Churchfield residents in Weems to move forward in 1898. They had a bit of work to do before the doors opened its welcoming arms.

Located just across the road from the Old Mount Jean School, the first organizational church meeting site at Gallain Fishermen's Hall was led by Reverend Levi Ball of Kilmarnock Calvary Baptist Church. Two acres of land stood at the ready having been purchased equally from and donated by Joe Gunther. Contractors Jake Swyna and Son were signed on. With horse and wagon secured, Edmond Gaskins and Willard Beane hauled the lumber from High Bank (location of Tides Inn Golf Lodge Complex) to the site. In turn, bricks and additional supplies from Weems were handled by Edmond Gaskins, Jessie Parks, and Alexander Henderson. A teacher in the community, Mrs. Lottie Thomas, suggested the name as Sharon Baptist Church from a facility she had attended in Baltimore.

Reverend Daniel Tucker served the congregation as its spiritual leader for 22 years. Under his leadership the Sunday school, Senior Choir, Young Men's Improvement Society, and missionary societies were formed. The Ladies' Auxiliary Missionary Society and the Sister's Guild Missionary Society came to the forefront as well. The following years of church growth produced many worthwhile organizations with focus upon "preschool preparatory, children's bible studies, recreation fellowship, adolescent and young adult fellowship, men's fellowship, and a Teen Focus Group." All of these worthwhile organizations were bolstered by the music of the Men's Choir and the Sharon Community Choir.

With the Reverend Levi Reese Ball as organizing minister, Sharon Baptist Church began its rise in Weems, Virginia. *Courtesy of Sharon Baptist Church archives.*

During a service on January 5, 1950, Marvis Beale motioned to usher Charles Laws that smoke was pouring into the church. Huge flames jutted out of the church belfry as a congregation of 200 members rushed outside with no injuries. They watched in disbelief as the huge bell cracked and fell. Even though the Kilmarnock Fire Department worked diligently, Sharon Baptist burned to the ground. With donations and proceeds from other churches, circles, and friends, the planning committee recommended building a cinder block church modeled after the original. Additional rear rooms appeared on either side of the structure. On January 1, 1952 befitting a new journey, a corner stone dedication service was held. Today through a succession of pastors and leader members, Sharon Baptist Church has served and continues to serve the community

for over 100 years. Standing with a 200 strong membership, its focus of "A Message for the Heart--A Mission for the Hands" resonates within their daily lives.

Congregational members stand near the ashes of Sharon Baptist Church in January of 1950. *Courtesy of Sharon Baptist Church archives.*

Today Sharon Baptist Church continues to celebrate its heritage and spirit of community. Their message focuses strongly on youth mentorship. *Author's photo.*

SHARON BAPTIST CHURCH FOUNDERS

Frank Wright	Jessie Parks
Elize Blackwell	Edmond Gaskins
Maria Blackwell	Herman Gaskins
John Blackwell	William Jones
Walker B. Byrd	Moses Waddy
George Fisher	

EDUCATION

With the 1870 Virginia Constitution stating "separate but equal" educational training for everyone, the earliest record of a "colored school house" emerged. The two acres of land sold by Josiah and Virginia Doggett to Issac Wiggins and Jacob Smith (north side of road from White Stone to Irvington) literally laid the groundwork to learn collectively. Heretofore, the schooling of elementary age children (grades 1-5) had taken place privately in homes or with community people in assist. Now old vacated buildings, lodge halls, and churches were called into service. Ministers took up teacher positions as well. In 1894 Mars Hill and some Eastern Branch citizens (Taylors Creek area) purchased land from Annie E. and William A. Ball in Weems and erected a one room school building. The teachers listed were: Hannah Pillard, Susan Williams, Robert Jackson, Carrie Bland, Alfreda Carter, Lottie Thompson, and Mrs. Hinton. This school later merged with Old Kilmarnock Elementary.

Although the strong need and desire to teach these youngsters was paramount in the black community, the Virginia framework for educational progress was slow and fraught with many difficulties. By 1906 only one half of the black student population was enrolled. There was no public high school or vocational formats as of yet. The school year consisted of only 125 days with the average student attendance as 71 days. Local citizens often supplemented monies for an extended year. Public bus transportation had not yet been provided.

Notably, Louise Beatrice Thompson Cheatham Taylor became the first Supervisor of Black Education in Lancaster County using her exceptional skills to work with and train teachers for 32 years. In 1936 she organized and became president of the first PTA. In 1932 Viola Winder Taylor became the first Home Economics teacher in the Northern Neck retiring in 1972. Narvel Wiggins became the first school bus driver in 1943 as Superintendent R. E. Brann declared public transportation for all. Mr. Wiggins charged a dollar per week per child with reduced fee for additional family members. A wealthy Pennsylvania Quaker, Miss Anna T. Jeanes (1822-1907), inherited a substantial family fortune. Intensely interested in aiding smaller less noticeable schools, she left "one million dollars" to fund them. By 1952 over 510 teachers had received training in the south through her gift. The needs and the people who addressed them was still a work in progress up to and beyond the September 1970 full integration of both students and teachers. But there was no denial. "Education as a means to achieve a better life" was a goal the residents of Churchfield in Weems did not take lightly. They would persevere and make it happen.

MOUNT JEAN (JEANES) ELEMENTARY SCHOOL
1930s

It was time to move. Gathering up mops, brooms, dust pans, and other supplies the walk from the Old Mount Jean School to the New Mount Jean School was short but uphill. Formerly located near the property of Sharon Baptist Church, this school debut would benefit greatly from a roster of dedicated teachers as well as excited parents and friends of the community. Learning coupled with love, compassion, and enthusiasm was to the forefront from the moment the doors opened.

Several delightful visits with Sandra Gaskins-Smyre and her mother gave way to valuable information about Mount Jean and its community. Her father, the late Mathews Gaskins, Sr., had attended both schools. His first grade teacher was Mrs. Viola Taylor.

She also taught Sandra high school Home Economics in later years. Now herself a 45 year career teacher in Lancaster County, Sandra shared her educational experience as one growing from the strong foundation of Mount Jean.

As both principal and sixth grade teacher at Mount Jean, Mrs. Elsie Byrd Nickens summoned the students by ringing the bell followed with the singing of "My Country Tis of Thee" and the recitation of the "Pledge of Allegiance." Math, science, reading, language arts, and history comprised the curriculum. The organized school league (similar to PTA) held monthly meetings to communicate student progress. Each grade averaged 15 pupils. Through their fund raising efforts, sixth grade students took a field trip to Washington, D. C., visiting the National Zoo, Smithsonian Institute, Washington Monument, Lincoln Memorial, and various federal buildings. Mr. Harvey Boyer, 4th and 5th grade teacher (1953-1960) as well as bus driver, showed a film of the trip at a PTA meeting. His wife also taught from 1948-1952. Other teachers from Sandra's school days were: Mrs. Ruth C. Ball, 1st and

Career educator in Lancaster County, Mrs. Sandra Gaskins-Smyre recounts her foundational journey at Mount Jean Elementary School. *Courtesy of Sandra Gaskins-Smyre.*

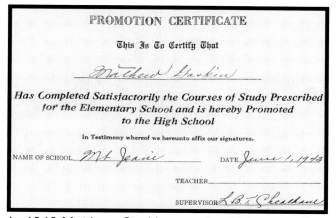

PROMOTION CERTIFICATE

This Is To Certify That

Matthew Gaskins

Has Completed Satisfactorily the Courses of Study Prescribed for the Elementary School and is hereby Promoted to the High School

In Testimony whereof we hereunto affix our signatures.

NAME OF SCHOOL *Mt Jeanie*   DATE *June 1, 1943*

TEACHER _____

SUPERVISOR *L.B.T. Cheatham*

In 1943 Matthew Gaskins received his promotion certificate from Mount Jean school to enter high school. *Courtesy of Sandra Gaskins-Smyre.*

2nd grade, and Mrs. Essie Elliot, 3rd grade. That they were phenomenal role models and success predictors in Sandra's eyes is very evident. After all, surviving Mrs. Nickens mandatory once-a-week book reading with accompanying report as well as her parent's question and answer sessions, led Sandra to double reading achievement scores by 6th grade.

Providing nutritious school meals were Mrs. Beatrice Gaskins (bus driver), Mrs. Julia Crockett (bus driver), Mrs. Gladys

The Mount Jean School Chorus: Top row from left to right. Row #1: Pearl Grimes, Hester Carter, Betty Hodge, Mrs. Chamberlain (music teacher), Frances Jones, Genevie Taylor, and Louise Beverly. Row #2: Florida Jones, Viola Carter, Ethel Carter, Elsie Nickens, Esther Taylor, Jaunita Beverly, Zenobia Carter, and A. J. Taylor (teacher). Row #3: Gladys Carter, Mary Greene, Bernice Grimes, Sadie Smith, Hortense Smith, Carrie Carter, Elsie Henderson, and Frank Carter. Row #4: Lorenzo Cottman, Vestelia Fisher, Jessie Gaskins, Mary Laws, Joseph Lewis, Cora Greene, Dorothy Johnson, Myrtle Jones, Mildred Doyns, Elsie Sanders, Mary Bell (future teacher at Mount Jean), and Ann Lewis. Row #5: James Taylor, Lawrence Hodge, and Robert Jones. *Courtesy of Sandra Gaskins-Smyre.*

Wilson, and Mrs. Justine Johnson. The janitor, Josh Wright, maintained an immaculate school. Before recess activities of softball, baseball, jump rope, marbles, and hopscotch, the students helped gather wood for the stoves. The annual Spring Opera with homemade costumes proved to be a highlight at Mount Jean. The school up the hill remained productive until the latter part of the 1930s. It had completed its mission of passing on morals and values through church attendance, community pride, and love of learning.

This 1953 Ford bus was driven by Harvey Boyer for Mount Jean students. He also taught at the school. *Courtesy of Sandra Gaskins-Smyre.*

Former Mount Jean Elementary School has been converted to Lancaster County School Board offices. *Author's photo.*

WEEMS COMMUNITY CENTER TEEN SHOP
Early 1960s

Located in a central position in Churchfield, the Weems Community Center provided a need for the community and flourished under the entrepreneurship of its owner, Mathews Gaskins, Sr. A "one-stop shop" it sold commodities, provided services, and promoted entertainment. It gradually evolved as far as the youth of the area were concerned into a teen shop. Nearby neighbors (Hodges, Carter, Gaskins, Veney, Chewning, Crockett, Kamp, Ball, Yerby, Kane, Smith, Cain, Saunders, and Sanders) welcomed the convenience of purchasing groceries and general everyday items. Here one could also receive a good hair cut, play pool, enjoy the arcade machines, drop a coin in the juke box or pump gas. Extra bonuses included hot cooked lunches, sandwiches, homemade soup, and crab cakes on the weekend. Ever the helpmate, Beatrice Gaskins stood behind the counter during the week days while her husband fished menhaden in New Jersey and Louisiana. Sandra Gaskins-Smyre recalled filling in whenever she could. When her father returned on the weekends, he often supplemented their income by oystering in the Rappahannock in his boat "Little Bow Peep" tying up near the Gangplank on Carters Creek. Following a slowly decaying process, the Teen Shop was bulldozed in 2011.

Nearby the youth enjoyed Floyd Clark's skating rink and Charles's skating pond seasonally. Around the area where Salem Road is today other stores such as a hair dresser, cleaners, and a soda shop were open for business. Churchfield community events were ongoing with Sunday nights reserved for visiting and eating dinner together. Often on the menu was the prized bread pudding layered with grape jelly and meringue topping. Organized by Mathews Gaskins, the Weems Club enjoyed baseball games. Surely there was discussion among the women concerning The Lodge activities or updates on Mavis Jones' Savings Club for boys and girls. Sandra Gaskins-Smyre recalls even today these close knit community times that left plenty to be thankful for.

CAPTAIN MATHEWS "SONNY" GASKINS, SR.
1929-2007

Born to Cenni and Ulysses Gaskins, Sr. July of 1929, Mathews was truly a Weems hometown boy. Although his 38 years of nauti-cal voyages would take him far away to the Atlantic Ocean and Gulf of Mexico, he always returned to his home berth... Weems. Here he attended Mount Jean primary school and was honored as the 1947 class salutatorian at A. T. Wright High School. One year later he married his high school sweetheart Beatrice Weaver. His family would grow with the births of three daughters and five sons. He applied to their lives the same belief he had chosen to guide his path...affectionate firmness, self-discipline, and a strong belief in God.

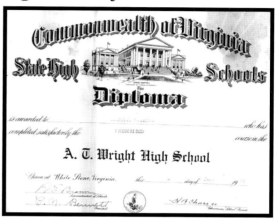

Commonwealth of Virginia High School Diploma awarded to Mathews Gaskins in June of 1947. He was the class salutatorian. *Courtesy of Sandra Gaskins-Smyre.*

The area provided job sources of oystering, fishing, and crabbing in over-lapping seasons, but menhaden fishing would become the joy of Mathews' life. Under the urging of his mentor, Captain George Jones, he studied and passed the oral and written examination for a Captain's license in 1965. He successfully completed 26 years of captainship aboard fishing steamers such as "Tiny Tim" and worked for the firms of Smith, Seacoast Products, and Zapata Haynie. In 1992 "Sonny" officially retired from thirty-eight years of working on the water, but he was not one to sit still. He fully

As a member of the planning committee, Mathews Gaskins unveils the A. T. Wright historical monument in honor of the principal of the county's first high school for African American students. *Courtesy of Sandra Gaskins-Smyre.*

appreciated his family life, operated Sonny's Lawn Service, and enjoyed sporting events until his passing in 2007.

A sudden end of spring rainstorm did not dampen my meeting in 2012 with his wife, Beatrice Gaskins. Residing in the home just down a ways from the former Weems Community Center location, she was surrounded by family pictures and past accomplishments of Captain Gaskins. We talked about the good times of the past noting that my father had called upon Ulysses Gaskins (Matthew's father) to join him in local carpentry work. Along with his wife, Cennie, Ulysses had supported five children also through his taxi service. His independent transport picked up and delivered groceries to families for a nominal fee. He, too, had passed a strong work ethic along the way.

It was notable that Beatrice still possessed energy and a will toward accomplishment. That she raised a large family alongside duties as a school bus driver, cafeteria cook, and Teen shop worker never seemed daunting. "That's just the way it was done in those times," she shared with a smile. "It's the end result that counts." It truly is, and she's satisfied to acknowledge the pleasure of completing her life's work on Weems hometown soil.

Menhaden fishing steamer "The Tiny Tim," with Captain Mathews, Sr. of Weems at the helm, is docked at Carters Creek at W. F. Morgan & Sons en route to Morgan City, Louisiana. *Courtesy of the Rappahannock Record and Sandra Gaskins-Smyre.*

Captain Mathews Gaskins is congratulated upon retirement by Tom Place, General Manager of Zapata Haynie in 1992. He had great pride in his career as well as his ownership in three boats: "The Little Bo Peep," "Sea Wolf," and "Please Bea Sonny." *Courtesy of Rappahannock Record.*

Left - Beatrice Weaver Gaskins cherishes the memories she and Mathews made raising their eight children in Weems. *Courtesy of Sandra Gaskins-Smyre.* Above - The homes in Greentown still retain a country like setting on Gaskins Road. *Courtesy of Norma Lumpkin.*

Photographed by Aubrey Bodine, Carters Creek in Weems, Virginia, envelopes a feeling of serenity on the water at day's end. *Used with permission by the Virginia Historical Society.*

PART V

OF HEART AND HAND

The springboard development of Weems Wharf in the 1900s and its surrounding community held to a strong continuum of growth through the 1990s. Seasonally and with few restrictions, the bountiful creek, river, and bay seafood offerings flowed as mainstay resources for the residents. Lucrative creekside oyster businesses morphed into abundant crab facilities. Fields of oyster boats filled every workable river space as the watermen staked out their favorite "oyster rock" to harvest. Crabbers skillfully maneuvered their long nets scooping up peelers and soft crabs to add to their laden "floats." Retailers flourished as "close at hand" community goods suppliers experiencing solid growth and healthy competitiveness. Family units held fast and took exceptional pride in the Weems area. The abundance of Lancaster County seafood resources was startling. In 1950, "more than 250,000 bushels of oysters, nearly 3,000,000 pounds of hard and soft crabs, and about 34,000,000 pounds of fish, counting menhaden was a dockside worth of about $1,250,000." The watermen's personal boat and gear investment had not been calculated. This was ultimately a "heyday" never to be replicated.

A waterman steadies his oysters in a bucket in preparation for sale on Weems Wharf. Local workboats, the Ashburn home, and oyster complex appear in the background. *From the collection of Dr. Henry J. Edmonds.*

Stanley Wilson shaft tongs for oysters at the mouth of Carters Creek. *Courtesy of Lois Kellum.*

An oysterman measures oysters by the bushel bucket on Weems Wharf. *Courtesy of Curtis Kellum.*

Oyster workboats are aligned on Weems Wharf at Richard Lumpkin's oyster house waiting to sell their oysters. *Dr. Henry J. Edmonds photo collection.*

From the onset, making a living on the water was precarious. Schooner captains hauling goods prided themselves on thriving against extreme weather elements, and reveled in their ability to counteract problematic situations through heart and hand. Ships sank regularly and were subsequently raised to carry on. Bringing the commodity to market was the goal with the reward of business outweighing the risk. Both owners and investors looked to the long term gain of the captain's natural expertise. Their exploits and close calls on the water were woven early on into the legendary Weems fabric.

Many men in Weems held the status of Captain. I knew one firsthand...my Grandfather Andrew Calvin Lumpkin (1881-1947). After years of transporting goods along the river and bay, he purchased an impressive two-mast schooner named the "Julia Hopkin." Built in the late 1800s she came to the open market from O. P. Roberts to settle an estate. The transaction took place on the corner of Broadway and Eastern Avenue in Baltimore, Maryland, about the outbreak of World War I. The purchase sum of $3,500 was a considerable amount for that time. During the summer months Captain Lumpkin sold produce grown on his farm off the deck of the schooner in the Baltimore Harbor. One trip a year was designated as a family vacation. My father often described the awe in being introduced to the "city lights" of Baltimore. The "Julia Hopkin" was to have a short stay. On the sixth of April in 1921, she was lost in the Chesapeake Bay near Cape Charles. Laden with 4,000 bushel of oyster shells, she ran helpless in a 50 to 60 mile gale and sank. All crew members were thankfully saved.

In his Rappahannock Record 1970s column "Bits n Pieces," Edgar McCrobie gave tribute to the theme of the Weems "everyman" on the

The beautiful schooner "Julia Hopkin" is loaded with cargo in Carters Creek. Andrew C. Lumpkin, Captain, stands in the foreground. *Author's photo and property.*

Andrew C. Lumpkin unloads watermelon and other produce for sale
at the dock. His son, "Boots," assists in the process. *Author's photo.*

water. It was a frigid winter's day in the late 1930s. A power boat,
the "Marion Oscar" owned by Oscar Ashburn & Son, sprung a leak
upon returning from an oyster shell delivery in Baltimore. Within
twenty minutes, the boat sank off Beach Creek in the Rappahannock River in frigid temperatures and dense fog. Securing a hatch
around his young crewman, Charles Tellis, and pushing him toward
shore, the Captain lashed himself to a few remaining feet of mast
and clung to life for 19 hours. R. L. Dodson and Lester Scott spotted him and built a blazing fire on shore to revive his nearly frozen
body. Sadly, Charles did not survive and was found several days
later half a mile up the Corotoman River from Wharton Grove. The
Captain was my Grandfather. His health declined rapidly and unable to tend crops on his seventeen acre farm at the head of Carters
Creek, he moved inland to a central Weems home for his last days.
If this had been his "finest hour" as representative of the fate of
many who lived and worked on the water, as McCrobie expressed,
it served as a reminder that "upon the water...man's spirit seems to
transcend above the oppressions and repressions of human folly."

Above - An abundance of oysters saw watermen in close water proximity vying for the "catch." *Used with permission by the Mariner's Museum;* Below - Watermen shaft tonging for oysters. Note the culling board astride the boat containing oysters. *Courtesy of Debbie Morgan.*

Following his father's path on the water, Raymond Calvin Lumpkin discusses the status of the local oyster catch with James Wharton, field agent for the United States Fish and Wildlife Service. *Baltimore Sun photograph.*

OYSTER ROW

The ability to make a goodly living upon the water ran through many Weems families. Some oyster/crab houses sprung up at the "foot" of home sites only to fade away after a season or two. Other individuals concentrated on shucking oysters or selling crabs independently at local levels. Additional seafood enterprises took hold and became very successful on a state wide level. Whatever their origins each business venture held promise with a story to relate.

R. H. LUMPKIN & SON

Early on Richard Henry Lumpkin (1891-1969), ten years younger than his brother Andrew, acquired a schooner, the "Florin Agnes," that carried wheat, corn, lumber, coal, fertilizer, and other goods to the Chesapeake Bay ports. He married a helpmate, Lottie Ashburn (1896-2000), who as a seventeen-year old bride "took to the helm" during storms, and cooked for the crew. After three exciting years on the water, Lottie retired to raise a family in Weems as well as become a bookkeeper in her husband's newly acquired seafood business known as the "Big L" brand. Shucking oysters at the Weems Wharf site in the early 1900s and packing and shipping in Kilmarnock, Richard became a highly successful entrepreneur, operating his buyer boat the "Fish Hawk" on the Rappahannock River for many years. His crab packing business (purchased from Max Bogen in 1946) became a part of Lancaster Seafoods, Inc., of which he was president. An unbearable tragedy for the couple occurred in August of 1950. A sudden storm on the Rappahannock sank the 16 foot runabout "Try Me" with their son, daughter-in-law, and three grandsons on board. The family was laid to rest at Claybrook Baptist church.

Neighbors and playmates (left to right) Donnie Self, Manley Lumpkin, Jr., Nelson Lee Lumpkin, and June Lakewood Lumpkin pose in Weems. *Courtesy of Donnie Self.*

Lottie Lumpkin at age 15. Mrs. Lumpkin celebrates her 104th birthday. *Both images courtesy of the Rappahannock Record.*

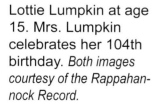

Packing oysters in the "Big L Brand" label can, Richard Lumpkin headed a lucrative business for many years. "Fish Hawk" was the name of his buyer boat. *Author's photo and property.*

In 1885 wooden barrels housed metal containers that held ten gallons of oysters. Ice was packed tightly in between. Two and a half and five gallon metal kidney shaped containers were also utilized. *Courtesy of Curtis Kellum.*

The "Fish Hawk," owned by Richard Lumpkin, is moored in the background on Carters Creek at Weems Wharf. To the left foreground the "Four Sisters" owned by Oscar Ashburn awaits another work day. Both men bought from local oyster tongers. E. I. Webb oyster complex is seen to the right. *Courtesy of Chase Webb Basilio.*

OSCAR ASHBURN & SON

It was a reunion within a reunion reminiscing with Marion Oscar Ashburn, Jr. (1929-2016) about Weems life experiences. Through the kindness of Virginia Lee (his sister) and Edmund Simpson, we enjoyed hours of back and forth at the cottage in Weems and a few days later at the annual Steamboat Era Museum crab feast. He reminded me of his Grandfather's Oscar A. Ashburn (1874-1972) seventy acre Weems farmland ownership adjacent to Wharton Grove. Uncle Oscar (as I addressed him) had not been one to tarry. A sprightly and cheerful man, he described Weems early on as billowing grain fields that shipped its product in sloops to neighboring areas. In time he operated an oyster business and store in Johns Neck near where Morgan's Seafood was once located. We laughed at the story of Oscar summoning his wife, Minnie, for cash for the register by tapping on the ceiling of their two story living quarters. He eventually purchased the Evan Owen lovely creek hill house in Weems. For thirty-four years he successfully operated an oyster and crab creek side facility known as Oscar Ashburn & Son.

During the winter, the company's buyer boat the "Four Sisters" could be seen in the Rappahannock River with four or five workboats moored alongside. Carried by swinging buckets from the top boat deck hull after weight assessment, the oysters were culled and brought to the company's cinder block facility in Carters Creek. Here about thirty

Minnie Belle Lumpkin married Oscar Ashburn in 1904. He listed his occupation as sailor and oysterman. In 1933 Oscar, along with son Marion L. Ashburn and brother Richard H. Lumpkin, purchased W. A. Doggett, Inc. By 1937 the Ashburns were the sole owners of the oyster business. *Courtesy of Virginia Lee Simpson.*

Wayland Doggett's store in 1910 was located in Johns Neck and incorporated in 1928. The general transactions were inclusive of buying and selling vegetables, automobile parts and accessories, and the selling of real estate and personal property. Doggett's oyster house sold a variety of seafood. From left to right: Bob Bryant, Fred Sadler, Ike Jones, Bill Gaines, and Dallas Warwick. *Courtesy of Rappahannock Record. Photo loaned by Mrs. Sandy Warwick.*

Oscar and Minnie Ashburn relocated their home and oyster business from Johns Neck to the Weems side of Carters Creek in the 1920s. Their son, Marion, remained active in the seafood business for many years. Here they celebrate their 50th wedding anniversary. *Courtesy of Virginia Lee Simpson.*

Oscar Ashburn residence in Weems. *Courtesy of Virginia Lee Simpson.*

Celebrating the Ashburn wedding anniversary are: Lemuel Ashburn and young Verlander girl (front), and (left to right) Raymond Lumpkin, Ida Louise Lumpkin, Frances Bell Ashburn, Elaine Lumpkin, Joyce Winstead, Johnny Walker, and Virginia Lee Ashburn. *Courtesy of Virginia Lee Simpson.*

workers skillfully shucked the oysters. Dumped onto stainless steel tables, the oysters were air blown to remove excess water. Deposited into quart and gallon cans, the earlier method of manually banging the tops on with a mallet was later replaced with machinery to compress them. Sold locally and shipped in trucks to the western part of Virginia, their brand became a respected

Readying for shipment a worker "skims" oysters into cans. *Courtesy of Curtis Kellum.*

product throughout the area. As a young girl, I was fascinated by the tons of oyster shells stacked like towering pyramids on the wide board planks near the wharf. Selling 90% of the shells for lime and keeping 10% to seed, Oscar Ashburn & Son utilized every means to remain operational all year. Haul-seining fishermen were also

tapped for their herring catch. These fish were packed in heavily salted wooden box-es and shipped by truck to customers. To supple-ment the inventory, the business also bought herring directly from other factories. Most of the oyster enterprises in Weems (more than twelve at one time on Carters Creek alone) operated in this fashion to varying degrees.

Left - Oyster shuckers stood in waist high wooden stalls to pry the oyster from its shell. Note the work imprint of the shucker's boots. *Courtesy of Curtis Kellum.* Right - Shucked oysters were placed in an elongated metal container and dumped on steel tables to be air blown. *Author's photo and property.*

Marion Oscar, Jr., shared that as a teenager he "wholeheartedly entered into every phase of the business." We talked a bit about the other side of the oyster business model...that of the man who rose early in every possible weather condition to head out to harvest his best day's catch. In a sturdy workboat powered by an automobile engine, two methods of oyster catch were utilized... shaft tong or patent tong. Manually griping two long poles of varying lengths with rake like attachments (giant scissors), the shaft tong procedure required strength and patience. The individual almost had to become one with the boat's motion to "sense" the prize within the waters. The patent tong weighed about 100 pounds with 4 inch teeth and was pulled by a winch or a winder apparatus powered by the boat engine. Although automatically retrieving oysters was considered a step-up, the watermen had to precisely time the up, down, and grappling motion to assure success. Later, an efficient dredging method pulled oysters in a basket with rake like bars powered by winders. No matter the method we agreed the energy applied to the oyster catch was remarkable.

Customarily, crabs were purchased from the watermen at the business docks. Categorized as green peeler, ripe peeler, and soft crab, they were measured by the dozen. Hard crabs were gauged by the bushel. Prices fluctuated, as they did for oysters, on the daily market catch. I learned, too, that Uncle Oscar had a dead rise boat named "Sylvia" that towed two or three skiffs to a crabbing site and waited off shore as watermen waded and caught crabs from the skiff bow. Alive in their "floats" the crabs were taken back to the crab houses and separated

Wooden floats on Weems Wharf await repair on shore near Wesley Ashburn's business. They will later be placed into the water, secured, and house both peelers and soft crabs to be readied for the seafood market. *Author's photo.*

A string of workboats show the productivity in Carters Creek in the 1940s. The Marion Ashburn, Sr. residence is to the left hilltop with the Milton Cross property to the far right. The framed oyster house will later be replaced by a cinderblock one.
Courtesy of Margery Nea.

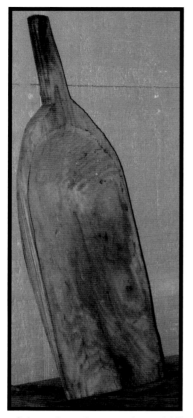

A handmade wooden skiff scooper used to bail out excess water. *Courtesy of Curtis Kellum.*

Another method used by watermen to trap peelers and hard crabs was wired baited crab pots. *Courtesy of Margery Nea.*

if need be. Peelers were placed in site floats to shed out. The soft crabs were packed in wooden boxes, covered with local seagrass, thoroughly iced down, and trucked to Roanoke for consumer use.

Aside from work, Weems offered excitements for Marion Oscar, Jr. both on the water and in the air. In particular, his 16 foot 1940s Chris Craft runabout named "Tantalizer of Weems" was a joy. Smooth and great to handle with the stern raising out of the water on sharp turns, he won many trophy cups during 4th of July Weems races. Although his father, Marion, Sr., never entered the sport he accepted a position as the "mandated passenger" and held on none too pleased with his son's daring maneuvers. Under the tutelage of pilot Joe Gunther, a Piper Cub Club was organized in Weems flying out of Currell's Field airstrip in Indiantown. Marion Oscar was among its 12 to 15 students. "I flew touch and go over Currell's pasture following farms and the shoreline to Kilmarnock. Familiarization of the area was the key. I practiced straight and low level turns, climbing and gliding, and take offs and landings. We all had a terrific experience."

Marion Oscar Ashburn, Jr. (on right) leaves Carters Creek with a nephew from Richmond in his Chris Craft boat "Tantalizer." This Racing Runabout was 16 feet long with speed upward to 44 miles per hour. *Courtesy of Marion O. Ashburn, Jr.*

Without question, Marion Oscar's attachment to the Weems area was still present although relocation to Florida afforded him few opportunities to visit. The three-storied exquisite home that welcomed his birth as well as that of his two sisters, Frances Bell and Virginia Lee, also sheltered his mother, Virginia Walker Ashburn, in her passing in 1948. With the cessation of his grandfather's business and sale to E. I. (Dutch) Webb the house was demolished. Oscar built a home for his wife and Granddaughters across from the Webb family on the main Weems road and lived there until his 98th year. After marrying and living in Weems for a short time, Marion Oscar enlisted in the Army for four years, reaching the rank of Sergeant. We agreed our Weems upbringing had been unique...almost idyllic. Could it be that "The Guiding Light" oyster can label of the Ashburn business was more than just a mere coincidence?

Above - A fish spotter after World War II, Joe Gunther organized the Piper Cub Club in Weems during the 1950s. *Courtesy of Alice Winstead..* Below - Home based in Currell's field in Weems, Marion Oscar's Piper Cub plane provided extensive hours of flight enjoyment in and around the Northern Neck area. *Courtesy of Marion O. Ashburn, Jr..*

| IF DUAL | | INSTRUMENT RADIO-HOOD LINK | SOLO | | REMARKS OR CERTIFICATION | TOTAL TIME |
INSTRUCTOR	AS STUDENT		NIGHT	DAY		
						18:10
				1:00	Check-out Neale E. Sanders 1216629	19:10
				:30	Landings + Take OFF	19:40
				1:25	X Country .	21:05
				:15	Take offs and Landings	21:20
				:20	" " "	21:40
				1:00	Straight and Level	22:40
				Marion Oscar Ashburn	TOTAL TIME
					SIGNATURE OF PILOT	

A portion of Marion Oscar's flight log. *Courtesy of Marion O. Ashburn, Jr.*

Far left - Virginia Walker Ashburn, mother of Marion Oscar, Jr., Frances Bell, and Virginia Lee, poses in her nurse's uniform. To the right - Marion Oscar Ashburn, Sr. and Jr. in early Weems days. *Both photos courtesy of Virginia Lee Simpson.*

Frances Bell and Virginia Lee Ashburn in front of their father's oyster house on Carters Creek. *Seafood magazine article.*

Cousins (left to right) Virginia Lee Ashburn, Raymond Lumpkin, Jr., and Frances Bell Ashburn on the steps of the Ashburn family home. *Courtesy of Virginia Lee Simpson.*

Marion Oscar Ashburn, Jr. and Jean Watts attended Kilmarnick High School and as a married couple lived in Weems for several years. *Courtesy of Virginia Lee Simpson.*

Elizabeth Ashburn, daughter of Marion Oscar and Jean, poses with namesake family outboard, "Little Beth." *Courtesy of Marion Oscar Ashburn, Jr.*

"The Guiding Light" brand label of Oscar Ashburn's oyster can denoted his faith based way of life. *Courtesy of Curtis Kellum.*

In this Aubrey Bodine photograph an oysterman manipulates shaft tongs on the Irvington side of Carters Creek. *Used with permission by the Mariner's Museum.*

W.F. MORGAN & SONS, INC.

The "life" of the oyster, crab, and fish business of W. F. Morgan & Sons began upon a tract of land in Johns Neck that had been previously owned by Wayland Doggett. Hailing from Crisfield, Virginia in 1927, Wilbur F. Morgan, Sr., was joined by his son Cranston and later by another son, Raymond, to establish a seafood business that would successfully generate a family legacy. During their formation years at the site, Wilbur, Sr., and Cranston developed the oyster business side while Raymond worked the fishing side of the venture. A second plant was operated in Ocran by the brothers as well.

Wilbur Franklin Morgan, Sr. (1981-1953) was the founder of W. F. Morgan & Sons seafood business located in Johns Neck. *Courtesy of Debbie Morgan.*

Undoubtedly, the family's ability to skillfully merge their talents was aided when Bill Morgan (Cranston's son) entered the oyster business garnering "Red Lobster" as a client. Bill also worked on the development of a "pillow pack" process to successfully freeze large orders of oysters for shipment to huge warehouses for restaurant use. Now with a third son, Wilbur, Jr., offering his talents as a bookkeeper, the business experienced expanded growth. By 1971 Bill became fully immersed at the Morgan packing site. In order to aid the many local shuckers a "hot shell shock " method was employed for ease of opening the shell. Baskets of oysters which had been placed in hot water moved along a conveyer line as the workers quickly opened them with shucking knives. Production heightened. With a declining fishing business (fewer catches by local watermen), the management declared that sector as "non-profitable" and steered the company towards growing the functionality of the oyster operation. A new packing house built in 1974 aided in that endeavor.

To the mid 1980s, W. F. Morgan & Sons was shipping oysters to a large customer base. During this time the original blue and white metal Morgan oyster can changed its appearance, later surfacing with red, green, and white miniature sailboat markings noting "The Pearl of the Oyster Industry." The company turned to "repacking" oysters, purchasing them from other sources to place in five gallon, one-half gallon, 8 ounce, 10 ounce, and 12 ounce cans for retail and trucking to customers. Smaller oyster units in quart and pint glass jars were available locally. When Cranston Morgan died in 1994, Bill and Wilbur, Jr. continued to work together until Wilbur's death in 1997. However, it would be Will (Bill's son) who joined his father in the soft crabbing business side bringing his skill set of computer technology to drive new business models. There couldn't have been more satisfying times at W. F. Morgan & Sons than these with Bill retaining his position as President and CEO from 1997 to 2005. The latter years saw growth in the expansion of two oyster hatcheries at Windmill Point and across the river. Also, pasteurized crab meat packed in an off-plant site had been added to the line along with breaded oysters. Additionally, a "value added process" emerged with a CO_2 tunnel that froze cooked crabs and packaged them for sale in wrapped cellophane. Using this process Oyster Rockefeller and Casino would also be offered. With many parts to its business to manage, W. F. Morgan & Sons prioritized its ventures and sold quality seafood to receptive consumers.

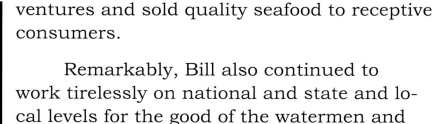

Remarkably, Bill also continued to work tirelessly on national and state and local levels for the good of the watermen and its industry. Twelve years of lobby effort in

William Cranston "Bill" Morgan (1949-2008), President and CEO of W. F. Morgan & Sons from 1997 to 2005, worked tirelessly to produce innovative and quality seafood products. *Courtesy of Debbie Morgan.*

Will Morgan handles a crab catch at the W. F. Morgan & Sons facility. *Courtesy of Debbie Morgan.*

Large trucks transported seafood locally as well as great distances from the Johns Neck site. *Courtesy of Debbie Morgan.*

Washington, D. C., led him to work on the Institute Shellfish Sanitation Conference, Shellfish Institute of America, National Pollution Research Council, and on the Steering Committee for the Hazard Critical Control Points (HACCP) for seafood safety. Possessing an innate speaking ability, Bill's energies were poured into positions on the Virginia Marine Advisory Committee, Rappahannock Preservation Society, Smithsonian Institute Advisory Committee on Marine issues, Virginia Seafood Council, as well as the Lancaster County Planning and Waterfront Overlay Committees for the Chesapeake Bay. Helpful to local watermen in obtaining their crab license card, he also spoke for the good of the whales and dolphins. With the

warm water bacterium "Vibrio Vulnificus" on the rise, he aided in obtaining the funding for testing of oyster products in the Chesapeake Bay. This disease would eventually greatly impact his business as well.

An interior view of the oyster shucking stalls at W. F. Morgan & Sons. *Courtesy of Debbie Morgan.*

Above left - A view of the seafood company's sanitation plant room. *Courtesy of Debbie Morgan.* Above right - Later issuance of "The Pearl of the Oyster Industry" oyster can was designed with miniature sailboats and a red, green and white color design for Morgan Oysters. *Author's photo and property.*

In September of 2003, tropical storm Isabel originated in the Atlantic Ocean off the west coast of Africa and reached the Northern Neck as a Category 2 (100 to 105 mph) storm. Virginia's businesses were hard hit with seventy-seven destroyed. W. F. Morgan & Sons was among them. With $75,000 worth of damage to the packing room and the onset of oyster season upon them, father and son continued to work at Joe Jenkins' packing house in Pass Christian, Mississippi. However, within two weeks their customer base had evaporated. A lucrative family business with nearly three-quarters of a century of productivity had come to an end.

The oyster plant complex of W. F. Morgan & Sons as situated on Carters Creek in Johns Neck. *Courtesy of Debbie Morgan.*

One warm autumn afternoon Debbie George Morgan generously shared the details of the W. F. Morgan & Sons story and reflected upon her own family history in the area as well. Her permanent home on the Weems side of Carters Creek (known early on as King's Grant) provided the backdrop for a portion of the land named "Green Point" by her Great-Grandfather Spencer George. The family property comprised a large tract of land to the present day Brickyard site which was sold to Captain Buck for $25.00. The George family has kept a goodly remainder of their Weems property holdings intact.

In the early 1900s brothers Spencer and Lawson George, Weems residents, sailed to Crisfield, Virginia to sell oysters. They returned with a load of watermelons and two new brides, sisters Emma and Maggie. Both families industriously set about with the men expanding their seafood business while their wives tended large garden areas. Lawson took up residence in a newly built home next to the corner brick store in Weems originally built by Peter Bittner. With the aid of horses, logs, chains, and ropes, Spencer moved his small one story mid-field home to the waterfront overlooking the oyster house. Later additions included a second story for bedrooms, a detached kitchen, and a backyard shed. Debbie shared that her great-grandfather Spencer and her grandfather Iredel operated an oyster house on the property comprised of a dock and a wooden oyster house. In later years the detached kitchen was used as a utility room and an incubator for chickens.

Left - Emma George, wife of Lawson George, settled in Weems as a young bride. *Courtesy of Debbie Morgan.* Right - Cousins, Debbie and Edward George, on the Weems property. Notice the oyster building complex in the background. *Courtesy of Debbie Morgan.*

Widowed for thirty-nine years, Grandmother Nellie became the matriarch of the family, sharing her cooking abilities with Weems neighbors. Debbie's parents, Louise and Franklin, also spent their years on the property. Franklin George worked for Standard Products/Humphreys Railways for many years as an engineer on a fish boat and later as the head manager for diesel products. After retiring from Standard Products, he would wake habitually at 5 am and cross the creek to Morgan Seafood to take the early soft crab shift to "dip" the crabs. This continuous two to three "dipping" hour process was a 24 hour procedure that placed the soft crab in open boxes which were refrigerated and iced for later shipment. His wife, Louise, held her own for many years, fishing and crabbing regularly on the creek and river. Singing in the Presbyterian Church choir, teaching Sunday school, and sharing food with her neighbors filled her days in the Weems community. Today Debbie Morgan happily resides in one of the three George family homes.

Louise and Franklin George enjoyed their years in the Weems community. *Courtesy of Debbie Morgan.*

WARWICK & ASHBURN
STINGRAY POINT SEAFOOD

Situated in Johns Neck on Carters Creek, the oyster business of Sandy Warwick and Jesse and Milton Ashburn began as a leased property in June 1935 from Wayland Doggett. Previously this property had been a tomato and herring cannery owned by Wayland's brother Benjamin.

Working weekly at Humphreys Railways for $15.00 and supplementing by crabbing along the shores, Sandy Warwick felt an established seafood business would be a better long term provider for his family. Known as Warwick & Ashburn, a new oyster venture was launched with thirty-five workers on board. They stood at wooden stalls and reached across long cement benches to shuck the oysters as bins from the waterside were emptied nearby. Two shell wheelers and two oyster carriers kept the shuckers in continuous supply. The skimming room shared a space with the ice house and was situated where the oysters were processed, packed, and shipped. The owners worked alongside during long and grueling 5 am to 7 pm days. Oysters sold for 75 cents per bushel and 60 cents per gallon. During its life span, the business burned and had to be re-built. Hurricane Hazel caused high damage to the premises in 1954. The W & A brand produced a quality product until its closure in 1971 due to the death of Jesse Ashburn and the illness of Sandy Warwick.

Mrs. Gracie Ashburn, Curtis Kellum's grandmother, shucked oysters at Warwick and Ashburn oyster house from the early 1930s to 1989. She carried her oyster knife, gloves and cracking iron in a homemade bag each day to work. Her gloves and finger stalls were also homemade and fashioned from canvas material. *Courtesy of Curtis Kellum.*

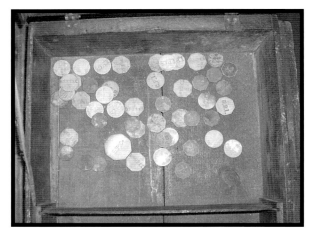

Oyster tokens were paid to the shuckers in place of money. They redeemed them at the company store to purchase merchandise. *Courtesy of Curtis Kellum.*

Established in 1936, the W. & A. brand (Warwick & Ashburn) oyster can touts "fresh oysters" with an inlay aerial view design of a lighthouse and single mast workboat. *Courtesy of Curtis Kellum.*

In the 1980s the business was purchased by Joseph S. and Phyllis M. Jenkins. Operating as Stingray Point Seafood, forty-five oyster shuckers, twelve crab shedders, and four staffers were employed. Seafood was purchased from local oystermen as well as suppliers on the James River, the Gulf Coast, and from North Carolina and Seattle, Washington. Nationwide sales saw pricing at this time of $7.00 to $16.00 a dozen for soft shells and $35.00 a gallon for oysters. After 1990 there was a significant overall decline in the oyster business.

WEEMS SEAFOOD COMPANY

A rather unorthodox wooden shed sat precariously over shallow water in Carters Creek to the left incline of Weems Wharf. Nearby several crab "floats" bobbed from side to side with small wakes from workboats. Inside the plank flooring supported a bench and stacks of thin wooden crates ready for soft crab shipment to commission men in Baltimore. This was the summer work setting for Earl Winstead and his son Lawrence as owners of the Weems Seafood Company. After wading for crabs in the Rappahannock River, I would often step carefully across the rickety wharf to sell a few soft crabs to Earl keeping several aside for supper. He kindly never turned me down.

From October to March the "Winstead Deluxe Brand" of oysters surfaced. Selling by the bushel for $2.50 to Captain Jim Wilder of Irvington, Earl was often accompanied by his son, Ben. After a twenty year career at Safeway in Kilmarnock, Ben retired only to return to the water complimenting his father's career. Purchasing a 36 foot Chesapeake Bay Deadrise named "Miss Vicky" (built by Marvin Stevens of Millenbeck), he crabbed and oystered begin-

The Weems Seafood Company delivered oysters to many sites in Virginia as well as Bristol, Tennessee, with Lawrence Winstead as the driver. A faint outline of the blue and white oyster can bearing the "Winstead Deluxe" label is seen on the driver side door. *Courtesy of Jean Robertson/Ben Winstead.*

Buying from local resources, Stanley Wilson (left) and Russell Winstead (right) of Weems noted their business as Winstead and Wilson "producers of fish, oysters, hard and soft crabs." Earl and Russell Winstead were brothers. *Courtesy of Lois Kellum.*

ning in 1980. Plentiful until later years when diseases (MSX and Dermo) struck the oysters, the Virginia Marine Resource Commission shut down the harvesting process for a time. Ben then turned to crab potting to make a living. Long hours and low pay prompted his decision to leave his labors on the water for good in 2006.

Earl Winstead on Weems Wharf with Russell Winstead's boat in the background. Earl's crab business would be short lived with the destruction caused by Hurricane Hazel in 1954. *Courtesy of Jean Winstead Robertson/John Wilson.*

Bessie and Earl Winstead's children (from left to right) Jack, Ben, Lois and Jean (Mary Kaye in front) enjoy an outing on Weems Wharf. Note the homemade float to the right used to wade for crabs on the "flats." *Courtesy of Ben Winstead.*

Hardworking and reliable, Ben Winstead held many jobs in the Weems Community. In addition to helpng my father in carpentry, he ploughed and tended local gardens. He's seen here on "Lucky" with neighbor Dale Sauer. *Courtesy of Ben Winstead.*

The Chesapeake Bay Deadrise "Miss Vicky" served Ben Winstead (center) well for twenty-six years of oystering, crabbing and crab potting. *Courtesy of Ben Winstead.*

Aboard his workboat on Carters Creek in 1958, Russell Winstead spent his lifetime working on the water. Crab floats can be seen in the background. The cinderblock building houses Texaco Marine. *Courtesy of Ben Winstead.*

Above left - Shuckers stand in cordoned off iron pipe spaces in A. T. Sisson's oyster house. Above right - Charles Johnson works with the large vats in the oyster packing room. Below - Weems Wharf creekside view of A. T. Sisson, Inc. oyster house in 1966. *Courtesy of David Cornwell.*

A.T. SISSON, INC.

A booming oyster business in the 1950s lured A. T. Sisson away from his job at the Irvington Fish and Oyster Company. He purchased a building from Herbert Pilch with a thirty year land lease from Oscar Dameron on Weems Wharf. A sturdy cinderblock oyster house was set up with bins for shucking and a skimming room for processing, packing, icing, and shipping the product. Thirty-six shuckers were employed. Oysters were obtained from local oysterman as well as buy-boat captains Frank Hudgins and Kenneth Rowe. Purchases were made from Maryland as well. In 1954 oysters were sold for $2.50 a bushel shelled and $4.50 for a gallon shucked. In contrast, when the business was sold in 1981 to Crockett Seafood in Irvington, the prices reached $15.00 a shell bushel and $20.00 in gallon form.

E. I. "DUTCH" WEBB & COMPANY

An enormous white cinderblock unit dominated a portion of the Weems Wharf scene in 1944. Destined to become "one of the most modern seafood plants along the Chesapeake Bay," its planning had been on the drawing board for about six years. No stranger to the seafood business E. I. "Dutch" Webb had followed in his father's (Ernest F. Webb) and uncle's (Ira W. Webb) footsteps. Both individuals had oyster companies of their own under the I. W. Webb and Dutch Cove brands.

In the center, "Dutch" Webb, with Stanley James (left), and Ernest Webb (right) attend an Oyster Convention in New Orleans. *Oyster Business Magazine.*

These brothers had married sisters Nettie and Maggie Thomas, whose family had established a tomato cannery in Weems. Their partnerships in life evolved into becoming active participants in the Weems community.

Interested in the seafood business as a teenager, "Dutch" began on a small scale buying crabs from local watermen to resell to consumers. Bolstered by the steady rise of seafood resources and consumption, his business grew rapidly. It seemed time to expand. The largest oyster com-

Early on Ernest Webb was a tank salesman at the Esso/Standard Oil Kilmarnock Plant. *Courtesy of Chase Webb Basilio.*

Maggie and Ernest Webb's home in Weems was located on the main road. Maggie Webb resided here until the age of 106. *Courtesy of Chase Webb Basilio.*

Margaret "Maggie" Webb watches great-grandchildren Carroll, Carter, and Chase enjoying the Weems area. *Courtesy of Chase Webb Basilio.*

plex ever to be built on Weems Wharf materialized under his direction. At its zenith, "Dutch" shipped oyster product to fifteen states and Canada under the highly regarded "Moonlight Bay" brand. He would remain operative in the oyster business for twenty-three years.

In the late 1950s, "Dutch" saw need for expansion across Carters Creek. He purchased the Oscar Ashburn & Son oyster business and cinderblock oyster facility. Originally belonging to Evan Owens, the stately Ashburn home on the hill was eventually torn down to make way for business equipment. The oyster house was reconfigured as a Tomahawk and Glastron fiberglass boat sales space. His son, "Sammy," worked as a salesman for the business that also featured Johnson motors. Both enterprises ceased full operation in the early 1960s. The cinderblock structure would house numerous businesses (Carter's Creek Marina, Gangplank Restaurant, Texaco Marine, and A. T. Sisson, Inc.) before it was demolished.

Shown here with his mother (Charlotte Hurst Webb), Maggie's grandson "Sammy" grew up in Weems. Charlotte served as Postmaster in Weems for fifteen years. *Courtesy of Chase Webb Basilio.*

It is the image of the "Moonlight Bay" oyster can logo that carries the legacy of the E. I. "Dutch" Webb & Company. A young boy sailing upon the waters in a canoe like oyster shell proudly holds a single oyster aloft for everyone to see. There was obviously great pride in accomplishment.

Workers surround the E. I. Webb & Company transport oyster truck. "Salt water oysters from the Chesapeake Bay...Weems, Virginia" can be faintly seen with the "Moonlight Bay" oyster can image as well. *Courtesy of Ben Winstead.*

Above - Sam Webb and R. C. "Sammy" Webb fill five gallon tins with oysters. *Courtesy of Chase Webb Basilio.* Left - The "Moonlight Bay" brand remains a coveted oyster can for collectors everywhere. *Courtesy of Curtis Kellum.*

Above - "Dutch" Webb poses in front of his boat and motor showroom in 1960. His business had greatly expanded. Right - "Sammy" and "Dutch" Webb enjoy a break from work. *Courtesy of Chase Webb Basilio.*

Full aerial view of Weems Wharf in 1958 with E. I. Webb & Company oyster complex seen near end of dock where the steamboats used to stop. Several smaller oyster houses are to the far left. Diagonally across Carters Creek is situated the cinderblock building that remained in use for many years. Other landmarks are: Oscar Ashburn home (far left), "Peck" Humphreys home (next land point), and Humphreys Railways (across the creek). *Courtesy of Chase Webb Basilio.*

With the E. I. Webb & Company packing house in the background, the moored workboats denote busy creek activity. In the foreground the "Miss Geneva" transported fishing parties and was owned by John Taylor. The next two work boats were owned by Otha Atkins and Wilbur Haydon. *Courtesy of Anne McClintock.*

OYSTER WORLD
WESLEY O. ASHBURN SEAFOOD

For nine years "Oyster World," owned and operated by Wilbur "Red" Cornwell, would function in three building sites on Weems Wharf beginning in 1980. His work path had held a steady succession of businesses in the area. "Cornwell Seafood" first surfaced with "Red" and his brother Jim conducting business out of an Irvington packing house. A short interim was spent working there with Benny Benson as well. "W. M. Cornwell" was another work site with partner J. P. Dize in Ditchley. About 1978 "Red" joined "Warwick and Ashburn." In 1977 this business had shucked over 80,000 bushel of oysters. Now "Red" eyed another opportunity. Buying out the lease from Frank McGinnis on Weems Wharf, he rented three large building sites from Ben Woodson previously occupied by "Dutch" Webb and launched "Oyster World."

Seafood trucks with the "Oyster World" logo transported oyster products from Weems Wharf to other areas. *Courtesy of David Cornwell.*

Over 80 shuckers were employed at one time with oysters purchased from 8 to 10 local watermen. Three drivers hauled 100 bushel daily to surrounding areas. Crabs shed out in eight tanks in the middle building site purchased from locals as well. The customer base reached as far as Virginia's Eastern Shore, Maryland, Louisiana, and Texas. The "shell stock" oysters found their way locally to Lee's Restaurant and Tri-Star Grocery located in Kilmarnock as well as Lowery's Restaurant in Tappahannock. Virginia Beach and Portsmouth were also sites inclusive of Oyster World sales.

Another smaller operational crab and oyster site at the bottom of the hill at Weems Wharf was operated by Wesley O. Ashburn.

A picturesque scene in 1992. Weems Wharf portrays a lovely tranquil setting. *Author's photo.*

His business accommodated 8 to 10 shuckers. Wesley bought locally as well as worked independently on the river. Both he and "Red" tapped into a booming seafood scenario. Wesley would pass away while working on the Rappahannock River near his business location. In 1989 with business issues overwhelming the operation, "Oyster World" would become the last commercial seafood undertaking on Weems Wharf. "Red" relocated to Kilmarnock and opened a retail business known as "Cornwell Seafood" for twenty years closing on Christmas Eve in 2012.

Looking towards the hill leading to Weems Wharf in
2004, the oyster houses slowly begin their decline.
Author's photo.

Representative of some of the oyster tins from Weems, Virginia, have found a home in the
Curtis Kellum Museum. *Courtesy of Curtis Kellum. Photo by Alice Winstead.*

Top row left to right - Oyster World ("Red" Cornwell), The Guiding Light (Oscar Ashburn & Son),
and Weems Seafood (Earl and Lawrence Winstead.)
Middle row left to right - Russell Kellum Seafood, Ellery Kellum, Bullis & Talbott (Oswell &
Henry), Harding Seafood Company, J. S. Norris & Son Packers, and W. F. Morgan & Sons.
Bottom row left to right - Wesley Ashburn, W. A. Warwick & Ashburn (Jesse and Milton), Abbott
Oysters, Lumpkin's Big L Brand (R. H. Lumpkin), J. M. Kellum, Moonlight Bay Brand ("Dutch"
Webb), and I. W. Webb.

CARTERS CREEK OYSTER HOUSES AND PACKING COMPANIES
WEEMS, VIRGINIA

W. A. Dameron Oyster Company (1900s)
Wayland Doggett Oyster Company
Joe McCarthy Oyster Company (1924)
Spencer George & Son (Iredel) Oyster Company (1909)
Charlie and Will Newbitt Oyster Company
Warwick & Ashburn Oyster Company (1935)
Ellery Kellum Oyster Company (1948)
Weems Seafood Company/Earl & Lawrence Winstead (1950s)
Emory Cross Oyster Company (Early 1900s)
John Kellum Oyster Company
Oscar Ashburn & Son (Marion) Oyster Company (1930s)
Richard H. Lumpkin Oyster Company (1916)
Abbott Brothers Oyster Company
W. F. Morgan & Sons Oyster Company (1927)
Blue Ribbon Oyster Company/Sam Winn
Grayson Hudson & Joe George Oyster Company
J. S. Norris & Son Oyster Company
Spencer & Iredel Oyster Company (1924)
Oyster World/ "Red" Cornwelll (1980)
Allie Harding Oyster Company (1924)
Westside Seafood Company/Benjamin Benson/Weems Resident/Irvington Location
Winstead & Wilson/Seafood Producers
Ira W. Webb Oyster Company (Late 1930s)
Russell Kellum Oyster Company
Ernest I. Webb Oyster Company
W. O. Ashburn Oyster Company (1980)
Stingray Point Seafood
E. I. "Dutch" Webb & Company (1944)
A. T. Sisson, Inc. (1950s)

TAYLORS CREEK OYSTER PACKING COMPANIES

Bullis & Talbott Oyster Company
Howard Conklin Seafood
Lynwood Talbott Oyster Company

WEEMS BEACH HOTEL

Whether it be lodging, food services, banking, or recreational activities, various businesses made their Weems entry for a time. Formerly the home of Mr. and Mrs. Ellery Cross and situated on Carters Creek with a primetime view, a tin roof farmhouse style structure housed a combination summer resort/hotel and restaurant. From 1890 to 1910 it was known as "Al Fresco." In 1933 Milton Cross, Ellery's son, operated the business as the "Weems Beach Hotel" with his wife, Thelma. Advertised as "clean, modern and homelike," summer guests from Richmond could swim in a netted shoreline spot, reserve an experienced captain for fishing, or enjoy refreshments while strolling on the dock. Repeat guests enjoyed its hospitality for sixteen years. The property was later renamed "Seabury Inn." In retirement, Milton Cross sold his interests to "Peck" Humphreys. Milton also served for fifteen and a half years as an inspector for the Commission of Fisheries. The dock behind his later home was built by my father, Raymond Lumpkin, and still houses rental berth for boats on Carters Creek.

Fashioned by Norma Lumpkin from oyster shells of the Chesapeake Bay, "Rivah Angels" have made their appearance in many local homes and throughout the Northern Neck area. *Photo by Norma Lumpkin.*

Above - A postcard of the Weems Beach Hotel, operated by Thelma and Milton Cross, shows farmhouse style lodging with access to water activities. *Compliments of Kilmarnock Museum.*

The Weems Beach Hotel provided guests with a personal "down home atmosphere" complete with home cooked meals. Notice the steps leading down to the bath houses on the right. *Dr. Henry J. Edmonds photo collection.*

Left - A section of the 1936 Milton Cross account from W. A. Dameron & Bros. store ledger shows a variety of food purchases for the meals served at Weems Beach Hotel. *Courtesy of Margery Nea.* Below - In later years Milton Cross moved from the farmhouse to a smaller dwelling. Note his house as well as the boat he used as Inspector for Commission of Fisheries. *Dr. Henry J. Edmonds photo collection.*

Right - Milton Cross at his last official day as Commissioner in March 1961. He was succeeded by Norman Ball. *Compliments of Rappahannock Record.* Above - Boat rental slips property of Milton Cross on Carters Creek. *Author's photo.*

THE GANGPLANK SEAFOOD RESTAURANT

By word of mouth in its beginning stages, the Gangplank at Weems cleverly advertised to "come to the end of Route 222 and eat all you can for $2.22." Operating from 5 to 9 pm daily, the white cinderblock structure was owned and operated by Thelma and Donald Doeppe from 1967 to 1980. Formerly Carter's Creek Marina, the restaurant attracted customers by foot, car, and boat. Although the "all you can eat" seafood buffet inclusive of fried oysters and steamed shrimp became the staple, the busy restaurant offered a full menu from appetizers to desserts as well as a children's dinner menu. The highest priced dinner of $5.25 presented a platter of crab cake, oysters, scallops, shrimp, filet of fish, soft crab, and deviled crab. Nightly long lines of customers watched the boat activity on Carters Creek and awaited their turn for a down home seafood delight. They were not disappointed.

Left to right - Restaurant ad from 1974. The menu expands in 1976. Restaurant ad from 1977. *All courtesy of Kilmarnock Museum.*

CHESAPEAKE NATIONAL BOAT 'N BANK

In 1969 a new style of banking housed in a white and blue fiberglass vessel launched its services along a 90 mile water stretch between the Rappahannock and Potomac Rivers. Inclusive of the 17 miles of Carters Creek inlets, this first floating bank in the nation cruised at 30 mph from pier to pier offering banking services to "an entirely new market of customers"...the watermen. The unique houseboat stopped in Weems at the Carter's Creek Marina and at

Johns Neck Texaco Dock with varying schedules. Bankers Douglas Monroe and Dudley Edson promoted this creative way to tap into the "cash only" watermen experience and give them convenient alternatives and incentives to bank with Chesapeake National. Keeping little cash on hand aboard the vessel, deposits were made to the nearest dry land branch with safety measures such as an alarm system and an armed guard in place. Seafood houses were encouraged to pay watermen by "special checks" void of service and checking account charges. Customized boat loans were also

Chesapeake National Bank

BOAT 'N BANK SCHEDULE

EFFECTIVE MONDAY, APRIL 14, 1969

WEEMS

At Carter's Creek Marina

DAILY: Monday thru Friday

9:00 a. m. to 2:00 p. m.

NORTH WEEMS

At John's Neck Texaco Dock

Wednesday and Friday

3:00 p. m. to 4:00 p. m.

Boat 'N Bank schedule. *Courtesy of Ben Winstead.*

offered at shows. During Christmas in 1972, the bank houseboat decorated with strings of lights cruised along the creek waterway with carolers aboard. By 1974 the houseboat was moored in Weems due to energy shortages. Used as a feature in boat shows, the floating bank continued to promote the availability of boat loans at Chesapeake National Bank until its closure in 1977.

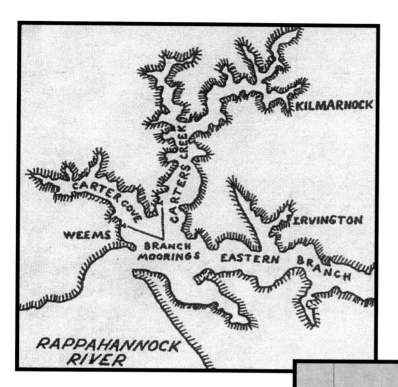

Top - Business water routes of the Chesapeake National Bank Boat. *Richmond Times Dispatch.* Middle - Moving upwards to 30 mph, the bank house-boat could move quickly from pier to pier conducting business. Here Dudley Edson greets a customer. *Richmond Times Dispatch.* Bottom - Part of the opening ceremonies of Chesapeake National Boat 'N Bank included appearances by Miss Virginia (Cherie Davis) and Sailor Bob. *Courtesy of Alice Winstead.*

WEEMS OUTBOARD RACES

The lure of racing workboats was always a "draw" on Carters Creek. Workmen enviably turned from long and tedious days on the water to challenges of speed and endurance of their craft against one another. The recreational aspect was sorely needed. Bragging rights lasted a lifetime. In September 1950, a newly organized Weems Racing Association sponsored the first power boat race held on Carters Creek. Four classes of outboard stock utility racers, three classes of inboard service runabouts, and one class of work boats comprised the race roster. Chairmen Ed Russell was assisted by Marion Ashburn (vice-chairman/treasurer) and Luther

Local watermen Raymond (left) and "Boots" Lumpkin display their identical skiffs and Johnson motors on Carters Creek. An oyster buyer boat is seen in the background. *Author's photo.*

"Boots" Lumpkin as secretary. The registration and food chairman, Russell Winstead, managed sandwiches and other foodstuffs on sale to the spectators as well as a crab steam for the drivers. Forty-five power boats entered the racing arena vying for trophies and award recognition. "Boots" Lumpkin took first place in the stock utilities outboard race on his deadrise the "Flying Saucer." Nearly twenty years later, he would watch among 500 spectators a "revival of the workboat racing tradition" in the Rappahannock River. Sponsored by the Rappahannock River Yacht Club, this Watermen's Day was complete with barbecue, speeches, and trophies handed out by Governor John Dalton. Seated on the stern rail of

A July 4, 1948 workboat race on Carters Creek provided great entertainment for everyone on shore. *Courtesy of Rappahannock Record.*

the "John Branford" among a field of 250 pleasure boats, "Boots" lamented that he couldn't give his skill one more try.

Just inside the mouth of Carters Creek the first of two Labor Day Regattas sponsored by the Carter's Creek Marina and sanctioned by the American Power Boat Association was held in 1967 and 1968. As sponsor Don Doeppe paid the race sanction fees and the required insurance money, R. Avery Dawley, Jr. of Kilmarnock served as chairman of events and pit manager for both years. Drivers from Virginia, Maryland, North Carolina, and Pennsylvania raced respectively in classes of A, B, C, and D utility runabouts and stock hydroplanes. Anxious to see a return of the sport to Carters Creek in nearly ten years, some 2,000 people were on hand watching from Weems Wharf and every available creek bank and shoreline. Intrigued by the skill involved in maneuvering the four lap race course, the crowd was treated to speeds upwards to 81 mph. Trophies (first, second, and third place) were awarded in eleven classes by Linda Reynolds…Miss Carters Creek. Prizes of lawn chair sets, coolers, and accessories for the drivers were also presented. An added attraction of a fifteen-minute sightseeing tour was offered by Wesley Jones of Weems. His amphibian airplane taxied passengers on and off shore at the Carter's Creek Marina.

Top left - The first American Power Boat Association race on Carters Creek drew crowds of spectators to Weems. Carter's Creek Marina is the building on the far left. Top right - A row of power boats align on Carters Creek in preparation for their race. These boats would "take off" from the edge of the shore. Left - A group of outboards are into their first lap of racing on Carters Creek as they pass Weems Wharf. Spectators are standing on a workboat near the A. T. Sisson, Inc. oyster house. *Courtesy of Raymond Lumpkin.*

Top - Readying for takeoff on Carters Creek, the sightseeing tour attracted many passengers. Weems Wharf is in the background. Rappahannock River bridge is seen in the distance. Right - Bertha Lumpkin took her first and only flight aboard the amphibian airplane on race day. She remarked "Weems is just as beautiful from the air as it is to walk upon its land." With her in front of the Lumpkin home are (left to right) great-grandsons Graham, Andrew, and Les Rose. *Author's photos.*

An avid boat racing fan and driver, my brother, Raymond Lumpkin, participated in running an underwater telephone line from the "pitts" launching area at the Gangplank Restaurant boat ramp to the oyster point at Weems Wharf. With a set form of communication, the officials and referee Bobby Jones from Williamsburg could monitor the progression of the race from Webb's oyster house, to the creek mouth, and around behind the Gangplank. It worked! The races were regulated without any difficulty.

In 1971 Raymond applied to obtain a permit for an Outboard Performance Craft race. Due to local complaints of excessive noise, destructive wake, and periods of inaccessibility to Carters Creek the permit was rejected. Not to be deterred he turned to racing independently along the east coast circuit for fifteen years eventually holding a world speed

Original flyer for the second Labor Day Regatta in 1968 on Carters Creek. *Courtesy of Raymond Lumpkin.*

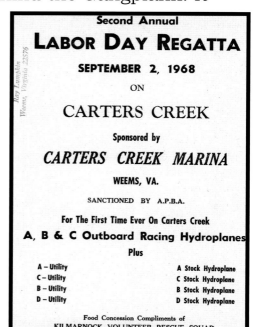

Ray Lumpkin
Weems, Virginia 22576

Second Annual

LABOR DAY REGATTA

SEPTEMBER 2, 1968

ON

CARTERS CREEK

Sponsored by

CARTERS CREEK MARINA

WEEMS, VA.

SANCTIONED BY A.P.B.A.

For The First Time Ever On Carters Creek

A, B & C Outboard Racing Hydroplanes

Plus

A – Utility	A Stock Hydroplane
C – Utility	C Stock Hydroplane
B – Utility	B Stock Hydroplane
D – Utility	D Stock Hydroplane

Food Concession Compliments of
KILMARNOCK VOLUNTEER RESCUE SQUAD.

record. In the fall of 2005, during a relapse of leukemia, Raymond purchased a twenty year old SST-120 super stock class tunnel boat with a V6 Mercury racing engine reminiscent of his earlier racing days. Its restoration was personally completed in two years and aptly named the "Hope Boat."

Much of Raymond's lifelong collection of memorabilia documenting the racing history of American Power Boat Association Region 4 may be accessed at the Calvert Marine Museum in Solomons, Maryland. His boating photos, slides, and taped memoir were helpful in the book publication of "Thrills and Spills" by Robert J. Hurry and Richard J. Dodds. Raymond's desire to race at high speed had its beginning on Carters Creek. There's no doubt he was never as fulfilled as when he caught that wave just right.

Dominance of sail and mechanical water power on the waters gradually evaporated for the independent watermen. Efficient replacements were waiting in the wings. No matter. The memory of the men who labored from dawn to dusk is on record. Vivid, too, are the times when families in Weems happily clambered aboard workboats to cheer on the Fourth of July boat races or catch fish "two to a line." For me it remains sitting on the bow of the "Gladys L" on a warm and still summer evening counting the red and green blinking lights on the way to our secluded cove on Carters Creek.

Left - A checkered flag signals the opening of the races on Carters Creek. *Courtesy of Raymond Lumpkin.* Below - Raymond Lumpkin races the "Gambler" on Carters Creek. *Courtesy of Norma Lumpkin.*

Ray Lumpkin (left) shares boat racing pointers with Les and Horace Rose in the 1970s. A "gas up" style convenience store is positioned at the end of the dock on Carters Creek. *Author's photo.*

Raymond Lumpkin participated in almost 300 races, winning 27 First Place trophies inclusive of Regional and National Championships. Serving as Referee, engine inspector, world record time trial inspector, and Regional Chairman for six years, Raymond proudly participated in this sport under his own initiative and without a sponsor. *Courtesy of Norma Lumpkin.*

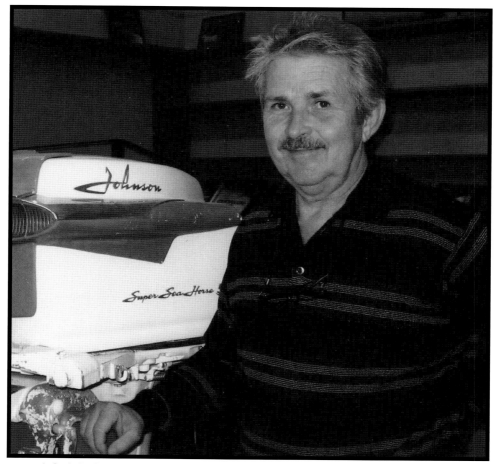

Raymond Calvin Lumpkin, Jr. (1944-2008) moved to Weems, Virginia in 1945. His retail work in the area included Colonial Hardware, Sears Roebuck Catalogue Store, Noah's Ark, and Second Chance Outboard on E-Bay. *Author's photo.*

Always hands on, at fifty-six years of age, Raymond Lumpkin purchased and restored a SST-120 super stock class tunnel boat. Named "The Hope Boat" it served, through his personal experiences, a way to draw attention to a good cause as well as to encourage others during life's difficult times. *Courtesy of Norma Lumpkin.*

Our cove on Carters Creek was a wonderful place to row, swim, fish, and enjoy just "being" upon the water. A small dock was built by my father to tie his workboat and a skiff. Before spring I repainted and caulked the skiff. My mother, brother, and I often held picnics on the bank. *Author's photo.*

Married in Calvary Methodist Church in Baltimore, Maryland, on January 1, 1936, Gladys Marie House Lumpkin and Raymond Calvin Lumpkin pose for their wedding portrait. *Author's photo.*

PART VI

THREADS OF OUR COMMUNITY

Many individuals and events exhibited Weems "staying power" impacting the community in both service and creative endeavors. They carried with them a stabilizing presence that captured a promise of longevity for the area. The threads of their stories weave a Weems presence always remembered and appreciated.

PEARSON'S STORE
GRAHAM LYELL PEARSON
1888-1964

It's still there...brick solid. The corner merchandise store facing Weems Road built by Peter Bittner and later conveyed to his son-in-law Graham Pearson. It was a profitable livelihood that stood the test of time. From its inception everything about the store was inviting. Its lined shelves of jars of cookies and candy, over the counter medicines, colorful yards of sewing fabric with sturdy shoes and boots to outfit an entire family were available. Huge wooden barrels placed strategically throughout the store were filled to the brim with dried beans, molasses, dried hominy, flour, corn meal, and brine pickles. A freezer stood to the side loaded with ice cream for hand dipped cones. Cases of soda pop were stacked nearby. Youngsters were especially drawn to an entertainment center with a popular pinball machine. The atmosphere was one of cordiality with a request to "come back tomorrow."

Bartering in Mr. Pearson's store was an ongoing practice. He genially accepted fresh made butter, eggs, and live hens in exchange for customer selected goods. Weights were calculated on brass hanging scales and measurements taken by the handy yard stick. Wire baskets full of fresh eggs sat on the checkout counter where an occasional "ding" might be heard when cash was available. Shirley Pearson Jett Walker recalled the daily walk from the family country home on the river bank to her father's store to join in the action. At ten years of age, she proudly became a "store helper" once selling an apron for 25 cents as a "markup" from the designated price.

During World War II, Mr. Pearson expanded the store to accommodate household furniture he had driven to Richmond to select from a furniture warehouse on 17th Street. A large truck backing up to the store signaled it was time to get the "first pick" of the elegant pieces. For many years the store maintained a steady service of offering stability of goods within walking distance. Mr. Pearson reluctantly closed the store in 1947 due to ill health. Although immediate family members were unable to continue the family tradition, the building would later host several retail grocery business owners--Richard Lumpkin and Carroll Davis. Today the property literally retains "cornerstone" status central to the Weems community.

This 1950s store structure was operated by Richard Lumpkin and also served as a bus stop for Weems children. The original Pearson's store was the main brick portion of this building. *Courtesy of Ben Winstead.*

CARROLL HOWARD DAVIS
1903-1981
DAVIS SUPER MARKET
1955-1981

Carroll Davis moved about at a fast pace with a wide smile on his face and the ever present Coca Cola at hand. Swapping jokes and pointing out the deals of the day atop the iced down drink cooler that fronted the store entrance with a series of "I declare, I declare" prefacing his remarks, Carroll Davis proudly and expertly held sway over his Weems Super Market business. His retail road had been long and winding successfully dovetailing his gregarious personality with the needs of the community members. Often referred to as the "Mayor of Weems," had the area been incorporated, he good naturedly merged his role as that of store owner and friend for forty-five years. Communicating with his two children, Carroll Davis Jr. and Pat Davis Hinton, filled in the details of their father's amazing "merchant of the area" style with their mother, Effie Irene Self Davis, alongside every step of the way. Their dual concept approach of hard work and genuine pleasantries hit the Weems community mark.

At twenty-five years of age Carroll Davis made his way from Rehoboth Church to Weems in 1928 seeking employment. His father had operated a business at Davis Mill Pond. No doubt he passed his retail skills on to his son. His entry into business at W. A. Dameron & Brother's store on Weems Wharf proved to be a successful matchup. Home to Carroll Davis and his family was the Weems two story top of the hill framed structure rented from the Dameron family. As a toddler Carroll, Jr. recalled baby-sitting time spent at the spacious Dameron home as well as the mysterious sloshing of water below the store planks where his parents worked. Years later, as a teen, Carroll, Jr. would wait on customers at the "Sam Thomas Store" (owned by the Dameron brothers and operated by Carroll, Sr.) systemically moving foodstuffs two shelves higher during tide surges.

In 1943 Carroll Davis entered a general merchandise business partnership with Hilton Carlson setting his eye upon opening a store in Johns Neck owned by W. I. Kellum. Several years later he became the sole store owner managing "live" chickens in coops or selling bulk lot food to customers that were not yet benefiting from refrigeration. The Davis family unit resided behind the Kellum store. Within two years Carroll, Sr. made an opportune criss-cross move back to Weems Wharf as operator of the Sam Thomas store. Facing the Carters Creek side, the store supplied early morning "gas up" for oyster boats along with watermen supplies and snacks. But the fast paced business was to be short lived. The limited point of land that had become Weems Wharf was about to respond to the "boom" of the oyster business. Plans for building expansive oyster houses became urgent with the promise of a lucrative industry in sight. The "Sam Thomas Store" became expendable. With nearly twenty years invested in the retail business, Carroll Davis would have to couple adaptability with persistence and turn elsewhere. Why not take another risk and rent the former Pearson/Lumpkin vacant brick store? Mid-Weems located and only a short walk from the post office this fledging business went one step further in offer-

ing "convenience store service goods" tailored specifically to the needs of surrounding families. This business operated about a decade. Then Carroll Davis purchased land from Milton Cross across the road from the home of Albert and Imogen Daniel. With the excitement of the emergence of a newly constructed white cinderblock building framed

Much pride was evident in the opening of the Davis Super Market in 1955 for Effie and Carroll Davis. Its staples and steady service were welcomed in the Weems community. *Courtesy of Stanley Kellum.*

by two large red Coca Cola signs that bore the words "Davis Super Market," Carroll Davis hit his retail stride with a win-win situation.

Large glass windows flanked the screen door entrance imprinted with Nolde's Breads and Cakes advertising. Two gasoline pumps stood off to the side and at the ready. Peeking around the large displays of rotating canned goods, bottled sodas, and weekly pricing posters customers eagerly geared up for the shopping experience. Once inside the 1,200 square foot space, the green and white floor tiles supported shelving stocked with the essentials--bread, milk, meats, penny candy, and drinks. A member of the Richfoods Association in Richmond, Virginia, Carroll Davis was a prudent weekly buyer. Special holiday turkey and ham orders were filled by advance individual request. The meat display storage box stood at the rear of the store and anchored the checkout counter. Ground hamburger, beef cuts, pork chops and other meats were on open display. With no in store water facilities, the Saturday evening ritual was dumping and cleaning the bottom of the meat box with a hose extended across the road to the Davis house.

Many welcomed jobs were provided for the people of the community. Pat Davis Hinton accepted the 50 cents an hour her father paid her (at age 12) to write down customers' grocery lists over the telephone, pile the goods in a grocery cart, bag, and hand them over to a licensed driver for delivery. Much to her father's bewilderment; however, she wandered off as much as she worked. David Hudson brought folks to and from Johns Neck by automobile to shop. Goldie Jordan Gregg assisted customers and managed limited store credit accounts from a large gray ledger. She was indispensible. Ben Winstead took his turn behind the checkout counter. My brother, Raymond, worked the meat sales section

Pat Davis checks out a customer at the Davis Super Market. *Courtesy of Stanley Kellum.*

and clean up. Children exchanged empty bottle deposits for confectionary delights. Donnie Self recalls trading an egg from his family's henhouse for a soft drink. Adults exchanged recipes and gossip. For twenty-six years Carroll Davis perfected this "hand and glove" community store warmth with jokes and stories delivered with a nod and a smile. At age 77, he passed away with nearly 50 years of business and service to the Weems area.

A "full service grocery store" was the goal of Sharon and Johnny Packett when they purchased the Davis Super Market in 1990 renting the building and equipment and changing the name to Weems Super Market. Packett had previously worked at the store site and after a nine year hiatus (U. S. Army and 3-M Business Products Sales), he re-stocked the shelves. As the McCrobie store had faded due to the surge of Carroll Davis' business so, too, would the Weems Super Market. Times had changed with accessibility to a variety of Kilmarnock's retail offerings. Later, Graham Pembroke purchasing the site as "Weems Turn Around," sought to re-create a country store atmosphere renovating the site with original paintings, sculptures, and art objects. With hopes that the convenience of food and gas for the community residents as well as garnering attraction from the local watermen would support a business, he, in turn, experienced a lack of market. In time, Lloyd Dilday purchased both the original Davis store and the Lumpkin store property as storage and office space for his growing Chesapeake Homes single and multi-family business. In 2013 Ben Williams purchased

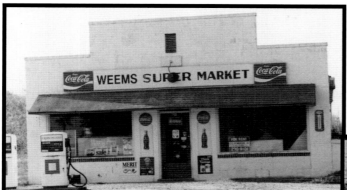

Left - In 1990 the Weems Super Market continued to serve Weems and surrounding areas. *Author's photo.* Below - The Weems Turn Around (original Carroll Davis store) was owned and operated by Graham Pembroke. Basic necessities were coupled with art and country style decor. *Courtesy of Rappahannock* Record.

both properties converting the original Davis Super Market into an amazingly creative home. Among his décor is a photograph of Carroll Davis standing proudly in front of a Coca Cola cartons display. Savor that image of an ever present smile and tip of the hat as one of the best of Weems recollections.

Many fond memories were made in the local Davis store. *Courtesy of Ben Winstead.*

DR. BENJAMIN HENRY BASCUM HUBBARD
1873-1940

If you ask around there are many Weems children bearing the name of "Benjamin." There is one I know of with the middle name "Hubbard." That would be my Aunt, Louise Hubbard Lumpkin, who was delivered at birth, as were so many in the community, by Dr. Benjamin Hubbard. Eventually establishing "one of the largest rural practices in Virginia," this energetic man maintained a passion for his work with an eye toward community service for forty-five years. Along the way he won the hearts of many grateful Weems patients. Among the tributes that poured in at his passing the words of Dr. D. H. Chamberlayne ultimately became his touchstone. "He was a true friend...gave liberally...carried sunshine into the sick room...gladdened the hearts of his patients...."

A product of Lancaster County Public Schools, Dr. Hubbard completed three years at William and Mary and graduated in 1895 from the Medical School of the University of Maryland in Baltimore. Next stop was home in White Stone, Virginia, to open a practice in the rear of the present day two story wooden framed Hubbard home. The lower office space and upper living quarters would serve for a while until a free standing fireproof office building emerged. With sectioned spaces for a general office, an examining room, and a waiting room, Dr. Hubbard maintained a highly successful medical practice renovating his office in 1915 and 1924. The building still stands at the White Stone business intersection. Devoting his last fifteen years of medical service to that of a United States Public Health Service surgeon, Dr. Hubbard also maintained membership in the Northern Neck Medical Society and the Medical Society of Virginia.

Dr. Hubbard's residence was located in White Stone, Virginia. His medical office was to the far right and separate from the main house. His practice spanned forty-five years. *Courtesy of Lloyd B. Hubbard, Jr.*

Over his lifetime Dr. Hubbard turned his energies to the development of many local business enterprises as well. Credits evolve displaying a menagerie of personal interests as President and Director of Taft Fish Company, President of Farmers' and Merchants' Bank and Trust Company, Director of the Bank of Lancaster, Vice-President of the Northern Neck Mutual Fire Association of Virginia to comprise a short list. He seemingly aligned his sight with a projected vision for White Stone in 1918 through the building of a "complex of structures" that housed various business and professional offices. A restaurant, auto parts store, upholstery shop, barber shop, and even an under-written Marlberry Shirt factory enterprise emerged along the way. Again, accolades upon Dr. Hubbard's passing gave way to acknowledgement as "one of the leaders of professional men in his Virginia district...an individual whose interest in his community was of great worth to contemporaries." Truly, Dr. Hubbard's legacy lies in his "best of care" to Weems and surrounding areas.

Dr. Benjamin H. B. Hubbard was recognized as a leading professional in his Virginia district. He extended his talents to enhance a better way of living to the communities about him. *Courtesy of Lloyd B. Hubbard, Jr.*

KATHARINE E. JONES
1902-1991

"Never enough room" was the lament in the quaint house on Weems Road, but the hundreds of artistic renderings that emerged from its enclosure would have one say "beg to differ." The artistic contributions of Katharine Jones still emerge today as hallmark palettes of color and design giving tribute to an area she loved.

Born in the Pimlico area of Baltimore near Riestertown Road, at eighteen years of age Katharine entered the Maryland Institute of Fine Arts at the Mount Royal Station in Baltimore. Founded in 1826, the present day Maryland Institute College of Art proved to be a firm training ground for her art training. Even today MICA has an outstanding alumni roster. After working at several department stores as a fashion illustrator for newspapers and advertising, Katharine made an independent move as a free lance artist. She continued this path turning her talented hand in later years to the creation of water color paintings, collages, ceramic plates, dishes, and jewelry.

That Weems became the artistic hearth for her work may perhaps be traced to a "chance" meeting with her future husband as a driver on a Baltimore trolley. Sixteen years her senior Virgil Washington Jones had been born in Irvington, Virginia. With a family history of two Jones brothers living on the Eastern Shore in the 1830s and building a raft to sail to purchase fifteen acres in Weems for $35 as a legacy, Virgil had followed several siblings to the Baltimore area for work. Perhaps the exclusive opportunity to build a home on two acres in Weems as a "new and satisfying career approach" appealed to the couple. Virgil began to oyster in the winter and pilot a Menhadden Steamer from May to October. Katherine turned to work in the acre garden of vegetables (beans, corn, strawberries, etc.) mastering the art of canning along the way. Two sons, Walter and Jack, were born to the union.

Katharine's artistic growth seemed to thrive in this new rural setting. Weems neighbors welcomed the personalized touch she provided to their daily lives. With a genuine interest and participation in community life, she water colored local scenes, poured molds to make gift pottery, and fashioned individualized jewelry all the while offering a helping hand when-

Virgil Washington Jones (1886-1957) built this home in Weems in 1930 from a Sears and Roebuck kit. A talented Merchant Marine Master Pilot, he navigated expertly through compass directions and engine speeds upon ocean, bay, and river waters. He also piloted the White Stone to Greyspoint Ferry. *Courtesy of Jack Jones.*

ever needed. Space did not confine her. Although the front and back porch were eventually enclosed and a small cinderblock work house became the laundry and drying area with a work bench/tool board and an art area, Mrs. Jones produced a tremendous amount of art throughout the years. All of this was accomplished through her son Jack's observation within a wonderful atmosphere of "creative disorder."

Jack and his mother pose in front of their home in the early 1960s. As a youngster growing up in the area, Jack embraced the natural surroundings. He often rode with his father in their low rise sixteen foot sharpie to harvest oysters on the river bed on the Corrotoman River. *Courtesy of Jack Jones.*

Top left - A ceramic candy dish designed by Katharine Jones. *Author's photo and property.* Top right - Mrs. Jones created this ceramic plate design of the "Miss Vicky" workboat owned by Ben Winstead. *Courtesy of Ben Winstead.* Bottom left - A personalized ceramic place setting fashioned by Mrs. Jones for the author's Kilmarnock High School graduation in 1954. *Author's photo and property.* Bottom right - The art hallmark of Mrs. Jones' work was varying forms of dogwood blossoms with her initials. *Author's photo and property.*

Foremost, among Mrs. Jones' achievements, was her desire for both informal and organized participation with other artists and lay people to promote the arts in and around the area. Jack recalls as a pre-schooler attending meetings in 1947 at the old Irvington School that eventually became the Rappahannock Art League founded in 1949. At six he was its youngest charter member. The first officers elected were: Miss Adelaide Noblett, Director; Mrs. Louis Jacobsen, Secretary/Treasurer; and Mrs. Virgil Jones, Advisor on all business matters. A small but impressive beginning in the Rappahannock Art League scrapbook lists Katharine Jones as "Virginia Artist 1951" (Virginia Museum Fine Arts) with her "Weems Wharf" entry that "captured the atmosphere of local in painting." During the 1950s she also hand painted luncheon sets that were sold through the Adam's store in Kilmarnock. By 1970 Mrs. Jones was elected President of Rappahannock Art League. A 1973 scrapbook segment honored her as "February Artist of the Month" with 43 paintings, crafts, ceramics, and jewelry to her credit. Two other Weems ladies, Imogen Daniel and Vivian Haydon, were also local artists submitting fine art work within the organization. Today the Rappahannock Art

Elizabeth Sykes (left) and Katharine Jones of the Rappahannock Art League oversee art entries taking place at the Lancaster County Public Library. *Courtesy of the Rappahannock Record.*

League operates as the oldest and largest visual arts organization in the area supporting art and fine craft with a 400 membership.

Continuing correspondence with Jack revealed his mother's talent for art forms mainly consisting of impressionistic water color

THREADS OF OUR COMMUNITY

Katharine Jones (left) and Vivian Haydon, Exhibition Chairman and President of the Rappahannock Art League, exhibited their art at the Historyland Festival at Warsaw. *Courtesy of Rappahannock Record.*

paintings depicting local scenes. She accepted commissions that supplemented ideas capturing her attention at a given time. He shared that many molds were poured and fired in two home kilns to fashion pottery and ceramic plates that facilitated a personalized artistic niche depicting one's home, pets, children, family, and boats. Many local businesses inclusive of The Tides Inn resort, Westland Marina, and shops in Irvington and Kilmarnock sold her work. Advertising once in the Rappahannock Record during Christmas season brought such overwhelming orders, she never repeated the request. Her publicity through "word of mouth" was indeed enough. Today many Weems residents hold dear pieces of Katharine Jones' art with "KEJ" imprinted upon a pink dogwood blossom. There couldn't have been a more perfect signature.

Left - A rendition of Mrs. Ben Woodson's wedding gown as sketched by Katharine Jones. *Courtesy of Margery Nea.* Above - Best Watercolor in a Southern Artistic Show was awarded to Mrs. Katharine Jones depicting a stream in Byrd Park. *Courtesy of Jack Jones.*

Top - A son's talent for the arts is seen in "Still Life" by Jack Jones in the 1960s. Bottom - This watercolor of Carters Creek, created in the mid 1950s, was one of many local scenes in Weems that Mrs. Jones kept in her collection. *Both photos courtesy of Jack Jones.*

GENERATIONAL BUS DRIVERS

If there was one warning issued to Weems school children every weekday morning, it had to be "please do not miss the bus." Within a rural setting there was little reliable school transportation in the early years. Unless a child was tutored at home, they walked or paddled a skiff across the creek to learn their lessons. When the school bus became a designated form of travel in the county, a steady means to enter the classroom on time was achieved. There were very few backups in the Weems community. Many of the fathers walked to Weems Wharf or a nearer home landing to begin work in the dawn hours. Mothers were busy tending to every aspect of homemaking. Weems children walked to the bus stop, rain or shine, laughingly craning their necks to shout out that the big yellow metal object was right around the corner.

For eighteen years the smiling face behind the wheel was Bessie Hall Winstead. Arriving in Weems at seventeen years of age, she met and married Earl Winstead in 1922. She worked at the tomato cannery, learned to can vegetables, and became one of the best cooks around. She raised a large family (Lawrence, Lois, Jean, Ben, Jack, and Mary Kaye), and contributed to the needs of the area she loved. But it was driving the school bus, attending to the needs of the children, and driving them safely back and forth that became her niche. We were the lucky ones. Many times I rounded the corner running at full tilt to catch Miss Bessie's bus. She almost always slowed down when she spotted you. Cranking back the cumbersome bus door, she'd smile and nod you inside. Phew! You were on your way! Winding around the Weems block, passing through Johns Neck, and

Mrs. Bessie Winstead transported children from Weems and surrounding areas to school for eighteen years. *Courtesy of Ben Winstead.*

Left - Weems students (left to right) Ella Mae Long, Billy Ward, and Jean Winstead rode Miss Bessie's bus regularly. Below right - Vernie Self (far right) gathers with Weems bus riders (from left to right) Barbara Lou Adkins, Elaine Lumpkin, and Betty Long. Ben Winstead (back left) and Billy Ward appear in the background. *Courtesy of Pat Hinton.*

with a short stop at McCrobie's store, Kilmarnock High School eventually came into view. School attendance was intact for another day.

Carrying the tradition, in turn, Bessie's daughter Lois Winstead Hudson and her daughter Patricia Hudson Gordon would meet the needs of Weems school children. Lois drove the bus for twelve years, and to date Patricia has thirty-nine years of service with continued appreciation for a job well done.

Lois Winstead Hudson, Bessie's daughter, continued the tradition of safe bus driving for many years. *Courtesy of Pat Gordon.*

Pat Winstead Gordon prides herself as the third generation of bus drivers in Weems. *Courtesy of Pat Gordon.*

Top left - Succeeding generations were grateful for the bus transport. Cousins (from left to right) Roger Wayne Lumpkin, Elaine Lumpkin, and Pat Lumpkin. Top center - Joyce Marie Winstead enjoyed riding in her father's Hudson automobile as well as riding to school in Aunt Bessie's bus. Top right - Friends in Weems (from left to right) Nan Ball, Elaine Lumpkin, Ida Louise Lumpkin, Raymond Lumpkin, and Mac Haydon enjoyed their upbringing in the community. *Author's photos.* Right - Neighbors Donnie Self and Frances Long shared a bus as well as a swing in their childhood Weems years. *Courtesy of Donnie Self.*

ROBERT P. MASON, SR.
1927-2013
LANCASTER COUNTY SHERIFF

Bulging photo scrapbooks of life in Weems and family history were generously shared one bright September morning by June Ward Mason (1924-2016). Her parents William (Willie) and Hilda Hutchings Ward raised four children in Weems. Coming full circle, June attended Weems School as did her mother. June's first job was working for Wilbur Davis at his machine shop on Weems Wharf creek side "keeping books" in the early

Willie and Hilda Ward raised their children, June, Sonny, Vera Mae, and Billy in the Weems community. Mr. Ward decorated the outdoor cedar tree for the Christmas holiday in the church yard for many years. *Courtesy of June Ward Mason.*

Sharing a wheelbarrow with a friend, Hilda Hutchings Ward (1901-1972) lived in Weems in what became in later years the Lumpkin property. The Brickyard on Carters Creek was located nearly behind this site. *Courtesy of June Ward Mason.*

1940s. With a wonderful view from the second story, she envisioned Weems as a "big family where everyone cared about you." She returned the sentiment when Mrs. Daniels, Postmaster, asked for a little extra help meeting the mail truck and putting up mail during heavy seasonal times.

Top left - Born in the same year (1924) June Ward and Lawrence Winstead shared a buggy ride in Weems. Top right - Friends in the 1940s (left to right), Boyd Ashburn, June Ward, "Red" Winegar, and Emma Robertson spent good times together. Bottom - "Red" Winegard and Vera Mae Ward later wed and made their home in Weems on the original Hutchings property.

June's move to Norfolk under the urging of a friend, Olive Haydon, resulted in meeting Bob Mason at a social event. After their marriage in 1945, they moved to Weems near her parent's home. Raising a family and working at Kilmarnock Service Shop and the state, Bob pursued his long time interest in law enforcement through studies at The Police Academy in Richmond, Virginia. June, who had sung in the Campbell Church choir at age 14, resumed her musical interests through playing the guitar, piano, and organ. In 1960 June supported her husband in his election bid for Sheriff of Lancaster County. Running against Sheriff Paul Treakle and John C. Bellows, Bob won the election and entered service in the community from 1960 to 1964. June recalled the family pride in this accomplishment.

As one of the "only locally elected constitution law enforcement officer of the Commonwealth of Virginia," Bob took his job responding as a primary enforcer to crime calls and citizen service calls very seriously. As sheriff, he also held responsibilities to secure jails and courtrooms, sequester jurors, maintain court papers, and promote local programs. During his tenure, Bob worked with Paige Robertson (jailer) who occupied an apartment in the Court House with his family. Emma Robertson was the onsite cook. Bob served with two deputies, Garland Forrester and Jimmy Brent. The tragic death of Deputy Jimmy Brent served as the most difficult and intense time of his service as sheriff.

Noting his abilities, the Virginia State Department of Corrections offered Bob a position as overseer of its jail division as state superintendent in 1964. For twenty-four years he served in this capacity in Richmond until retirement at Greyspoint near Deltaville. His service to Virginia is to be commended.

Born in Atlantic, North Carolina, to Preston and Meda Mason, Robert "Bob" Mason served in the United States Coast Guard until the end of World War II. He met June Ward in Portsmouth and after marriage moved to Weems in 1946. *Courtesy of June Ward Mason.*

GEORGE W. and CORNELIA M. VERLANDER MEMORIAL FOUNDATION

Owing to his rural upbringing in Weems and a positive educational and mentorship experience at White Stone High School, George Verlander (1914-1994) often thought of the importance of higher education in one's life. His journey as a graduate of the Merchant Marine Academy, subsequently, working aboard an oil tanker for Exxon after serving on ships during World War II and Korea, solidified this mode of thinking. Moving back to Weems, he put his ideas into motion at retirement and in 1969 began in earnest to grow wealth through the stock market. Meeting with a group of individuals at Wells Fargo in Kilmarnock, George set up a trust fund to initially help students in Weems (beginning in fifth grade) to identify and pursue an educational path. In 2001, at Cornelia's passing, this foundational gift went into effect. The results have been remarkable. Today some six hundred students of which 118 are college enrolled have benefited from his generosity.

Jack Neal, a member of the original investment group and George's friend, shared the groundwork for George Verlander's personal yet practical vision of furthering educational opportunity for Weems' students. Qualifications for this application would not be regulated to race, creed, or even the ability to sustain payment. Conditions invited anyone desirous of advanced education with the goal to "stay the course" as welcomed participants. Indeed, students with varying abilities who worked hard and looked to future participation as a citizen of the community were encouraged to apply through the Verlander Foundation.

"Giving back" became the goal for both George and Cornelia who had no children of their own. What began as a means to "exert a positive and lasting influence upon the young people of Weems" has now expanded its reach to students throughout Lancaster County. Within its fifteenth year, the Verlander Foundation has developed many innovative and progressive opportunities. In effect in Lancaster High School for eight years has been a program mentoring and training high school students for future college or life career decisions. With a 95% success rate, "Career Coach" has focused to prepare "for employment, postsecondary education and enrollment in formal career pathways." Dual enrollment courses are stressed as means to earn college credits during high school at no additional cost. Many of these advanced placement courses are

George and Cornelia Verlander (shown here on their wedding day) worked through their foundation to provide educational funds through many venues for students from Weems and extension into Lancaster County. *Courtesy of Jack Neal.*

available on-line. Alternative career choices are bolstered through vocational education at the Northern Neck Technical Center in Warsaw. Verlander Foundation funding is the financial mainstream for these endeavors.

Programs continue to grow. The Dexter C. Rumsey scholarship is a special venue to recruit local students to extend their talents into the teaching field for the Lancaster County area. College endowments are in place at James Madison University, Virginia

Tech, Radford, University of Virginia, Old Dominion University, and Virginia Commonwealth University. Additionally, Rappahannock Community College students have benefited greatly from scholarships through the Verlander Foundation. In 2011 the Chancellor's Awards for Leadership in Philanthropy from the Virginia Foundation for Community College Education recognized the Verlander Foundation for its invaluable contribution.

That scholarships have exceeded the million dollar mark to further educate Weems and Lancaster County students would, in all probability, astound George Verlander. Perhaps it is we who should be astounded. After a satisfying career, this quietly unpretentious man who returned to Weems to settle back into a peaceful country lifestyle desired to explore lifetime possibilities for others.

MAY MEIGS OLDS
1869-1969

She answered to the name "Topsy" early on for her lively and precocious manner. Born in Washington, D. C. in 1869, Mrs. Olds (as I knew her) was central to histories of presidents and extraordinary happenings. Not unlike her Weems entry in the late 1940s. Furniture, boxes, paintings, and books made their way through the lawn of part of the original Corotoman estate of Robert "King" Carter. With a smile and a wave of her hand, Mrs. Olds motioned me to join the commotion. I did. That would be the first of many visits to talk just about everything.

May "Topsy" Olds married Henry Olds in 1891. A well-known ornithologist, he had lectured, studied the musical warbling of birds, and written

May "Topsy" Olds displays a landscape portrait of Weems. *Courtesy of The News Leader. Photo by Isabel Gough.*

One of the many watercolor bird sketches of Mrs. Olds. *Courtesy of Chase Webb Basilio.*

articles about many species. May Olds painted the slides for his lectures. She continued to work in oils and later watercolors producing birds and landscape scenes for nearly sixty years. Much of her work produced in Weems was graciously giv-

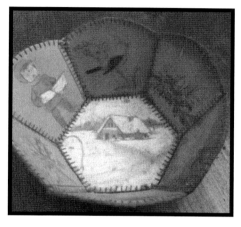

Left - Watercolor Christmas images are painted upon light leather and handsewn for this personalized Christmas container from Mrs. Olds. Right - The view of the Rappahannock River from Mrs. Olds window. *Author's photos and property.*

en to many neighbors. There's no doubt Mrs. Olds found happiness observing the land, its creatures, and the waters that flowed past her window in Weems.

A RETURN TO THE WATER

Gather together any number of individuals who lived in Weems and instinctively there is a story that bonded them to the area. With that thought in mind, Charles Haydon's crab and oyster presence upon Carters Creek and the Corotomon River today reveals a unique and interesting

Grandpa Wilbur Haydon's buy boat named the Charles L. around 1953. *Courtesy of Charles Haydon.*

Grandma Vivian Haydon and Uncle Mac sitting on a crab float around 1943. *Courtesy of Charles Haydon.*

circumstance. Let's say he lived the best of both worlds at the same time.

As a Weems youngster, Charles had the opportunity to spend weekends and summers interacting with his father and Grandfather Wiley in their crab and oyster business ventures in Bundick Wharf on the Coan River. During the week, he lived close to Grandfather Haydon learning about Carters Creek and the Rappahannock River. Those first twelve years made quite an impression. So much so that in retirement from Dominion Power, Charles made an important decision. Buying a complete waterman's inventory of boat, truck, crab pots, and existing license, he returned to the water. Six years later finds him still happily pursuing the path of his father and grandfathers. "It's really something inside me I just can't shake. Getting up early and going on the creek...it's my heart."

Left - Maternal Grandfather, Wiley Bryant, holding Charles with neighbor Russell Winstead in Weems around 1953. An oyster truck appears in the background. Center - With the remains of the Levin T. Buck brickyard in 1953 in the background, Charles with Grandfather Wiley approach the foot wharf on Carters Creek. Right - Aboard his twenty-one foot workboat, Charles Haydon regularly sets out 80 to 140 crab pots along Carters Creek and Corrotoman River. It's time well spent in a community that continues to "give him more." *Courtesy of Charles Haydon.*

VINTAGE WEEMS

A look back one more time at early life in Weems still fascinates us all. Folks simply had the ability to "make do." Harsh winters found foodstuffs stacked in containers around the attic chimney. The coolness of wells freshened up milk and butter in the summer heat. Fired up wood stoves produced quantities of hoe cakes, cornbread, sweet potatoes, fried chicken, and mountains of biscuits smothered in churned butter. Sausage and pork chops were stored in grease jars for quick reheating aboard the oyster boats. Miss Winnie could be spotted paddling her skiff out to the bound stakes catching fish and soft crabs seasonally. Oysters were harvested manually in the winter. Up the road chickens were purchased from Herbert and Lavinia George's farm. The Ball family homestead offered fresh milk. Matt Donahoe regularly pedaled beef around the community. A wagon filled with fresh grown garden vegetables made the rounds from Greentown. Mr. Grimes hawked fresh fish by wagon. Weems operated as the perfection of a modern day "Farmers Market" minus the booths. The all day corn grinding trip to Kamps Mill outside Kilmarnock was coordinated with a neighbor who had a horse and wagon. Dresses were fashioned from colorful feedback sacks with white sacks sewn together as bed sheets. Many residents built their home with help from talented neighbors. Bartering and swapping goods and services was the norm.

Youngsters spent their time wading for soft crabs, fishing off the end of the pier, swimming in the cove, or investigating the shoreline to see what the tide brought in. Competitive games were played well into the evening. Baseball, lawn croquet, hide-n-seek, marbles, and hopscotch rounded out the neighborhood fun. Lightening bug chasing? Just about anywhere. An entrepreneurial spirit existed as well. Sales of wild cornfield cress and asparagus bunches growing along the creek bank were coveted finds. Spring flowers fashioned Mother's Day corsages. Holly, pine cones, berries, and mistletoe were top of the line Christmas sales. No matter that some of these items were gathered from the local customer base. Weems belonged to everyone.

A WEEMS CHRISTMAS

During the winter children in Weems fervently wished for a white-out snow storm. With wooden sleds underarm, youngsters moved like determined voyagers to test their sledding skills on Miss Lena's Hill. Like sleek magnets they were drawn to the slope, checked out the iciest path, and hurled themselves through the biting air with undisguised fear of the abrupt stop at the bottom. What a ride! Several sheep who had not sought the warmth of the crib house glanced nonchalantly as if to wonder what all the whoops and hollers were all about. On cue snow wall mounds be-

Left - A heavy snow blanketed the Weems community in the early 1950s. Shown here is the residence of Gladys and Raymond Lumpkin. *Courtesy of Norma Lumpkin.* Right - Lena Diller's Hill was the designated snow sledding stop in Weems. Sheep regularly grazed on the slope. *Courtesy of Pat Hinton.* Below - Sleigh riders in 1942 (left to right) Walter Jones, Sonny (Francis) Ward, and Marvin Earl Blake take a much needed break. *Courtesy of Ben Winstead.*

gan to take shape. Teams formed. Ducking and weaving the packed snowballs whizzing through the air became an art form. Lunch time with warm ups beside the floor furnace and a change of overhauls and jackets briefly slowed down the action. Only wintery darkness brought the snow gusto to an end.

It was forever Christmas in Weems. Families approached the season as a well oiled celebration machine. With natural wealth in abundance, the perfect pine or cedar tree stood as a dazzling work of art in the living room. Several strings of lights set the backdrop for homemade paper decorations, mounds of tinsel, twirling stars, and elaborately winged angels. Wreaths of running cedar and ber-

Left - Awaiting Santa's arrival in 1971 at Campbell Memorial Presbyterian Church are Bonnie Rae Lumpkin, Andrew Rose, Graham Rose, Les Rose, Collin Lumpkin (foreground) with other Weems children. Right - Reacting to Santa is Graham Rose (left) and sharing their wishes in front of Santa are Andrew and Les Rose. Joyce and Fletcher Brown appear on the right. Below - Cousins (left to right) Bonnie, Andrew, Les, Graham, and Collin enjoy a Weems Christmas with their grandmother Gladys Lumpkin. *Author's photos.*

In 2012 the "Weems Warriors" met at Campbell Memorial Presbyterian Church to celebrate Christmas through story and song. Front row (left to right) Louise George, Ben Winstead, June Mason, Betty Davis, Betsy Bussells, and Anne Long McClintock. Second row (left to right) Alice Winstead, Debbie Morgan, Peggy Allen, Meredith Brent, Page Pembroke Rudolph, Vera Mae Winegar, Mary Kaye Brent, and Sheila Newman. Third row (left to right) Audrey Ward, Dorothy Carr, Walter Winegar, Walter Carr, Billy Ward, and Patrick Newman. Also present were Laura Hall, Emma Robertson, Mary Ritz, Delores James Carnes, Mildred James, Stanley James III, and Gordon Winfield. *Church photo. Courtesy of Ben and Alice Winstead.*

ries hung upon the door. Frosted glass window panes glowed with scores of candles. Meals were carefully planned well ahead from start to finish. Cookies, pies, fruit cakes, puddings, salt ham, sweet potatoes, and oyster stuffed turkeys awaited on cue. Each Weems home became part of a magical Christmas portrait.

Santa Claus had a personal interest in Weems children. Somehow during his home and church visits, he knew them by name and by deed. They listened intently to reminders that good grades and school conduct as well as home helpfulness were very important. By the time the apples and oranges tucked within a red woven stocking had been handed out, emotions ran strong. No doubt a long and sleepless but wonderful Christmas Eve was at hand.

An early Christmas morning produced a flurry of unwrapping presents. With unstoppable energy Weems children propelled themselves from house to house for gift exchanges. They were not above tossing homemade nut and bolt firecrackers on tin roofs along the way. Sumptuous Christmas midday meals pressed families, neighbors, and friends together in a harmonious mindset where only stories with happy endings are written. Standing majestically in the churchyard to witness it all was the cedar tree that had traditionally signaled the beginning of the Weems Christmas celebration. Only hours before everyone had clasped hands and sung familiar carols underneath its brightly lit branches. If there was hope in the air, this was the defining moment for us all.

Christmas card painted by Mrs. Olds. *Author's photo and property.*

EPILOGUE

All is quiet save the wind, traveling past homes and down the hill toward Weems Wharf. Gone are the myriad of boats, oyster and crab houses, and the bustle of human activity. The land built upon oyster shells seems much smaller now. Gulls swoop in and about, crying as they arch over a cloudless sky. Tufts of grass sway in tandem. A few vessels lean steadily against the remaining wooden wharves. A subtle movement of the waters of Carters Creek draws your eye toward the mouth of the Rappahannock River. Waves on the water's surface catch reflections of voices and images of long ago. The spirit of Weems lives on; upon the rise and fall of the tide.

REFERENCES

PART I ~ TIME BEFORE US

BOOKS

Brown, Katherine L. Robert "King" Carter. Staunton, VA: Lot's Wife Publishing, 2010.

Brown, Katherine L. Sorrells, Nancy T. Christ Church Lancaster County, VA. Staunton, VA: Lot's Wife Publishing, 2001.

Horn, James. Adapting to a New World. Williamsburg, VA: University of North Carolina Press, 1994.

Isaac, Rhys. The Transformation of Virginia 1740-1790. Williamsburg, VA: University of North Carolina Press, 1988.

Jett, Carolyn H. Lancaster County, Virginia Where the River Meets the Bay. The Lancaster County History Book Committee (in association with) The Mary Ball Washington Museum and Library: Lancaster County, VA, 2003.

Kaliban, Maral S. Clarke County. Charleston, SC: Arcadia Publishing, 2011.

Roundtree, Helen C. The Powhatan Indians of Virginia. University of Oklahoma Press: Noman, 1989.

Salmon, John S. A Guidebook to Virginia's Historical Markers. Charlottesville, VA: University of Virginia Press, 1994.

CORRESPONDENCE

Robert Teagle <rteagle@christchurch1735.org>

Sarah Whiting swhiting@preservationvirginia.org

INTERNET/WORLD WIDE WEB

"About Historic Preservation Easements." Department of Historic Resources, Easement Policies. Virginia Department of Historic Resources, 7 June 2015. Web. Winter 2015.

"Robert "King" Carter of Corotoman (1663-1732)." Historic Christ Church. Foundation for Historic Christ Church, n.d. Web. Winter 2014.

http://www.encyclopediavirginia.org/Carter_Robert_ca_1664-1732

http://www.christchurch1735.org/history/john_carter.html

http://www.vahistorical.org/dynasties/robertcarter.html

http://www.christchurch1735.org/history/corotoman.html

MAGAZINE ARTICLES

Bemiss, Samuel M. "Colonel Robert (King) Carter of Lancaster County." Northern Neck of Virginia Historical Society.

"Carter's Corotoman." Northern Neck of Virginia Historical Magazine. Montross, VA: 2005.

Carter, Robert Randolph. Transcribed by Greg Williams. "A Journal of our Pilgrimage to the Northern Neck." Northern Neck of Virginia Magazine. December 1995 XLV: 1:5197-5211.

"Easement Strengthened For Corrotoman Site." Historic Ventures. Spring 2011:7.

Fishburne, Jr. Junius. "A Future For Corotoman!" Virginia Historic Landmarks Commission.

Goodwin, Conrad H. "Colonel Carter's Mansion Dwelling Burnt." Northern Neck Historical Magazine. Montross, VA: 1978.

"The Mystery of Corotoman." Sunday Magazine News Edition. (Undated.)

Wayland, John Walter. "Christ Church, Lancaster County." The Virginia Magazine. Vol. X. No. 2: October 1902.

Wharton, James. "Spinning House." Lancaster Heritage: July 1972.

NEWSPAPER ARTICLES

Cavedo, Brad. "One Big Question Is Why Corotoman Was Built?" Richmond Times Dispatch. August 19, 1979.

"DAR" Marks Historic Tree." Kilmarnock, VA: Rappahannock Record. April 15, 1975.

Gough, Isabel. "King Carter House Study Ends For Now." The Richmond News Leader. December 5, 1979.

Gough, Isabel. "Robert Carter Is Her King." The Richmond News Leader. November 20, 1981.

Gough, Isabel. "Part-Time Historian Theorizes on Va. Ruins." The News Leader. March 26, 1957.

Hinton-Valdrighi, Lisa. "King Carter's six-acre home base purchased by preservation group." Kilmarnock, VA: Rappahannock Record. 19 October, 2000.

Kreiser, Barnette. "17th Century Corotoman Site Studied." Northern Neck News. November 29, 1979.

Kreiser, Barnette. "Dig Begins At Corotoman." Northern Neck News. July 1977.

Latane III, Lawrence. "Antiquities group buys mansion site." Richmond Times-Dispatch. Fall 2000.

Ortado, Caroline. "King Carter Dig Halted For Winter." Kilmarnock, VA: Rappahannock Record. November 8, 1979.

"Storms and winds fell trees, damage homes, cause power outages…" Kilmarnock, VA: Rappahannock Record. April 15, 1999.

Wharton, James. "Corotoman, Home of the Carters." Kilmarnock, VA: Rappahannock Record: 1948.

Wharton, James. "King Carter Cedar Lane." Weems, VA: Lancaster Heritage #16: January 1974.

NEWSLETTERS

Weems Village Newsletters

REPORTS

Bulletin of County Historical Society. Volume 35. 1998.

Hudgins, Carter L. "Archaeology In The "KING"S" Realm: A Summary Report of 1977 Survey At Corotoman With A Proposal For The 1979 Season." Virginia Research Center for Archaeology. Williamsburg, VA: January 30, 1979.

RESEARCH AREAS

Christ Church Museum and Research Room

Department of Historic Resources Commonwealth of Virginia

Rappahannock Record

Virginia Historical Society

TOUR

Kelly, Ann. Corotoman Grounds. 2013.

∽◦∼

PART II ~ RENEWAL OF THE LAND

BOOKS/BOOKLETS

Dameron & Bros Store Daybook Volumes/Original/1933-1935; 1935-1940/Margery Nea.

Dameron & Bros Fish Books/Original/1926/Margery Nea.

Dameron & Bros Order Book/Original/October, November 1937/Margery Nea.

Dameron & Bros Dry Goods & Groceries/Original/1927,1928/Margery Nea.

Jett, Carolyn H. Lancaster County, Virginia…Where the River Meets the Bay. The Lancaster County History Book Committee: 2003.

Holly, David C. T. Tidewater By Steamboat…A Saga of the Chesapeake. Baltimore: The Johns Hopkins +University Press and The Calvert Marine Museum: 1991.

McClintock, Anne Long. We Are Who We Are Because Steamboats were. Steamboat Era Museum. 2014.

Miller, Donald Lane. Campbell Memorial Presbyterian Church Weems, VA. CSMP: 1989.

Record of C.O.D. Parcels Received For Delivery. Weems, VA. 1938/39.

Rowell, W. W. Laws of Virginia Relating to Fisheries of Tidal Waters. Richmond: The Commission of Fisheries of Virginia, 1930.

Superintendent's Book of Condensed Records. Campbell Memorial Presbyterian Church: October 1901-02.

Wilson, John C. Virginia's Northern Neck…a pictorial history. Norfolk/VA Beach: Donning Company Publishers: 1984.

CORRESPONDENCE

Dameron, J. O. Personal Letter. Weems, VA. April 23, 1909.

Dameron, Margery. Personal Letter. Weems, VA. March 1932.

Jones, Jack. Weems Memories. 2013.

INTERNET/WORLD WIDE WEB

http://www.stfranciskilmarnock.org/id11.html

http://www.thehouseandhomemagazine.com/Articles/Vol1No6/HollyBall/tabid/197/

http://www.steamboateramuseum.org/html/era.html

http://www.findagrave.com

DOCUMENTS

Edmonds, Margery. "History of Campbell Memorial Church."

Lattimore, Wilson. Nea, Anne Meade. "Roots Paper Cultural Diversity." November 28, 1994.

Sydner, R. C. Land Record. Dameron. "Sloop Landing Point." August 6. 1886. Margery Nea.

ESTATE PAPERS

Edmonds, Henry Jr. Dr.

Edmonds, Henry J. III

INTERVIEW

Self, Donald. Weems Memories. 2014.

MAGAZINE ARTICLE

La Gorce. Editor. "History Keeps House In Virginia." *The National Geographic Magazine*. April 1956: p. 473.

NEWSLETTERS

Edmonds, Margery. "Church Notes." 1989.

Edmonds, Margery. "Weems Story." Weems Villager. 1997.

Weems Villager. "Selected Weems Topics." 1999, 2007.

NEWSPAPER ARTICLES

"About Virginia Citizen." Irvington, VA: 1891-1921.

Burgess, Robert H. "Memories of River Steamers Live On." *Rappahannock Record.*

Burgess, Robert H. "Steamboat Once Sailed The Rappahannock River." *The Virginian-Pilot.* December 4, 1955.

Burgess, Robert H. "Steamboat Passing Thirty Years Ago Marks End of Romantic River Era." *Northern Neck News.* March 1, 1962.

Crockford, Hamilton. "Old-Timer Who Enjoys Life Tells Of Steamboats on Rappahannock." The *Richmond Times Dispatch.* February 24, 19--.

Dameron-Jones Wedding Article. June 26, 1902.

Dodson, Clarence Mrs. "Happy Memories of Steamboat Days." *Rappahannock Record.*

Farmer, John Reverend. "Reflections: Steamboats and camp meetings." *Rappahannock Record.* July 9, 2009.

Leverton, G. H. "Old Eastern Shore Steamboat Landings." *Baltimore Sun.* July 17, 1956.

McCrobie, Edgar J. "Bits and Pieces." *Rappahannock Record.* August 14, 1975.

McDonald, W. Lee. Editor. *Virginia Citizen.* Irvington, VA. January 1900, March 1901, August 2, 1901, June 29, 1902, February 1902, April 1903, May 1903, August 24, 1903, November 1903, May 19, 1905, May 26, 1905, August 11, 1905, August 2, 1907, May 8, 1908, August 21, 1908, May 1908, August 13, 1909, August 27, 1909, October 1909, June 1910, August 5, 1910.

Northern Neck News. March 30, 1978.

Rappahannock Record. "Weems Church Is Concentrated."

Rappahannock Record. *"Church Celebrates 90th Anniversary."*

Rappahannock Record. *"Women of Church Honor Mrs. Edmonds."* Weems, VA.

Rappahannock Record. "Dr. Edmonds Dies At His Home Here." Kilmarnock, VA. June 13. 1969.

Rappahannock Record. "Mrs. J. O. Dameron Dies at Age 88." Weems, VA. February 21, 1966.

Rappahannock Record. "Funeral Today for J. O. Dameron." Weems, VA. September 15, 1949.

Reid, H. "Steamboat Yesterday: "It Meant Way of Life For Tidewater Folk." *Times-Herald.* Newport News. December 24, 1955.

Reid, H. "Steamboat Yesterday: "Drummer, Joke Target, Rode Rivers." *Times-Herald.* Newport News. January 7, 1958.

Reid, H. "Steamboat Yesterday: "Wharf, Church Were Social Centers." *Times-Herald.* Newport News. December 21, 1955.

Reid H. "Steamboat Yesterday: "Frequently Ladies Whooped It Up." *Times-Herald*. Newport News. January 14, 1956.

Reid, H. "Steamboat Yesterday: "Shark Smiled When He Hooked You." *Times-Herald*. Newport News: January 21, 1956.

Reid, H. "Steamboat Yesterday: "Hard Times, Autos Hurt Service, Storm Ends It." *Times-Herald*. Newport News. January 28, 1956.

Richmond Times Dispatch. January 17, 1922.

Sanders, Thomas. "An Appreciation." *Rappahannock Record*: October 3, 1940.

Special Correspondent. "Miss M. M. Dameron Queen of Holly Ball." Heathsville, VA: December 28, 1933.

Stump, William. "The Bay's Biggest Fish Story." *Baltimore Sun*.

Tims, Jane. "A Closer Look." *Rappahannock Record*.

Wilson, John. Editor. "A New School Year…Records of the Past." 1928.

Wilson, John. "A life of sailing, problem-solving and assistance." *Vintage Profile*.

PAMPHLETS

Campbell Memorial Presbyterian Church. "Resurrection and Thanksgiving For Mary Meade Dameron Woodson." Weems, VA: February 1, 2000.

Campbell Memorial Presbyterian Church. "Celebration of Life of Henry Jeter Edmonds IV." Weems, VA: April 30, 2014.

Committee on Church History. "A Brief History of Campbell Memorial Presbyterian Church." 1964.

Virginia Historical Society. "Summer homes and historical points along the routes of The Weems Steamboat Company." Baltimore, Williams and Wilkins Co. Press.

PERSONAL RECALLS/ORAL AND WRITTEN

Cockrell, Genevieve Webb. Memories. 2000.

George, Louise. Memories. 2000

James, Bertha. Memories. 2000.

James, Mildred. Memories. 2000.

James, Stanley. Memories. 2000

Lumpkin, Gladys M. Potomac Steamboat Trips. 2000.

Mason, June Ward. Memories. 2000.

Nea, Margery Dameron. Dameron Family. 2013/2014.

Robertson, Emma Hodges. Memories. 2000.

Winegar, Vera Mae. Memories. 2000.

Winstead, Thomas "Ben". Memories. 2000.

REPORTS

Edmonds, Brainard B. "The Life and Times of John A. Palmer." The Bulletin of Northumberland County Historical Society.

Long, Jack. "Family Group Records."

Sickel, Jeannette. "Minutes From Worker's Council."

Williams, Lynn. "Lancaster County Deed." 2013.

TOURS

Hudnall, Eugene "Bud". The Clifton House. 2013.

McClintock, Anne Long. Steamboat Era Museum Exhibits: Weems Tomato Cannery, Wharton Grove, Potomac Steamboat. 2013, 2014.

<hr>

PART III ~   WE EMERGE

BOOKS/BOOKLETS

Wharton, Henry Marvin. Pulpit, Pew, and Platform. Wharton, Barron Company, 1891.

Wharton, Henry Marvin. Messages of Mercy. Sunday School Board of Southern Baptist Convention, 1927.

Wharton, James. Where'd The Name Come From? Weems, Virginia: The Occasional Press, 1983.

Wilson, John C. Virginia Northern Neck…a pictorial history. Norfolk/Virginia Beach: Donning Publisher, 1984.

DOCUMENTS

Lancaster County Courthouse Records. The Luttrell Farmhouse.

Post Office Department Office of the First Assistant Postmaster General. Sept. 25, 1886.

INTERNET/WORLD WIDE WEB

http://www.aboutusps.com/publications/pub100pdf

INTERVIEWS

Merrick, Leigh. Luttrell Farmhouse. 2014.

Self, Donald. Weems Memories. 2014.

MAGAZINE ARTICLES

Brann, Raymond E. "Lancaster County Public Schools. Virginia and the Virginia County." September 1952.

Chowning, Larry S. "Pick, peel, can and cook 'em." *The Rivah Magazine*. August 2003: pages 52-55, 57.

Sadler, Otis K. Colonel. "Post Office in Lancaster County." *Northern Neck Historical Magazine*. Dec.1952: Vol. 11, No. 1.

The Confederate Philatelist. "Mail Routes of Counties of Northern Neck of Virginia." 1982: May-June.

Wharton, James. "The Great Wharton Grove Camp Meetings." *The Commonwealth*. Richmond, VA. December 1951: 47, 48, 100-102.

NEWSLETTERS

Long, Jack. "A good place to grow up." Weems Villager. 2002.

Merrick, Leigh. "The Luttrell Farmhouse."

NEWSPAPER ARTICLES

Hathaway, Peggy. "Up in smoke: Weems Community Hall is burned, but memories linger." *Rappahannock Record*.   June 27, 1996.

Lee, John. "Far away places appeal to Pembroke, Esso officer." *Richmond News Leader*.

Rappahannock Record.   "Neill Shultz Earns the Eagle." 1997.

Rappahannock Record. "Weems Gets Its Welcome Sign." May 15, 1997.

Richmond News Leader. "One room school house adapts to the needs of the individual child." 1968.

Sitnik, Marsha. "Wharton Grove: A Local Camp Meeting Revisited." *Rappahannock Record*. May 24, 2007.

Spaven, Bill. "Mothers work to save school." *Richmond Times Dispatch*. June 16, 1968.

Wilson, John C. "A century ago camp meetings set the tone for creativity at Wharton Grove 'cathedral'." *Rappahannock Record*. March 26, 1992.

PERSONAL RECALL/ORAL AND WRITTEN

Haydon, Charles. The Pembroke House. 2014.

Hindman, Illa. Weems School. 2012.

Hudson, Lois, Ben Winstead, Carroll Davis, Jr., Walter Lee Harding. Thomas Tomato Cannery. 2010.

Jackson, Jayne. Weems Elementary School. 2013

Pembroke, Jr. Graham. Notes. 2005.

Winstead, Ben. Growing up in Weems. 2011.

Winstead, Alice and Ben. Weems Topics. 2012-2015.

RECORDS

Official Souvenir Program of Tri-centennial Celebration Lancaster County, Virginia. (1652-1952).

TOURS

Nelson, Jean. Wharton Grove. 2013.

Rudolph, Page Pembroke. Brickyard. 2014.

—∞—

PART IV ~ OUR WIDENING PATHS

BOOKS

Cowling, Dorothy Norris C. Historical Notes on Life and Achievement of Blacks Lancaster County and State 1619-1974. Lancaster County African American Historical Society: 1991.

Frye, John. The Men All Singing. The Story of Menhaden Fishing. Norfolk/Virginia Beach: Donning Company Publishers. 1978.

Jett. Carolyn H. Lancaster County, Virginia. Where the River Meets the Bay. The Lancaster County History Book Committee. The Mary Ball Washington Museum and Library. Lancaster, Virginia: 2003.

CORRESPONDENCE

Hayden, Essie L. Claybrook Baptist Church History. 2012.

Jones, Maurice. Grisby's Store. 2006.

Moss, Elaine Lumpkin. Claybrook Baptist Church History/ Photographs. 2015.

Simpson, Virginia Lee Ashburn. Claybrook Baptist Church History/Photographs. 2015.

INTERNET/WORLD WIDE WEB

http://shipbuildinghistory.com/history/shipyards/inactive/humphreys.htm

http://kellumseafood.com/sustain.asp

http://www.governor.virginia.gov/news/viewRelease.cfm?id=1936.

http://newswatch.nationalgeographic.com/2014/07/31oysters-in-the-bay

MAGAZINE ARTICLES

"Carter's Corotoman." *Northern Neck of Virginia Historical Magazine*. December 2005.

Chowning, Larry. "Splitting Pairs." National Fisherman. 2013.

"Oysters and Kellum Seafood's New Generation." *Chesapeake Currents*. Fall 2008.

"Rotation system pays off with bountiful oyster harvest." *The Virginian Pilot*. 2011.

"The Humphreys Railways, Inc." "Standard Products Company, Inc." *Virginia and the Virginia County*. September 1952.

"The Humphreys Railways: Total Marine Capabilities For Four Generations." Advertisement.

NEWSPAPERS

"Capt. And Ship Sail." *Rappahannock Record*.

"Fish Boat Captain Retires." *Rappahannock Record*. 1992.

McCrobie, Edgar J. "Bits and Pieces." *Rappahannock Record*. 1970.

Tims, Jane. "A Closer Look." "Humphreys Railways." *Rappahannock Record*. June 2005.

Tims, Jane. "A Closer Look." "Menhaden Fishing." *Rappahannock Record*. 2004.

Springston, Rex. "State's oyster harvest hits highest level in 25 years." *Richmond Times Dispatch*. 2013.

ORAL/WRITTEN HISTORY

Boyer, Harvey. Mount Jean Elementary School. 2012.

Dixon, Jr., Henry E. Menhaden Fish Spotting. 2012.

Kellum, Jimmy. Menhaden Fishing. 2012.

Kellum, Lois. Sauer's Texaco Service. 2012.

McCrobie, Winnie. McCrobie Family History/Family Album/McCrobie. 2012, 2015.

Smyre-Gaskins,Sandra. Mount Jean Elementary School. 2012.

PAMPHLETS

"A Homegoing Celebration Tribute to the Life of Retired Captain Mathews Gaskins, Sr."

Conklin, Addie (compiled). "A History of the Wesley Presbyterian Church. 1921-1981."

Rose, Brenda. "History of Weems."

"Sharon Baptist Church Celebrating 100 Years 1898-1998."

"Wesley Presbyterian Church Weems, Virginia 1981-1991."

Wharton, James. "Where'd The Name Come From?" Weems, Virginia. *The Occasional Press:* 1983.

PERSONAL INTERVIEWS

Dunaway, Cosby E. Weems and Johns Neck History. 2013.

Gaskins, Beatrice. Weems Community Center/Teen Shop. 2012.

Jones, Clarence. Weems Calvary Pentecostal Tabernacle. 2016.

Kellum, Bill and Joe. Kellum's Seafood. 2015.

Kellum, Lois and Curtis. Johns Neck History/Claybrook Baptist Church History.

Kellum, Lynn. Humphreys Railways/Photographs. 2013.

Merrick Leigh. Weems History and Photographs. 2015.

Smithers Collin. Indiantown and Airfield. 2013.

Smyre, Sandra Gaskins. Churchfield/Greentown History. 2012, 2015.

RESEARCH

Virginia Historical Society

TOURS

Kellum, Bill. Kellum Oyster House. 2017.

Lois and Curtis Kellum. Johns Neck History/Weems Waterman Memorabilia. 2014.

⟨∘⟩

PART V ~ OF HEART AND HAND

BOOKS/BOOKLETS

Hurry, Robert J. and Richard J. Dobbs. Thrills and Spills (The Golden Era of Powerboat Racing in Southern Maryland.)

CORRESPONDENCE

Lumpkin, Raymond Calvin Jr. The Hope Boat. 2007.

Wood, Thelma. Gangplank Restaurant. 2006.

INTERNET/WORLD WIDE WEB

"Who's Who in Boat Racing." http://boatracingfacts.com/forums/showpost. 28 August 2008.

INTERVIEWS

Ashburn, Marion Oscar Jr. Growing Up in Weems. July 26; 27. 2013.

Basilio, Chase Webb. Thomas and Webb Families. E. I. Webb Oysters. 2014.

Cornwell, David. Oyster World. 2015.

Kellum, Curtis. John Neck. Oyster History. 2013.

Lumpkin, Bertha. Julia Hopkin. 1974.

Lumpkin, Raymond Calvin Jr. Weems Boat Racing. 2006.

Morgan, Deborah George. W. F. Morgan and Sons. Weems Memories. 2015.

Simpson, Virginia Lee Ashburn. Weems Memories. 2013.

Winstead, Ben. Growing up in Weems. 2014.

MAGAZINE ARTICLES

Curlett, Jack. "Crab-meat Packing."

Chilton, Collin W., and H. C. Treakle. "Lancaster's Seafood Resources of River and Bay."

Edmonds, H. J. Mrs. "Taverns, Inns, and Hotels."

"Floating a Loan." Boating Industry. January 1975.

"New Plant for Webb." 1950.

Style Magazine. August 2015.

NEWSLETTER

Winstead, Ben. The Weems Villager. "Oysters." 2006.

NEWSPAPER ARTICLES

"Boat Notes." Virginia Citizen. November 26, 1909, Image 3.

"Boat Races at Weems." Rappahannock Record. September 7;14, 1950.

"Boats to Race on Carters Creek Monday." Rappahannock Record. 1967.

Cavedo, Brad. "After 20-Year Lapse, Watermen Race Again." Richmond Times Dispatch. 1981.

"Charles Tellis Drowns in River." Rappahannock Record. August 14, 1975.

"Entire family drowned in Rappahannock River." Rappahannock Record. August 10 and 17, 1950.

"First Regatta Held at Weems." Rappahannock Record. 1967.

Loving, Rush. "Bank to Launch Boat Branch." Richmond Times Dispatch. 1967.

McCrobie, Edgar. "Bits and Pieces." Rappahannock Record.

Powell-Naber, Robin. "Lottie Lumpkin celebrates her 104th." Rappahannock Record.

"Regatta Held At Weems." Rappahannock Record. 1968.

"Resolutions. Andrew Lumpkin." Rappahannock Record. 1947.

"Weems Brick Yard." Advertisement. Virginia and the Virginia County. September 1952.

"Weems Before 1900." Rappahannock Record. Kilmarnock ,VA.

ORAL/WRITTEN HISTORY

Jenkins, Joe. Stingray Point Seafood. 2006.

Lumpkin, Norma. Gangplank Restaurant. Boat Racing. 2015.

Sisson, A. T. A. T. Sisson Oysters, Inc. 2006.

Warwick and Ashburn Seafood. 2006.

PAMPHLETS

Campbell Memorial Church. "Celebration for the Life of Raymond Calvin Lumpkin." August 9, 2008.

Claybrook Baptist Church. "In Loving Memory of Lottie A. Lumpkin." 2000.

TAPE

Kellum, Woodrow B. Working on the Water. 2004.

<hr>

PART VI ~ THREADS OF OUR COMMUNITY

BOOKS/BOOKLETS

Encyclopedia of Biography. "Hubbard, Benjamin Henry Bascum, M. D." page 232.

McKenney, Elizabeth B. "History of the Town of White Stone Lancaster County, Virginia." Whitestone, VA: HS Printing & Stationery, Inc.

CORRESPONDENCE

Davis, Carroll Jr. January 2016.

INTERNET/WORLD WIDE WEB

www.ches-homes/aboutus.html/

http://www.lancastersheriff.net/programs_services.html

vassheriff.org/sheriffs-resources/sheriffs-offices-respon.

webpmt.usps.gov

MAGAZINE ARTICLES

Rappahannock Community College. "George Verlander." May 11, 2010.

Thomasson, Audrey. Rappahannock Record. "Career Coach Guides Students on Future Paths."

NEWSLETTER

Weems Village Newsletter. "Graham Lyell Pearson's Store."

NEWSPAPER ARTICLES

Gough, Isabel. The News Leader. "Woman's Hobby Is Painting." February 3, 1958.

McCrobie, Edgar. Rappahannock Record. "Profile Margaret Olds Benedict."

McCrobie, Edgar. Rappahannock Record. "Profile Carroll Howard Davis."

Rappahannock Record. G. T. Ashburn Obituary.

Rappahannock Record. Carroll H. Davis Obituary.

Rappahannock Record. "Packett's Purchase Davis Super Market."

Rappahannock Record. "Verlander Foundation Is Recognized For College Scholarship Philanthropy." May 5, 2011.

Rappahannock Record. "Verlander Foundation Pledges Additional $500,000 for Scholarships at Rappahannock." June 3, 2010.

Rappahannock Record. "Weems Has A New Country Store."

ORAL/WRITTEN HISTORY

Davis, Carroll Jr. "Weems Memories." "Carroll Davis Store." 2013, 2015.

Hinton, Patricia Davis. "Weems Memories." "Carroll Davis Store."

Hubbard, B. H. "B. H. B. Hubbard, M.D." 2014.

Jones, Jack. "Weems Memories." "Katharine & Virgil Jones." Letters 2013.

Mason, Robert. "Sheriff of Lancaster County."

Neal, Graham "Jack". "Verlander Memorial Foundation." January 2016.

Neal, Graham "Jack". "Verlander Foundation Fact Sheet."

Weems Residents. "Christmas Stories." December 2013.

Weems Residents. "Oral History of Weems." 2000.

PERSONAL INTERVIEWS

Haydon, Charles. "Weems Memories & Family History." 2014.

Mason, June Ward. "Weems Memories" & "Ward Family History." 2013.

Self, Donnie. "Weems Memories & Family History." 2013.

TAPE

James, Stanley Jr., Robertson, Emma, Winstead, Ben. "Weems Memories 30s & 40s."

TOURS

Hubbard, Lloyd B. Dr. Hubbard's Office. 2014.

Williams, Ben. Weems House Tour. 2013.